WHOBEDA'S GUIDE

TO

BASIC ASTROLOGY

Marcha Fox
B.S. Physics, Dipl. IAA

Kalliope Rising Press

Burnet, Texas

For information pertaining to bulk or instructor discounts contact the publisher through their website www.KalliopeRisingPress.com or email info@KalliopeRisingPress.com.

Kalliope Rising Press
P.O. Box 23
Burnet, Texas 78611

Copyright © 2013 - 2015 by Marcha Fox

First Printing: October 2015

Cover: Cathedrale de Strasbourg Horloge Astronomique photo by Didier B licensed under terms of Creative Commons (Wikipedia)

Cover and interior design by the author

ISBN-10-0988333589
ISBN-13-978-0-9883335-8-1

Publisher's Cataloging-In-Publication Data
(Prepared by The Donohue Group, Inc.)

Names: Fox, Marcha.
Title: Whobeda's guide to basic astrology / Marcha Fox, B.S. Physics, Dipl. IAA.
Other Titles: Who better's guide to basic astrology
Description: Burnet, Texas : Kalliope Rising Press, [2015]
Identifiers: ISBN 978-0-9883335-8-1 | ISBN 0-9883335-8-9 | ISBN 978-1-310-41454-1 (ebook)
Subjects: LCSH: Astrology--Handbooks, manuals, etc.
Classification: LCC BF1708.1 .F69 2015 (print) | LCC BF1708.1 (ebook) | DDC 133.5--dc23

OTHER BOOKS BY MARCHA FOX

The Asteroid Archetypes: A Primer

Lilith: Dark Maid of the Sith

Astrological Influences in Effect at the Time of the Three Major NASA Accidents

Definitive Guide to Astrological Reports

With Ena Stanley

Astrology's Basics: Examining the Chart's Structure

DEDICATION

To all those skeptics who think that astrology is no more than myth and superstition. As someone who was once an unbeliever myself, I invite you to study it personally to discover for yourself whether or not it works. You can't make this stuff up.

For those who want a scientific explanation, I recommend a careful study of quantum mechanics. Physicists themselves cannot agree on exactly what the influence of an observer is. Furthermore, it would be career suicide for any of them to investigate anything outside the prevailing views, even if they could find funding. As a physics major myself, I believe the answer lies in one of the many mysteries of quantum mechanics.

To quote Bruce Rosenblum and Fred Kuttner, physicist authors of the *Quantum Enigma*, "When experts can't agree, you can choose your expert. Or speculate on your own."

QED

TABLE OF CONTENTS

TABLES

FIGURES

WHY ASTROLOGY?

The other day I was listening to a song by Coldplay and the opening lyrics struck me as being very applicable to astrology. Here is what they say:

You're in control. Is there anywhere you want to go?
You're in control. Is there anything you want to know?
The future's for discovering
The space in which we're traveling....

This is where astrology really shines. The space in which we're traveling is influenced by the planets. By finding out what forces are at work in your life at any given time you know better what the appropriate action is. You're really in control more than you may think, even if circumstances around you are in utter chaos. Some of the hardest times in my life when everything was going wrong, the things that I could actually control were going just fine. Knowing what to expect can make a tremendous difference in your reaction to adversity. Otherwise, you may take it all personally where, in reality, it's just the prevailing cosmic energy or perhaps one of the planets giving you a bad time (usually Pluto or Saturn).

We are all here on Earth to learn, grow and progress but sometimes we wander into a blind alley, make a really big mistake, or simply feel lost. This is when astrology can come to the rescue and explain the lesson you're supposed to learn and offer some possible approaches to resolve whatever happens to be bothering you. It's also comforting to know that there really is a plan for your life and that you're truly a child of the Universe which will provide you with whatever you need, including answers.

ZODIAC SIGNS

Before getting into the personality descriptions of the various Signs of the Zodiac, it's important to understand that there is more than one Zodiac! The one most commonly used in modern (or western) astrology is known as the *Tropical Zodiac*. This system is connected to the Earth's relationship to the Sun and delineates the seasons. The Cardinal Signs *(Aries, Cancer, Libra, Capricorn)* relate to specific cosmic events that mark the turning of the seasons. The Sun goes into Aries at the Spring Equinox; Cancer at the Summer Solstice; Libra at the Fall Equinox; and Capricorn at the Winter Solstice. (These seasons are, of course, reversed if you live in the Southern Hemisphere.)

These events are characterized by the Sun's position with respect to the Earth, or vice versa, however you choose to look at it. If you look at a globe you'll notice that the Equator surrounds the largest circumference with the Tropic of Cancer 23° north and the Tropic of Capricorn 23° south. This area is, not surprisingly, known as the Tropic Zone and the only area on Earth where the Sun is ever directly overhead. For the Equator, this occurs on both the Spring and Fall Equinox. For the Tropic of Cancer, the Sun is directly overhead at the Summer Solstice and for the Tropic of Capricorn, the Sun is directly overhead at the Winter Solstice. And this is why it's referred to as the Tropical Zodiac.

However, if Mars is in Sagittarius using the Tropical Zodiac and you go outside and look at the constellation Sagittarius, guess what? It might not be there but is more likely to be back in Scorpio somewhere. This is because the stars and constellations use the *Sidereal Zodiac* which differs from the Tropical Zodiac by about 23 degrees, though this isn't related to the 23 degrees mentioned above, just a coincidence; it will eventually change while the tilt of the Earth's axis hopefully won't anytime soon. At one time these two zodiacs lined up together, but due to a phenomenon known as precession, the Tropical Zodiac has crept backwards over the centuries. Another zodiac used by some astrologers is known as the Whole Sky zodiac, which incorporates more constellations.

Each system has its merits and all seem to "work" in their own way. One way to look at it is that the Tropical Zodiac relates to your current sojourn on Earth whereas the Sidereal Zodiac relates to your souls' relationship to the cosmos. Planets in a particular sign of the Tropical Zodiac express themselves in a specific way as their energies blend together, but a planet's location within a given constellation as a whole also implies numerous implications for a person's life.

SUN SIGNS

Nearly everyone on Earth, at least if they're in a civilized country, knows their Sun Sign. Some of them may not know it correctly, but they at least are aware of the concept. In my experience those who may think they're a different sign than they actually are were born right on a cusp. The Sun does not conveniently change Signs at Midnight Greenwich Mean Time but can occur at any time on slightly different dates, given that our calendar is not perfect. For example, someone born on September 22 could be either a Virgo or a Libra, depending on the time, and someone born on July 23 could be a Cancer or a Leo.

Oddly enough for these people, in some years the Sun may not even be in your Sign on your calendar birthday. Many of you who have gotten Solar Return reports, which is your REAL birthday, when the Sun returns to its Natal position, have noticed how this often does not occur on what you consider your birthday.

Thus, if you've noticed that some Horoscope columns list you as one Sign while others say something different, you should have an astrologer run your chart for your birth time and find out, once and for all. Of course if you don't know your birth time, then it's a bit more difficult, though astrologers do have ways of rectifying your birth time based on key life events.

Some have noted that the Sun has a neutral energy of his own, that his position in your Natal Chart simply highlights/reflects the energy of that Sign. I agree and it is certainly born out by experience.

Your Sun Sign defines your core, *i.e.*, your basic nature and essence, and is one of the major determinants in your personality. Obviously you've noticed that everyone is different, however, even those with the same Sign, so clearly the Sun alone does not determine everything. The astrological indicators which provide the foundation for your basic nature include your *Sun Sign, Moon Sign* and *Ascendant*.

In case you're not familiar with the Ascendant, it's the zodiac sign which was on the eastern horizon at the moment you were born and is key in defining your outward appearance and personality. Your Moon sign is the major determinant of your emotional nature. This section applies to both your Sun Sign *and* Ascendant. Just remember that your Sun Sign represents who you are at the core while your Ascendant is the personality you show to the world. If they're the same, you will be a strong representation of your particular Sign.

The following are somewhat tongue-in-cheek descriptions based on a lifetime of observation. Bear in mind that these represent the Sign operating on its own without any mitigating factors, as if the Sun, Moon and Ascendant as well as all the planets and asteroids were also in that Sign when you were born. For some people that is actually the case and they are a very true representation of their Sign, but most people are a unique and complex blend of the Sun, Moon, Ascendant as well as all the planets, asteroids, and various other entities, some not even tangible, within your birth chart. So take the following with the proverbial "grain of salt" though you should recognize the essence as something you can relate to, not only in yourself but those around you.

Ω Ω Ω

Accolades for Aries...

♈ Aries: The Ram

March 21 – April 20
Ruling Planet: Mars

How many Martians do you know? Okay, so it's a bit of a stretch. Just because you're ruled by Mars doesn't mean you're a Martian. But if you know any Aries, you've got to admit there are numerous times that you truly believed that they came from another planet. An unfriendly one. One like those the science fiction horror writers invent, where its inhabitants have totally destroyed their own world so now they're after ours.

Remember that alien in the mother-ship at the conclusion of the movie, "Independence Day?" The one that kind of cocked its head in disbelief before Will Smith and Jeff Goldblume blew its insidious, alien butt to the great unknown? You know that look? The one that says, "Who the hell are you, dumb ass, and why are you in my space station?" Well, if you've seen a look like that lately, its owner was probably an Aries.

I'm not saying Aries are unfriendly. Quite the contrary, they can be very outgoing and seem like your best buddy in the entire universe, but that only lasts as long as you're on their side and not giving them any flack. If you make the mistake of crossing one, you may be the one who wakes up in the great unknown. They're officially personified by a Ram and, believe me, that symbolism is as accurate as comparing a Capricorn to a mountain-climbing goat. Never turn your back on a Ram or you might find out the hard way just how much damage those horns really can do.

Aries, as you can probably guess, is a Fire sign. Its natives are born between March 21 - April 20 and love attention as well as excitement and if there isn't any they'll make their own. The louder and more disruptive the better. The original redneck was probably an Aries. I don't know if an Aries invented the rifle, but I would bet, statistically, they own more firearms than any other sign. After all, Mars *is* the god of war. Furthermore, they live in the 1st House of Personality and definitely have a sense of self. (That may be the biggest understatement that I make all year.)

This is not to say that Aries are not lovable. Male or female, they possess a refreshing honesty and charm that's hard to resist. Even if its because they'll say what no one else would dare and couldn't care less if someone was offended. But amazingly, they're really quite sensitive, so be cautious in how personal you get if you're brave enough to return their insults. They'll admire your spunk to a certain level, then respond pretty much like the Queen of Hearts in *Alice in Wonderland* and take off your head. All this aside, most of your genuine heroes are Aries. They'll run into that burning building to rescue someone's Chihuahua without a second thought.

They can really tell stories, or especially jokes that will dissipate any shades of boredom in a nanosecond. They have little, if any, concept of time and are perpetually late. Some years ago as a manager I had an Aries supervisor who reported to me. She was late to virtually every staff meeting we ever had and then invariably needed to leave early. Fire signs all seem to think that time itself is subject to their control. They're impulsive and witty but, unless they have an Earth sign for their

5

ascendant or Moon, they're probably not punctual and likewise somewhat remiss at completing projects.

Nonetheless, they tend to be natural leaders because, like most cardinal signs, they love to be in charge, so in most cases they'll find one of their vast minions to do the real work. Aries love new beginnings. For the guys particularly, if their life ever becomes intolerable they have no problem packing up whatever they can fit in their car or truck and driving off into the sunset in search of new adventures rather than deal with messes that are far too complicated to hold their interest.

Many years ago I lived next door to a family where both parents were Aries. Hardly a day would pass that the wife didn't send over one of her many children to borrow something. But whenever there was an emergency or we needed help of any sort, the husband was there. The bigger the emergency, the more help you got. Usually their car would be in the driveway with all the doors flung wide open where the kids got out and scattered but neither parent would notice or care about this unimportant detail. It annoyed the hell out of me, Ms. Capricorn/Virgo Ascendant, but now I see the humor in it. Things like closing car doors just don't show up on an Aries' radar.

There is definitely a place for Aries in this world. They'll take on dragons or any other problem they can solve with a sword, sparing the rest of us the trouble. These natural warriors, unlike the rest of us, don't mind a little blood on their boots. After all, their favorite color is probably red for a reason.

So the next time you're in trouble, you'll probably encounter an Aries in one form or another. It will either be that impulsive hero saving your butt or the one kicking it, depending on which side of the situation you fall out on. Either way, you've gotta love 'em for that knack they have for livening up what can sometimes be a pretty drab world, even if they think the rest of us are (forgive the term but it's how they think) pussies.

Attitude: Kill 'em all and let God sort 'em out.

Ω Ω Ω

More than the usual bull. . .

♉ 𝒯aurus: 𝒯he ℬull

April 21 - May 21
Ruling Planet: Venus

People born under the sign of Taurus the Bull come into this world between April 21 - May 21. They are native to the zodiacal 2nd House of possessions, finances, comforts and pleasures. This is not to say that Bulls are materialistic, but you can bet that their bank account is solid and their possessions are generally of the highest quality. Simply put, they like nice stuff. They're particularly fond of clothing that is soft and comfortable. They also like good food. "Who doesn't?" you ask, but Bulls are particularly fond of gourmet quality food and fine wines. They'll not only know what wine to have with what main course, but also the best year and vineyard. Besides that they'll also know where to buy it for the best price.

Many Bulls love to cook, and perhaps ancillary to that, they love to garden as well. If they don't have their own little plot of land they feel lost. Not surprisingly, Taurus is an Earth sign, which definitely contributes to their strong practical side. Their ruling planet, Venus, no doubt pushes them toward an affinity for the finer things in life. If you've ever seen a picture of some medieval lord attired in fur, massive rings and sitting at the head of a table spread with every imaginable food, a goblet clenched in his raised hand, then you have seen a Taurus in his glory.

But don't mistake him for the cretin at the local tavern bellowing, *"Aye, wench, another flagon of ale!"* No, Taurus is the one sniffing the cork of the best wine west of the Rhine.

If the average person on the street were asked to name a Taurean trait, more than likely they'd mention stubbornness. While this is somewhat apparent in all Fixed signs, Bulls have perfected it to an art form. They don't make a lot of noise about it and are often rather quiet and reserved, but the chances of them changing their position is slightly less than winning the Texas lottery. They may seem to move somewhat slowly at times but don't mistake it for standing still. Like a glacier, they will move over the top of anything, and I mean *anything*, in their way.

Bulls come in all shapes and sizes but there seems to be one trait that stands out and that's their eyes. No matter what color or shape they are, there is a certain look about them that is peculiar to Taurus. If their eyes are blue or green, it's part mischief, part humor, part amusement and part teasing, kind of like they're saying *"I know something you don't know."* If their eyes are brown, they often have a liquid, peaceful, bemused quality, kind of like a, well, like a cow.

Most of the Bulls I have known were very nice people. They were gentle, honest, kind, trustworthy and brimming with common sense. They didn't move very quickly but they moved steadily in the right direction. They were hard workers, practical with their personal affairs and loyal to their friends, employer and family.

The few I've known that were NOT nice people must have had some major affliction in their chart, but amazingly the negative examples also seemed to have common characteristics that were the opposite polarity from those mentioned above. In other words they were lazy, mooched off of anyone willing to accommodate them, were sneaky and secretive and would stab you in the back in a second if there was something to be gained by it. Some of you may recognize those as Scorpio traits. Since Scorpio is Taurus' polar sign and therefore their 7th house of relationships, it's not surprising that this behavior can arise in dealing with people in their life. (If that doesn't make sense, keep reading because it should make more sense when you get to the house section.)

There doesn't seem to be anything in between, they're either really nice or really jerks slinging about a lot of, well, you know, that Bull stuff. And I'll tell you what, if you ever come up against a Bull, be prepared to lose. In their slow, methodical, devious way they will eventually git you. In spades. Do NOT turn your back on a Bull anymore than a Ram or you will be sorry. *Really* sorry. It takes quite a bit to get a Bull riled up but when you do, look out. And chances are any Taurean will never forget it if you hurt them in any way. Conversely, a Bull will also be a loyal friend forever unless you give him or her cause to act otherwise.

Taurus is probably one of the strongest signs in the Zodiac, meaning your chances of winning against one are probably not worth the risk. They make good friends and bad enemies, generally give very good, practical advice that you should seriously consider.

If you only remember one thing, let it be that no matter who you are or what your sign may be, knocking heads with a Bull is an experience you'd do well to avoid.

Attitude: The only thing better than money is land. Lots and lots of land.

[Pun intended]

Ω Ω Ω

Jumping Gemini, it's the Twins!

♊ Gemini: The Twins

May 22 - June 21
Ruling Planet: Mercury

You wouldn't think that two people could fit in one body, but these folks do it all the time. Gemini natives are one of only three astrological Signs represented by human beings. However, in this case, one is not enough so we have Twins. Gemini natives are born between May 22 - June 21 and are born under an Air Sign, which is obvious if you've ever known one. They not only could talk the proverbial ear off of a horse but could do it while engaged in some other activity, such as solving the Grand Unified Theory that eluded Einstein.

The Twins reside in the zodiacal 3rd House of the intellect, and in their case the House has many very large rooms. Every Gemini I have ever known was brilliant. At least two of them earned a PhD. The only reason more of them don't get there is that the one thing they have a hard time doing is focusing on one thing. That is why they're represented by twins, because no single person could ever do or even *think* all the things they can accomplish over their lunch hour alone. The only problem is for all they do, the actual act of finishing something is often lost in the shuffle because they're never finished gathering data.

Mercury, master of communications, rules these hyperactive individuals. And communicate they do, at the speed of light. They are multi-talented, know something about just about everything, and are disgustingly competent at most anything they attempt.

Except possibly relationships. Most Twins would probably be better off if they simply stuck with their alter-ego for companionship and forgot about even trying to get along with another ordinary human, especially in an intimate relationship. Of course they could always get together with another Gemini but then there would be four of them, which has some interesting implications, though I'm not sure that would qualify as a relationship. More like group therapy, which is crazy enough that it might actually work.

Seriously, Gemini's get bored so easily they seldom pair up with an ordinary human. At the least, they are drawn to someone quite different than themselves, usually from another culture. (I suspect this is because their Natural 7th House cusp of relationships is in Sagittarius, which is all about long distance travel, other cultures, ideologies, mind expansion and the like.) Sometimes such a coupling works and sometimes it's a complete train wreck. And I mean *Train Wreck* to the tune of things like international domestic kidnapping scenarios and the like.

This is not necessarily a fluke because I know personally of two Gemini's (count them, *one...two.*) who wound up living that situation. I kid you not. Gemini may abhor boredom but that kind of situation even stresses a Twin. One thing about them, though, when a relationship is clearly dead they will move on as quickly as they do with any other activity. Not that being a Mutable Air sign makes them fickle, but when they've had enough they simply walk away, brushing their hands together as if to say, "Oh, well, win a few, lose a few. *Next...*"

This is not to say they're insensitive because they're not. They have feelings like everyone else, but since they thrive on data and move at the speed of light, they simply get over it so fast that no one can actually tell they've been affected. They're not inclined toward sloppy sentimentalism unless they're tempered by something like a Cancer Moon. They remember birthdays and anniversaries better than anyone I've ever seen (except possibly Virgos) and are very considerate about sending cards and little gifts to their friends, even when they're in the middle of writing their PhD dissertation on something like the electro-chemical properties of squirrel dung. They stay so busy and accomplish so much it leaves the rest of us with our heads spinning. It seems they don't concentrate on anything for long, but somehow, in these little, bitty segments of time they spend on each interest they manage to put together some incredible accomplishments, kind of like those pictures you see of life-size castles built with Legos.

Two personalities or sometimes more are a given with Gemini. You may not see all sides of a Twin, even if you're married to one, unless you see him or her in all possible arenas. For example, your Twin may be a real soft touch at home but a despot at work. Two jobs or major interests are common such as an advanced degree in some scientific discipline and then a consuming hobby on the side such as amateur radio. Occasionally their personalities are so diverse that they embrace two diametrically opposed moral standards and truly believe in both, making them prime material as politicians. Don't mistake this for the same behavior as Librans who try in their infinite fairness to see both sides of an issue. The Twins can go beyond understanding to living and believing two mutually exclusive value sets.

Twins are very comfortable with the concept of two lives. This helps them avoid boredom and is also an escape mechanism if one of their lives becomes tedious or too demanding. Being a Mutable sign, change is not only accepted but embraced or in some cases sought. They don't do this on purpose to annoy or deceive, it's just how they are. To them this is normal and they may have a hard time understanding those who have a single personality and more concentrated interests. They also tend to believe that when they leave one life for their backup plan, whatever the reason or length of time involved may be, that everything in life #1 grinds to a screeching halt and will be exactly the same when they return. They are entirely oblivious to the fact that they might be missed or things might change while they're away.

I don't know whether you'd call it courageous or impulsive, but once they set their mind on something they jump on it like a duck on a June bug. Moss does not grow under their feet. They don't have any particular "look" in common, other than the fact they usually talk and move rather quickly. I don't think I've ever known a Gemini who was seriously overweight, probably because they have the metabolism of a hummingbird or forget to eat. Either that or they manage to squeeze a fitness program into that crazy schedule of theirs.

Gemini natives generally make dedicated parents and somehow find time for their children, though they often won't do the same for their spouse.

11

This might be because the kids can move fast enough to keep up with them and they're much more fun. There is also the Progression factor, where many Twins will have progressed into Cancer by the time they become parents, adding to the nurturing instinct.

You'll never be bored around a Gemini unless they move so fast that they seem like a blur, kind of like watching a ceiling fan. They're also fast with witty remarks, so fast that you might not understand the quip until the next hour or even day. Nonetheless, their enthusiasm for life can be quite inspiring and you're bound to learn a lot by simply listening to them.

Just one bit of advice if you want to try and keep up with one: be prepared to consume a lot of caffeine.

Attitude: Let's be logical...

Ω Ω Ω

Get a grip on the Crab...

♋ Cancer: The Crab

June 22 – July 22
Ruling Planet: Moon

Cancer the Crab natives are born between June 22 and July 22 and are ruled by the Moon. Since the Moon rules everyone's emotions, these folks have a double whammy. Furthermore, as you may have assumed, they're a Water Sign, meaning that they live in a sea of emotion, similar to that of their fellow water-dwellers, Pisces. Unlike Fish, however, Crabs are a Cardinal Sign, meaning they like to be in charge. They go after what they want, with a vengeance, if necessary.

Don't be fooled by their sensitivity, Crabs are much stronger than they appear and are well represented by a creature with a hard shell and soft interior. If you've ever had anything to do with an actual crab, you know that those sea faring crustaceans have claws that are not to be trifled with. Likewise, people born under this Sign.

Crabs represent the zodiacal 4th House which comprises the home environment and everything we need to be comfortable. Along those lines, everyone has known someone at one time or another who never seemed to know how to cut the umbilical cord. Someone who lived at home until they were forty or so, or had to ask Mom for her exalted advice on every decision, whether it was what to study in graduate school or perhaps what to have for lunch. Male Crabs especially tend to be quite close to their mothers and often qualify as "sensitive guys." This is not to say that they are wussie in any way, unless you happen to affix that label to folks like Terry O'Quinn of *Lost*, Harrison Ford, or Tom Hanks. O. J. Simpson also was born under this sign, so give that some thought. On the other hand, if you've ever seen the TV show *Home Improvement* and remember Tim's assistant, Al, he's a pretty good example of a Cancer male, albeit significantly more dysfunctional than the norm.

Male crabs tend to be a bit moodier than others of their gender, which can drive their actions for good or ill; some need to be careful to avoid being whiney. As a rule, they make good friends to both men and women and usually have a sympathetic ear. Their Cardinal properties coupled with their natural people skills often escort them to fairly high career places, though they are generally fairly modest about their accomplishments. They also can be quite happy remaining single, apparently getting enough from their career and their relationship with good ol' Mom.

However, if your mother's sign is Cancer you could be in trouble. She will grip you in that claw of hers and never, and I mean never, let go. She will smother you with hugs and kisses every time she sees you and most likely do the same for your friends. If you try to ignore or neglect her she will not be above using guilt to bring you into line. In a nutshell (or perhaps a crab shell) they are terrifically affectionate but expect you to reciprocate. They'll love you to pieces and be very resistant to their young leaving the nest. For those of you old enough to remember *The Andy Griffith Show* back in the 60s, Aunt Bea was a pretty classic example of a Cancer woman. They do hate to see their babies grow up.

One dichotomy most female Crabs display, however, is that regardless of how dedicated they are to their families, their housekeeping skills are generally pretty lacking unless they have some Virgo in their chart. They may improve with age, particularly as they progress into Leo, but for the most part keeping a nice, neat house is not high on their agenda. Just because their first love is their children doesn't mean they never leave the nest themselves. No, they usually have other interests outside of the home and often have successful careers. In spite of all that Water, they are quite dependable and hardworking. That, coupled with their affectionate nature, makes them highly valued in the workplace. They not only do a good job, but serve as the resident Mother, giving everyone their daily ration of hugs and good, solid, maternal advice, and as required, kicks in the butt. But look out, those claws might latch onto you, too.

Conversely, Crabs do make great children. I have a son with a Cancer Ascendant who's married to a native Crab. They live a few miles from me and wander in and out of my place like housecats. He calls me almost every day and if I need anything, they are there with a smile, and I imagine if anyone takes care of me in my old age, it will be them.

Cancers tend to be creative and enjoy expressing their many emotions artistically. They will share these talents freely and derive a lot of satisfaction from their efforts. They are good-hearted and generous, though they do manifest various moods on a fairly regular basis with the worst manifestation a tendency to be a bit querulous. Remember, they're ruled by the Moon, which moves about through the signs much faster than the other planets. However, this is also why they can relate to others so well, because they experience such a variety of feelings themselves. I dare say that I have genuinely liked most of the Crabs I have known.

Anyone who doesn't have a Crab somewhere in the family or close associations is missing something. While every Sign has much to offer, particularly in their positive manifestations, there is something endearing about Crabs that epitomizes what family is really all about. That claw hooked into your rear end may be annoying at times, but somehow it's also quite nice to know that someone really cares. In today's world, those qualities Crabs come by so naturally are rapidly heading for the endangered species list. So the next time a Crab gives you a big hug, don't wince or wiggle away. Rather stop and enjoy it for what it is. Unbeknownst to you, that Crab could be the best friend that you have.

Attitude: Gimme a hug!

Ω Ω Ω

Let's hear it for Leo!

♌ *Leo: The Lion*

July 23 – August 23
Ruling Planet: The Sun

Leos, like the King of Beasts who represents them, have a natural grace and regal bearing that is hard to miss. It's amazingly cat-like, particularly in Lionesses, and is wont to be imitated by others of their gender. Whether they are walking, swimming, or especially dancing, there is a noticeable willowy movement about them of which they are amazingly unaware. At least the movement part. Not so, the regal bearing. There really is something discernibly different about them that bespeaks royalty and they know it, though they don't flaunt it in an ostentatious way. It's like they know they don't have to prove anything to anyone, but simply deserve attention as a matter of course.

While other Fire Signs tend to believe *"it's all about me"* Leo takes this to the next level; they not only believe that they're the center of their *own* universe but the center of *yours* as well. After all, Leo is ruled by the Sun, placing them figuratively in the center of the solar system. They like nice things and usually get them, not necessarily through their own efforts, but usually through someone who recognizes their royal status and pays appropriate homage. They accept it graciously enough, but never question whether or not they deserve it or whether or not you should have spent your grocery money on those dozen roses. For those things that they do get for themselves, they know where to get them and love to tell tales of their shopping exploits. If you want to know a good place to buy something, ask a Leo.

A bit egocentric but not usually selfish, they like to give as well as receive and will shower their loved ones with little gifts and tokens of kindness on a regular basis. Be sure to show your appreciation when they do because they're really quite sensitive and tender-hearted regardless of how confident they may appear. If their feelings are hurt they're inclined to retreat and hide for a while, licking their wounds, either until the offender apologizes or their need for attention demands they come out.

None of anything said so far was intended to imply that Leos are lazy. While the image of a well-fed lion lounging in the light of its ruling planet may seem to lean in that direction, don't forget that the nap was much deserved after a hard morning chasing antelope. They know how to work and usually do a good job. Being royalty, they have a strong sense of pride and therefore do things correctly, which naturally elevates them to a position where they are somehow at the center of things. They thrive on attention, they like to talk and being a Fixed Sign, they see little reason for change other than to improve their standard of living.

Leo resides in the 5th House of creativity, children, investments, entertainment and love affairs. As expected, they excel in all these and then some. They are born between July 23 and August 23, when their ruling planet is hot and sultry. They likewise seem to possess more than their share of sex appeal, are strong, protective parents and express their creativity in numerous unique ways. They also tend to be very fond of animals and generally treat their pets as if they were human.

Leo has a bit of the Fire Sign temper, but it's expressed in their own dignified way. When an Aries loses his temper people run for cover; with Sagittarius they're mesmerized by the display of energy, but not particularly impressed; and with Leo they tend to listen sympathetically and then find a way to figuratively pet the kitty so he's happy again. No matter what got them riled up, it seems that they were somehow justified and it should be corrected, no matter what the cost. With anyone else you'd tell them to get over it, but somehow a Leo with all that royal blood deserves better.

Lions can have a strong sense of justice and if they're wronged they don't sit there quietly and accept it. This is when the claws come out and if you listen carefully you'll hear a low growl. They don't always make a lot of noise when they're angry, but they will seldom ignore it and if you're the target, don't be surprised if you're pounced upon when you're least expecting it.

You can spot a Leo at a party by looking for the one with a small entourage of admirers. Regardless of what their specific features may be, there's something sexy about them. They may not be doing anything any more profound than sipping a glass of wine, but those that don't know them think they're a celebrity and those who do are waiting for them to become one. Other Fire Signs have groupies, too, but Aries is telling the stories and Sagittarius is probably delivering a detailed travel log of their latest trip abroad or other exploits. Meanwhile, Leo only has to project their natural charm and charisma to attract admirers far and wide. People will meet them once and remember them forever.

If you only remember one thing about Leos then remember this: No matter how gracious and royal they may seem, there is more there than a kitty cat. Don't ever put yourself in a position to be reminded that they are well represented by the King of Beasts.

Attitude: It's good to be king (or queen).

Ω Ω Ω

Perfection. The ultimate solution...

♍ ᐯirgo: ᐧᐤhe ᐧᐧᐧaiden

August 24 – September 22
Ruling Planet: Mercury

Virgos are born between August 24 to September 22 and reside in the zodiacal 6th House of work, health and pets. What this fails to tell you is that Virgos are the only ones in the known universe who know how to do things exactly right. I kid you not. Virgos are perfectionists to a fault and will let you know in a heartbeat, thanks to being ruled by Mercury, that those pitiful efforts of yours are flawed, inferior and probably beyond any hope of redemption. If only they could run the world, everything would be just fine. Environmental problems would go away, politicians would cease to lie, wars end and budgets balance. All we need to do is listen and do what they say and a perfect world could be ours.

Yeah, right.

Of course they hide behind this diminutive symbol of a maiden which would imply that they're the nicest people in the world. And they can fool you into believing that for a while. Being driven by their quest for perfection, they have impeccable manners and can be exceptionally polite, leading you to believe that they're some of the nicest and best

17

educated people you've ever met. But after you've known them for a while, the "constructive criticism" begins and before you know it they've torn you to shreds. All with a smile, of course. Your first clue should have been that *"I'm Surrounded by Idiots"* bumper sticker on their perfectly groomed car, old though it may be.

Needless to say they're meticulous in everything they do. Their clothes always match and their closets are better organized than any given clothing rack at *Lord and Taylor*. If their home appears less than perfect in any way, it could be because they got frustrated trying to get everything in order and ran out of shelves, drawers, cabinets and closet space. You've probably known people who are "secret slobs." Their house appears spotless, but if you open a cabinet or closet you risk being buried in debris that has been haphazardly stashed out of sight. Virgos can be "secret neat freaks." Their closets, drawers, *etc.* will be all lined up perfectly but when they run out of storage space, they just leave the rest of the stuff lying around wherever. Being perfectionists, if they can't do it exactly right, they don't do it at all. With their great memories, they always seem to be able to find what they want and will somehow make it your fault if you can't find something they left out for lack of a proper storage space.

Along these lines, they also tend to be clean freaks. One of my children is a Virgo and he would go on cleaning frenzies where he'd organize the pantry or scrub out the microwave. Believe me that was NOT normal behavior for a teenager. They'll change their clothes as often as necessary so they look neat and clean, yet some of them have a remarkable earthy side (they're an Earth Sign, by the way) in that they can find a significant amount of humor in body sounds of all varieties. Another art form, I suppose, since they can be quite creative and talented in the arts.

Being an Earth Sign they are practical and their picky nature makes them careful shoppers who always balance their checkbook. They make great accountants or any other profession that gets down and dirty with details. Their memories are like a steel trap, particularly for anything you ever did that was wrong or offended them. In spite of being able to dish out criticism, they are very sensitive themselves and get their feelings hurt easily. Earth Signs don't talk about their feelings much, but they have them, and can nurse a grudge for a long time (you too, Taurus and Capricorn).

Since their powers of observation are so astute, they can find something wrong with virtually anything. If there's a misspelled word in a thousand-page document, they'll find it. If someone is a minute late they'll say something. If they're on hold too long, the grocery store runs out of a sale item, or a meal doesn't measure up some one will hear about it. Since the world is so hopelessly imperfect they have a target rich environment for their critical eye and plenty to complain about. And love every minute of it.

Of course since they're perfect, nothing is ever their fault. If they admitted they'd done something wrong their entire world would collapse. There will always be an excuse and a means to blame the problem, no matter how small, on someone else. This does not go well with that someone else is their boss and Virgos have a real propensity for problems in that area. They're smart, honest to a fault, and work hard, but they often don't seem to get ahead because they absolutely can't play the schmoozing game they need to in order to get there, at least not for an extended amount of time or during a crisis.

Residing in that 6th House, they are exceptionally hard workers and, as masters of detail, can be handy to have around in the workplace, that is if you can stand all that griping about everyone who doesn't quite make muster. As you can imagine, they make great auditors, which endears them even more to their coworkers. Related to this is the fact that Virgo tends to be somewhat resistant to obtaining a higher education. This is for various reasons.

First of all, as perfectionists they like to think they already know everything worth knowing. Thus, they are also nearly phobic about admitting when they don't know something, to themselves as well as others, for the same reason. Then, on top of that, to actually enroll in school they'd have to admit *imperfection*. Should they get past all this and actually enroll, *then* they'd expect themselves to get straight "A's" and feel like a failure if they didn't. So you see their dilemma if they don't find a field of study where they can ace every class. Test anxiety is very common for these folks since they're as hard on themselves as everyone else.

Another 6th House characteristic is the love of animals of all kinds. In fact, they're quite inclined to like their pets more than the people in their life. After all, a dog is only a dog and a cat only a cat so the expectations for their behavior are much lower, plus animals don't pass personal judgment on people or get tired of listening to their tales of woe and other frustrations. Along with trying to attain perfection is their search for the Fountain of Youth. Virgos are particularly health conscious and will generally eat a reasonably healthy diet and have more than the usual number of bottles of vitamins in the cupboard. Since they go around the better part of the time worried, frustrated and/or annoyed by all the problems in the world, they're inclined to have blood pressure problems. Nonetheless, they're reliable, hard working, loyal and generally fine folks to be around. Just don't take it too personally when they tell you that shirt really doesn't quite go with that pair of pants.

Okay, so I'm being pretty hard on these folks. Maybe it's my own Virgo Ascendant coming out. Or deep-seeded resentments from my own childhood, which was spent with two Virgo parents who carefully pointed out my every flaw. Of course that was for my own good, so that I could eliminate my many faults, though it didn't work out that way. In all fairness, Virgos are their own worst critic and are usually too hard on themselves, as well. Perfectionism is a heavy load to carry. What they need to realize is that while they see it as a virtue, the rest of the world views it as a fault. Virgos should bear that in mind the next time they're dishing out some unsolicited, constructive criticism and get another one of those looks.

Attitude: I'm surrounded by idiots.

Ω Ω Ω

The leanings of Libra. . .

♎ Libra: The Scales

September 23 - October 23
Ruling Planet: Venus

Libra is the only astrological sign represented by an inanimate object, in this case a balance scale. All the others are animals or people of one sort or another. This has got to tell you something right off the bat. To say they're unbalanced isn't quite correct, because there isn't a single other group that tries harder to keep on an even keel. But let's just say they do about as well at that as Virgos do at being perfect.

Our "scaley" friends are born between September 23 and October 23 and are ruled by Venus. Now right there's a major clue. Factor in the Element of Air and the Modality of Cardinal and you have someone who loves everyone, or wants to at least try, talks a lot and wants to be in charge whenever possible. Sounds pretty ideal, doesn't it? And actually, Libras generally are pretty nice people. And that's because they want everyone to be happy. Everyone has a story to tell and Libra does an exceptional job of being able to relate to people so well that they manage to understand just about everyone. This is not to say they *agree* with everyone, but they do a very good job of figuratively "walking a mile in someone else's moccasins" and being nonjudgmental. I don't care if you're Mother Theresa or an ax murderer Libra could probably get along with either.

Libras live in the 7th House of relationships and unless they're involved in one or more, they're lost. They not only can't stand contention, but want everyone to get along. They may appear two-faced to some because they seldom take sides. Rather they listen to both and will try and facilitate an agreement wherever possible. Being an Air sign, logic prevails, but Fire and Water signs are often less than enchanted with their efforts to bring resolution to a problem. Those that aren't comfortable talking about some issues likewise won't appreciate it, even though Libra is only striving for everyone to be heard, understand one another and play happily in the same sandbox.

Ironically, Libras often have a very difficult time talking about their own emotional issues. Astrologically they're somewhat caught between a rock and a hard place because they require a relationship to feel fulfilled, yet when any kind of emotional crisis comes up they are incapable of discussing it and will retreat and deny and generally avoid discussing their feelings at all costs. They can be supremely logical about everyone else's problems, but their own are insurmountable.

Maybe they feel like they shouldn't have any problems because they're so good at helping others solve theirs. Or maybe their identify is so tied up in others that they feel genuinely threatened when a disagreement arises. More likely, they can't figure out how to be "fair" when they're one of the parties. They know what they want, which is in conflict to the other party, making them feel as previously mentioned between that proverbial rock and a hard place. When placed in this kind of situation, they will either ignore it entirely or, if they react at all, be a text book case of passive aggression. If they have heavy Gemini influences, the two personalities will come into play and you can imagine what that would be like to deal with.

Many of the Libras I have known have been blond, at least in childhood if not as an adult. And some of them are blond in the figurative sense, too, i.e. reference the "blond joke" of your choice. Some of the females tend to be "air heads" but this can be balanced with an Earth-based Moon sign or ascendant. If there are heavy Water Sign influences they're likely to be quite emotional and if there are several Fire Sign influences they'll have a temper and be slightly more glitzy than usual. Generally, they're well liked, however, because they are non-controversial. To be so would require taking a single stand on something, which they are loath to do.

Along those same lines, they can also be indecisive because they're so busy weighing all the pros and cons. I'm not saying they're a bunch of abuliacs, but they're more likely to lean in that direction than any of the other signs. (Taurus may take their time, but they do eventually decide and won't budge once they do; Gemini decides, it's just that they change their mind so much it gives the impression that they don't. With Pisces, it's not so much that they're indecisive as that they probably really don't care and want *you* to decide.)

Since Libras at some point in their life will Progress into Scorpio, the secretive nature of that Sign may lend them a partial solution to their dilemma, meaning they may then take sides but do so in a covert manner. In other words, they'll agree with one person, but never admit it openly, especially to anyone with opposing views with whom they also agree, at least at the time.

What a tangled web we weave...

Don't forget, however, that they really don't see it that way, though they do attempt to agree with everyone, even those with diametrically opposed views. And to repeat, those who disagree with each other and have a Libra in the middle are both likely to be unhappy with the Libra. This is because he or she seems to be siding with the other, introducing discord which in turn will drive the Libra back to the negotiation table or a stiff drink, whichever seems more efficacious at the time. For someone who tries to keep peace all the time, they have a remarkably difficult life.

What the rest of us need to remember is that they really do mean well. They want everyone to be happy and are just trying to help. To simplify your own life, you may want to avoid confiding too much in your Libra friends. Or at the least, make sure that they aren't acquainted with any of your enemies. If such should occur, take my word for it, that one or both of you is probably going to wind up in a rubber room. Don't say I didn't try to warn you.

Attitude: It isn't fair.

Ω Ω Ω

Scoping out Scorpio. . .

♏ Scorpio: The Scorpion

October 24 - November 22
Ruling Planet: Pluto (anciently Mars)

Scorpios are born between October 24 and November 22 and reside in the zodiacal 8th House of sex, death and other people's money. You think I'm kidding. I'm not. There really is a House that covers those areas and Scorpio is the ruling sign. Think of all the Scorpios you know and I'll bet you'll be able to name at least one who truly belong there. The others either have mitigating aspects which soften their demeanor, channel their energy in more positive ways, or simply maintain a better façade. For example, Julia Roberts, Meg Ryan, Jamie Lee Curtis and Sally Field are Scorpios. So are John Cleese, Danny DeVito, Kevin Kline and Leonardo DiCaprio. Likewise, General David Petraeus and Bill Gates. So far so good. Then we have Hillary Clinton. My ex. And Charles Manson.

Get the idea? These people know how to get what they want, whether or not it's in a socially acceptable fashion, and if you give it some thought you should be able to associate each of them with at least one of the 8th House categories without too much trouble. The 8th is also the house of transformations, which definitely fits Gates, and possibly by ex, who certainly transformed me into a, uh, not so nice person. Okay, I admit you ladies may not find Cleese or DeVito a sex symbol or know my ex; if that's the case maybe you can put them in the "death" category, *i.e.* you'd rather die.

23

On the other hand if you've ever seen the old 80s classic, "Ruthless People," DeVito was a perfect example of his birth sign as someone who married for money then tries to kill her off. And then there's Cleese as Archie in *"A Fish Called Wanda"* where he got the girl (Jamie Lee Curtis) away from Otto, played by fellow Scorpion, Kevin Kline. Maybe that's a bit of a push, but you get the idea; they certainly were convincing in those roles.

Scorpio is represented by the scorpion, grey lizard or eagle, depending on the Scorpio in question. They can soar with the eagles, like many of the examples above, crawl with the lizards or sting like a scorpion. Granted most of them are wonderful people, but consider yourself warned with regard to that handful of individuals who aren't quite so civilized. Besides, the darker side is much more interesting. So let's go there. Much of this derives from the fact that their ruling planet is Pluto. God of the Underworld. Not a nice person. Secrets are their natural domain. They'll have plenty of their own and a tremendous interest in yours. And don't think for a minute that you can keep them tightly locked away. Scorpios have this sixth sense that guides them right, straight to the heart of anything covert, the juicier the better. They probably invented blackmail, even if they do it with a smile.

Most Scorpios have a libido that competes with the output from Hoover Dam and sex appeal that emanates like Chernobyl. If you don't believe that, look back at some of the names at the top. No, it doesn't have to be dark and sultry, but it's there, no matter how innocent the package. Unless they direct that energy elsewhere, they need sex like Taurus needs land, Libra needs fairness and Capricorn needs status. If they're not getting what they need, expect them to be either very sulky or very grumpy. In extreme cases it might even fuel their natural ruthlessness to a drive for power that makes others' heads spin. That energy has to go somewhere, and the Moon Sign and Ascendant can give some clue where. I knew a Scorpio manager who had a large, ceramic urn in his office that said *"Ashes of Former Employees"*. I'm not sure that anyone ever had the nerve to look inside to see whether or not it was a joke.

It's interesting that Scorpio is a Water Sign. The other water signs make sense, *i.e.* Pisces the Fish and Cancer the Crab. Scorpions as well as gray lizards, the last I checked, lived in the desert and eagles usually live in the mountains, though they do like to fish. There is no question that Scorpios are driven by their emotions, but they're significantly different than the others. Fish may nip at you (even though some of them are like piranha) and the Crab may pinch you with his or her claw trying to hang on, but Scorpio can put you out for the count with one sting of the tail.

About the only sign that is consistently stronger is Taurus, and that's questionable. As polar opposites in the Zodiac, both are Fixed signs that can wait a long, long time to wreak that revenge. In other words, if you tangle with a Scorpio you are likely to be stung sooner or later. They don't like to lose. And while they have deep emotions, they will use them differently than Fish or Crabs. They get hurt like anyone else, but in most cases these folks believe in the old adage, *"Don't get mad, get even."* And if that's the case they'll use that emotional energy to get it, no matter what the cost. As previously mentioned, they're a Fixed Sign, meaning they're not likely to get over it anytime soon and all you have to remember about Water Signs is that their namesake sculpted the Grand Canyon.

The third major element of their resident House is death. This includes inheritances. And this, of course, ties into the "other people's money" part. This is not to say that they're lazy, but if they can latch on to someone else's assets they will in a second. My experience with Scorpios has included a sucking sensation on my wallet. What's theirs is theirs, and what's yours is theirs. I have seen a Scorpio actually open and close their fingers at the sight of $1,000.00 dollars in cash. Like Taurus, their polar sign, and Leo a square away, they like nice things and if they can get someone else to give them what they want, they won't hesitate to take it. They're intense and have a remarkable amount of charisma. They usually don't hesitate to speak their mind, unless it's to their advantage to remain silent. Remember what I said earlier about secrets. They make extremely good friends and equally fierce enemies; you decide which side you want to be on.

One other thing about Pluto you need to know is that it rules obsession. Depending on where it is in your Natal Chart or which House it's transiting at the time, you could find yourself obsessing on the affected areas. As their ruling planet, Scorpios need to guard themselves carefully to avoid obsessions that lead to addictions, bankruptcy, or other self-defeating behaviors. Getting themselves set on a negative path is what can make the difference between a grey lizard and an eagle. Another difference can be whether they derive energy from pity or admiration. This dysfunctionality is not a problem exclusive to Scorpios, but since they can do obsession so well, they need to be extra careful. They like power and will take it wherever they find it, albeit gently, which could manifest as either the perfect victim or a tyrant, depending on their motivation.

Remember that none of this is intended to say that (most) Scorpios are not nice people. They just have a hidden side, perhaps even from themselves. You may never see it, but the potential is there. They're very kind and giving to those they care about and make very dedicated parents. However, one important thing to remember if you're in a relationship with a Scorpio is that just because they smack you upside the head with that tail occasionally doesn't necessarily mean they don't love you. That reaction may be lightning fast, like stepping on a scorpion in the middle of the night. Just make sure you never make the switch permanently over to those they disdain or perceive as an enemy. If you do, you're bound to get stung sooner or later. It may take a while, but rest assured the surety is right up there with death and taxes.

Attitude: A sucker is born every minute.

Ω Ω Ω

There's something about Sagittarius. . .

♐ Sagittarius: The Archer

November 23 - December 21
Ruling Planet: Jupiter

Those born under the sign of Sagittarius come into this life between November 23 and December 21. As a Mutable Fire Sign they tend to be all over the map. Literally, since Sagittarius is what the 9th House of long distance travel, legal matters, beliefs (including politics and religion) and higher education calls home. Foreign cultures and microcosms fascinate them, particularly those that involve celebrities such as actors or astronauts.

Like all Fire Signs, Sagittarians have, shall we say, a strong ego. Throw Jupiter on there as a ruling planet and you have one that can easily become over-inflated. Perhaps the reason they're represented by an Archer is a subtle reminder albeit warning that an appropriately placed arrow could quickly render them into a state of rapid decompression, kind of like a balloon.

Conversely, they like to take pot shots at people, in a figurative if not literal sense. Archers like to think that they're smarter than the rest of us and in many cases they are. They don't live in the House of higher education for nothing. Even those with only a mediocre education have the knack of projecting a persona that bespeaks someone who has a high degree of knowledge. They may even be able to convince you that they do, but often it is no more than a bunch of, well, hot air. They're not actually lying, because in most cases they really believe that they're exceptionally intelligent. But before you place any bets, much less do something like hire this person, make sure their references check out.

There are exceptions, of course, particularly if they have a Moon or Ascendant in an Earth Sign such as Taurus. The heavy emotional punch of the Water Signs as an Ascendant or Moon could likewise cause some conflicts. Fire and Water. Do the math. Otherwise they may start to come down to Earth when they progress into Capricorn. If they have heavy Air influences and spend a significant amount of time in Sagittarius before they get to Capricorn, say their late twenties, they're probably going to have a lot of damage to undo before settling down in life.

They are likely to be experts on some esoterical subject such as the mating habits of the dung beetle, which leads you to believe that they must be well versed in more mundane subjects as well. Not so. Much like Gemini's, a single subject doesn't hold their attention for long so they'll have all these trivial bits of knowledge they carry around that they picked up on the History Channel for the express purpose of impressing people like you. Aries believe they're invincible, Leos believe they're royalty and Sagittarians believe they're intellectually superior. Key word here is *believe*. It's up to you to figure out whether or not this is true.

Jupiter tends to expand anything it touches and usually not in a bad way. It's the planet of luck and is usually prominent in those who do things like win the lottery. Similarly, Sagittarians tend to be lucky, but conversely they also tend to be clumsy. Not good for someone toting a bow and arrow. If you wonder what it's like to be an Archer you can come close by taking in more than your usual amount of caffeine. If you don't do caffeine and don't plan to, you can get the same idea from an old CD that skips or gets stuck. They may think they're clever and witty but from your side of the conversation there seem to be huge chunks missing. Trust

27

me, it isn't you that's missing something. It's this same lack of attention to detail that will cause them to trip over something in plain sight, fall off a roof or drive into a wall. *Ooops.*

They may also express their intellectual superiority by waxing philosophical and expressing ideologies that are more accurately labeled as *idiotogies*. Note that besides legal matters, politics are also included in the 9th House. Politicians--need I say more? A slightly less illustrious occupation than these in which they'd also excel would be a con man, which is only a slightly less civilized version of the same thing.

Nonetheless, they usually attract large circles of friends, though they are seldom that close to any one person. They can be very entertaining, particularly at a party, but they're not exactly known for delivering on their promises or persevering to the end of that huge project, though they may come in quite handy during the brainstorming phase. Several of their friends exist simply because they were duped into thinking that the Sagittarian is smart or important and that it is to their advantage to cultivate such friends for future reference. Thus, these people tend to deserve each other and play many silly games back and forth before one or the other wises up or gets tired and moves on.

All in all, Sagittarians are a handful. They can be exceptionally bright and if they use their natural abilities and apply some common sense and perseverance they can accomplish amazing things. Just make sure you check those references and think twice before turning your back on someone represented by an Archer. They're depicted with the bow and arrow for a reason and whatever it is, don't take any chances on finding out why the hard way.

Attitude: Sometimes I amaze even myself.

Ω Ω Ω

A salute to Capricorn...

♑ Capricorn: The Goat

December 22 - January 20
Ruling Planet: Saturn

Capricorns are born between December 22 - January 20. For those in the Northern Hemisphere, that is the darkest, coldest time of year. As if that's not bad enough, these unfortunate souls are ruled by Saturn, the most serious, wizened, staunch and even stuffy planet we know of and so aptly personified by that decrepit Father Time seen so often around New Years. No wonder people get drunk on New Years Eve. And as a friend of mine so often remarks to those with a negative spin, "It must suck to be you."

In response, I must admit that, yes, indeed it does. And I can say that with authority because I'm a Capricorn.

The astrological icon for Capricorn is the goat, or more specifically the sea goat. And no doubt the expression "old goat" originated to describe a Capricorn. We are grumpy, mean, serious, taciturn, authoritarian, power hungry, social climbers.

And proud of it, I might add.

We reside in the zodiacal 10th House of community standing and all that hoopla. We like to feel important. We don't necessarily like a lot of attention or fanfare, but we want to be appreciated and respected and we don't mind working hard to get there. After all, goats are known for climbing mountains. (They're also known for eating tin cans and the neighbor's tulips, but we won't go there. Actually, goats are picky eaters. I know because I had one once. Her name was Geraldine and she and my ex didn't get along. He'd be out there milking her at o'dark:30 in 20 below weather and when he was done she'd look him in the eye and deliberately put her foot in the bucket. We didn't have her for long. Oddly enough, that really was typical Capricorn behavior....)

If you look in a Capricorn's closet, most likely you'll see a lot of black. This isn't because the light is out, but because we like wearing dark colors. I don't know why. Maybe it goes back to being born in the dead of winter, though I'm not sure that's it, either, because with Christmas and the other holidays around that time you'd think we'd like red and green. Which, actually, I do. But I do wear a lot of black. And look good in it, too, which is kind of scary. Believe me, I get more compliments when I wear black than any other color, and of course that reinforces it. It has other advantages as well. It doesn't show dirt and it hides those extra pounds I put on between Thanksgiving and New Years. Yes, if there's one thing we are, it's practical. Saturn sees to that.

In case you haven't already guessed, we're also known for our dark sense of humor. At least we have one, buried though it may be, and we do know how to use it. I can't tell a joke as well as an Aries or Aquarius and the laughs I evoke aren't the hee-haw, knee-slapping kind of wit, but I can make people laugh when they need it most. Like in the middle of a long, dry meeting, at tax time or even a funeral. Those times when you don't know whether to laugh or cry are when I'll make you laugh. As an Earth sign, I'm more comfortable with cool logic than outward displays of emotions. I have them but don't like to admit it. So when situations get tense, I try to lighten things up.

There have been times when there's this wet stuff leaking from my eyes and I'll be accused of crying but I'll firmly declare that it's my allergies, contact lenses or the jalapeno juice I got on my hands fixing dinner. I was at a farewell luncheon in a Mexican restaurant for someone I'd worked with for roughly ten years and we became very good friends. A couple of times I could feel it coming on, but when the conversation started getting too sentimental I simply declared to everyone present not to go there and then pretended it was the hot sauce. Since I was the boss I could do that.

Lots of us are bosses, by the way. We're hardworking, dependable and barring a troublesome ascendant, usually pretty low maintenance as an employee. We also don't mind responsibility, so usually wind up with plenty. We seldom have anything handed to us. That's the way it is when you're ruled by Saturn, but we also have the tenacity and perseverance it takes to wear others down and eventually get where we want to go. And that about sums it up.

I'm not sure this qualifies as a salute, but then there are numerous definitions of "salute," some of which can't be included here. But the fact of the matter is that Capricorns carry more than their share of the weight of the world and do it well, in spite of the creaky joints we inevitably acquire as we age. I guess that's the price we pay for climbing all those mountains.

So the next time you're at some festive event, find a Capricorn and give that goat a great, big smile. Better yet, a hug, if you dare. If you don't know where to find one, try that person in the corner working frantically on a laptop, even if it's their daughter's wedding. And if that doesn't work, try that one over there with the Edgar Allen Poe smile. You know, the one over there. The one all dressed in black.

Attitude: Nothing beats the view at the top.

Ω Ω Ω

A toast to Aquarius...

♒ *Aquarius: The Water Bearer*

January 21 - February 18
Ruling Planet: Uranus
(Ancient Ruler - Saturn)

Aquarians are born between January 21 - February 18 and reside in the zodiacal 11th House of friends, groups, hopes and wishes. Their modern Sign Ruler is Uranus, planet of unexpected events, surprises, disruptions, sudden change, breaking free, pathfinding and when required, rebellion. Of course people make a lot of bad jokes about this planet's name, largely because they don't know how to pronounce it properly, which is yur-*on*-us. I have to admit that I've gotten a few laughs out of it myself, especially with an article put out by NASA some years ago. If you read no more than the title, i.e., "NASA's Hubble Discovers New Rings and Moons Around Uranus," I'm sure you'll understand why I found it amusing, tacky though it may be, but I digress. Traditional astrology which dates back prior to the discovery of Uranus assigned Saturn as the ruler of Aquarius, which is where they get their hardworking, dependable nature. However, most Aquarians have a certain spark and need for freedom that defies Saturn's restrictive and conventional nature.

Those of us who have been around for about a half-century or so remember being serenaded back in the 60s that we were at the "dawning of the Age of Aquarius." This song was written for a play in which the actors and actresses in one particular scene ditched all their clothes and stood on stage completely in the buff. As I recall, it was banned in Boston, which was a lot less liberal then than it is now. Mardi Gras, which is held every year when the Sun is in Aquarius, also somehow reflects the same basic idea.

I don't know how familiar you are with *Mardi Gras*, but it generally personifies any form of decadence known to mankind. It originated as the last, big bash before the period observed by the Catholic Church called Lent, which starts the next day, Ash Wednesday. From then until Easter they're supposed to abstain from various pleasantries so they make sure they get all they can the day before, which translated from the French becomes, "Fat Tuesday." And this celebration, which has been going on for centuries, has duly captured the undisciplined and spontaneous spirit of Aquarius taken to the extreme.

So what exactly constitutes an Aquarian? Are they really that weird? Does the fact that they're ruled by Uranus reflect in their daily lives? In my professional opinion, I would say yes, but that is not to say that they all thrive on decadence or are not delightful; quite the contrary. There are exceptions, of course, but any sign taken to the extreme is going to result in someone who is seriously weird.

Aquarians tend to be "people persons." They thrive on interaction with others and dislike being alone. These are the folks that turn on the TV or radio when they're home alone because they don't like too much quiet. Being into people and group interactions, their lives are dedicated to others and humanitarian causes. Of course there are numerous ways this manifests itself. Someone who's exceptionally interested in others can also be the local Gossip Guru. If you know a family, neighborhood or office gossip, there's a good chance they've got some strong Aquarian in their chart. This person will always know exactly what is going on in everyone's life and actually be interested in it. Undoubtedly, an Aquarian invented soap operas, probably because there wasn't enough going on in their own life, so they had to make something up.

As an Air Sign they tell great stories, often embellishing them with expressions and gestures that make them the life of the party. In fact, it's probably *their* party. Aquarians tend to be the heart of any group, often being the one who brought it together in the first place.

Aquarians are also the ones who'll dedicate their lives to some cause for the betterment of mankind. The 30 years I spent as an Aquarian I was borderline obsessively involved with groups.

[NOTE:--Okay, I know at this point some of you are really wondering how I spent 30 years as an Aquarian when I already admitted I was a Capricorn. Granted, that's gotta sound even weirder than you already believe astrologers are in the first place. No, I'm not talking about some previous life and I promise I'm not making this up. It happens to everyone. Really. Trust me. It will start to make sense when you get to the section on Progressed Charts.]

Sorry for digressing, *again*. It's got to be that Gemini Moon of mine. Anyway, to continue, during that time I put an astounding amount of time into community service-type activities. I did everything from serve as a Boy Scout Merit Badge Counselor to a public affairs director for a church, all without any kind of pay or credit other than the personal rewards for being involved. I would work 8 hours in my day job and then come home at night, feed the family and then spend several more hours in the evening on these other projects. And I actually wondered why everyone else wasn't as dedicated as I. And said so, endearing me to any number of people—not!

Now that I've stepped out of Aquarius into Pisces, I couldn't care less about any of that stuff and my family gives me all the group interaction I need. But Aquarians need to be part of a group. Not society as a whole, because they're usually unconventional if not rebels of one sort or another, but they require an identity that goes outside themselves and connects with others, even if they're far from the mainstream.

Aquarius is a Fixed sign, *i.e.*, one of those that resists change. This is interesting since their ruling planet is the planet of surprises, change, rebellion, and unexpected events. It also rules innovation and inventions. So this appears a bit of a dichotomy until you think about it in a more personal manner. These people do not change who and what they are. What you see is what you get. Oftentimes they have very unconventional, even rebellious, ideas. These ideas are not going to

33

change anytime soon. And they'd rather attempt to change the entire world to fit their view of it than change themselves. So while they may be agents of change, they are not going to change as individuals. What this means to you is if you're related to an Aquarius or in a relationship with one is don't waste your time or breath trying to get them to change. It ain't gonna happen.

What greater personification of an agent of change than a wizard or some other magical being, such as Tinkerbell waving her magic wand? Many Aquarians even have a certain look about them--a slant to their eyes, pointy ears, or upward slope to their nose-- which makes them easy to imagine in an elf's cap. They often dress a bit differently, also, like the social rebels they are, perhaps mixing patterns or colors that most people wouldn't even put together in the washing machine. Some people flat-out can't match their clothes because they aren't artistic, were never taught the basics of color coordination by their mothers or in some cases are male, but Aquarians do it on purpose to show they're different. (If they have a conservative ascendant this won't be the case. However, someone with an Aquarius ascendant might, since your ascendant determines your outward appearance.)

The thing to remember is that these are the very folks who are looking out for the world, at least their small corner in it, and will do what they can to change it as required. Just never themselves.

Attitude: I'll drink to that!

Ω Ω Ω

The world according to Pisces. . .

♓ Pisces: The Fishes

February 19 - March 20
Ruling Planet: Neptune
(Ancient Ruler - Jupiter)

Pisces are born between February 19 - March 20 and are represented by the 12th House, which comprises the collective consciousness, transcendence, and other hidden elements. It also relates to inner struggles, anxiety, cares and limitations as well as prisons, convents and hospitals, implying seclusion and limitation.

And more than likely insanity, though no one wants to come right out and say so. However, I'm trying to tell it like it is, so I'll go ahead and say it because it needs to be said. This is not to say that all Pisces are not nice people. Most of them are. Nonetheless, to use a favorite expression of a good friend of mine, (okay, a VERY good friend...) *"they're not wrapped too tight."* (My Virgo ascendant tells me that grammatically that should be "tightly", but you get the idea.)

This is most likely because they are a Water sign and therefore usually drowning in a sea of emotions. These people feel things that normal people only have nightmares about. And being as they're drowning most of the time, they're short on oxygen to the brain and more than likely waterlogged, so therefore don't think the same as the rest of us. This is not to say that they're stupid, only that everything looks different under water.

If you've ever really looked at a fish tank or into a brook or stream, you know that water distorts things. This is because the index of refraction of water if different than air. Have you ever stepped into a stream that looks like it's only a foot or so deep and the water came up to your thighs or even higher? Welcome to the world of Pisces. And even though all of us are made up of 90% water or so, our fishy friends must be 95%. Something must explain why they're like they are, because they are definitely different.

Appropriately enough, these folks are ruled by the planet, Neptune. The symbol for this planet is easier to remember than most because it looks like Neptune's trident. So the fishes of the Zodiac are ruled by Neptune, which ought to be pretty easy to remember for those of you who are trying to learn this stuff. Neptune influences fantasies, dreams, imagination, intuition and, on the negative side, deception. In a nutshell, kind of like looking at everything through a wall of water. If you've ever really fallen for a really big lie, you can bet that Neptune was messing with your chart somewhere.

Female Pisceans contain more water than most people and therefore leak a lot, usually in the form of tears. They cry when they're sad, they cry when they're happy, they cry when they're angry and they cry because they can't find their other aqua sock. Even the males of the species are

35

a bit more sentimental than those native to other signs. Male fish epitomize the "Mr. Sensitive Guy" description quite well and make great friends because of it. However, their emotionalism is shown more in their deep reaction to situations that Air or Earth signs would shrug off. Male and female fish alike are very intuitive, often to the point of being psychic.

Pisces is also a Mutable sign, meaning that they're adaptable. At least that's the polite term. Unstable would be another possibility, depending on the other aspects in their chart. Throw a Cancer moon or a Scorpio ascendant at a fish and you'd better get busy building an ark. You'll need it to save yourself from drowning with them in that sea of emotion. If they have a Mutable Grand Cross or Grand Water Trine, look out. Run, don't walk, to the nearest exit. At their best they can be caring, nurturing and intuitively meet your every need. At their worst, they'll read your thoughts and use them against you to deceive and use you in every imaginable way.

Since Pisceans reside in the Universal 12th House which includes the Land of Nirvana, they are frequently driven by the need to merge with the collective consciousness or seek emotional or spiritual highs. This can include a tendency toward alcohol or drug abuse, though this need is often expressed in less destructive ways. In fact, there is nothing more determined than a Pisces who knows what he or she wants. Many of them seek these glimpses of another existence through such things as yoga. Other routes are possible via seemingly worldly activities. These can include extreme sports, whether it happens to be running marathons or mountain climbing.

Some even seek their thrills via their career, such as in the military or other high-risk occupation, or simply immerse themselves in learning. Escape through novels and movies are also a favorite. The chosen area for expression will be apparent by other aspects in their chart, such as their Moon sign, placement of Mars, Jupiter and so forth. They aren't necessarily competitive *per se*; more likely they're simply trying to prove something to themselves that will result in some kind of a buzz.

At any rate, life with a Pisces will never be dull. Fish are hard to know. What you see is not what you get. They don't deliberately try to deceive you, they just have to put on a facade to survive on dry land and are probably totally different than you think. No matter how much of a hard-ass they make out to be, I promise you they're not. However, don't think that Pisceans are weak because they're emotional. Remember that sharks and piranha are also fish. They're very persistent and masters at using emotional manipulation to get what they want.

If you know a Pisces who doesn't fit this description at all, there are a couple possible explanations. First of all, if they have a Moon, Ascendant or stellium in one or more Earth signs they'll appear much more normal since they'll be spending at least part of their time out of the water, on a figurative island, so to speak. Heavy Air sign influences will probably only make them talk more, which usually confirms the statement above about their not being "wrapped too tight." Air in water creates bubbles and you'll see lots of them. Fire signs...well, you know how it is with fire and water. And if they have more water signs in their Big Three, (i.e. Sun Sign, Moon Sign and Ascendant), that would have the same basic affect as adding a surfactant to water. Forget the ark and build a spaceship.

The other primary reason that a native Pisces may not fit this description is because they have progressed into Aries (see section on Progressed Charts if you haven't already). There are no signs that are more diverse than Pisces and Aries and when they make the switch it's likely to be like black and white, night and day, Dr. Jekyll and Mr. Hyde. No doubt the Sirens in Greek mythology were Pisceans making the transition to Aries.

Conversely, when someone progresses into Pisces they will likewise find themselves in an entirely new space. In other words, someone can go from a genuine bad ass war hero to someone who gets sentimental over some pretty silly stuff. I've seen it happen and it's scary. Really scary. Finding yourself suddenly afloat in a sea of emotion can be a daunting experience. Trust me, I've been there.

Coming or going, Pisces is a different place to be. If you must be around a Pisces, or if you happen to be one yourself, either by birth or progression, all I can recommend is a strong lifejacket, swimming lessons and in extreme cases a SCUBA tank. Just know that at some point you're going to get wet, either because they're crying on your shoulder or they're holding you under water. It may still not be too late to build that ark...

Attitude: Visualize whirled peas.

☽ MOON SIGNS

Your Moon Sign drives your emotions and how you react to them based on the sign the Moon was in when you were born. The Moon moves quickly, spending about two and a half days in each zodiac sign and thus can be in more than one sign on a given day. If you were born on one of those days when it changed signs you need your birth time to know for certain what your Moon Sign is, though it is often fairly easy to figure out based on your emotional nature.

If your Moon Sign is not compatible with your Sun Sign or extremely different, you will be a bit of a dichotomy. For example, in the simplest terms, if you're an Aries with a Pisces Moon, you will be a compassionate warrior; if you're a Capricorn with a Libra Moon you'll be a fair authority figure; if you're a Taurus with a Gemini Moon you'll be set in your ways but willing to listen logically; you may be a patient, easy going Pisces but if you have a Leo Moon you'll surprise everyone with an occasional flare of temper when you're upset, etc.

In other words, the sign placement of your Moon will give you an emotional nature that reflects the general characteristics of that sign. What follow are some brief descriptions of how the Moon might act in respective signs.

You'll notice an occasional mention of a "progressed" Moon Sign. You need to read the section on progressed charts to fully understand that statement but the short version is that your Moon Sign changes every two and a half years. This makes a considerable difference in your emotional nature but few know what is going on when it occurs. Sometimes it's not that noticeable and others it is, particularly if the Moon Sign is substantially different by nature than your Sun Sign or Natal Moon. For example, if you're usually a logical, unemotional sort of person who suddenly finds him or herself being overly sentimental or crying more than usual, the odds are quite high that your Moon Sign just changed into a Water Sign such as Cancer or Pisces. I have given that information to more than one client over the years who was tremendously relieved there was a reason for it and that they were not going off the deep end.

That is why I share this information, so you'll understand yourself better as well as how to use the astronomical influences in a way that promote your growth and well-being.

Ω Ω Ω

♈ Aries Moon

If you have an Aries Moon, either natally or by progression, more than likely you are an outgoing person. At least that's what you're called in polite company. Chances are you're called something else behind your back. You're a natural show-off and when you really get on to something, you'll ride it until you either fall off or it drops dead beneath you.

You have lots of friends, or at least you think you do, though only a select few people really know you. You don't like disappointments and if they occur, you'll blame everyone and everything, including the dog, other than accept the blame yourself. The thought that you could do something wrong is incomprehensible and shakes you to the core. You're impulsive and make a career of hating yourself in the morning. You tend to burn your bridges and then be totally surprised when this bites you later.

If your Sun Sign is an Earth element, an Aries Moon will give you what it takes to walk over the top of anyone who gets in your way while you're pursuing your many goals and ambitions. If your Sun is in an Air element, it will make your more aggressive in a verbal sense, which usually alienates you from those who could possibly help you. It also contributes to you being even more likely to offer your opinion before you figure out whether or not it is backed up by logic.

For those with their Sun in a Water element, an Aries Moon will give you yet another emotional dimension. Rather than react with a show of humble emotion to a disappointing event you're more likely to strike out at everyone and everything first. Then when you realize that everyone either has their hands over their ears or has left the scene, you'll back-pedal to a "woe is me!" stance and try to garner all the sympathy you can.

If you Sun Sign is a Fire element, an Aries Moon will simply give you a bit more punch and exacerbate those over-stated qualities you already know how to exploit. You're likely to be considered egocentric and a high maintenance individual, so if you want to maintain any friendships or positive relationships you'll have to realize that your glorious presence alone is not necessarily enough to sustain them. Make it a point to LISTEN once in a while and at least try to become a part of someone else's world.

When emotionally aroused, in polite company you are considered "spirited" and possibly "eccentric" while is less formal circles you are feared for your temper and ego-centricity. A vast majority of people may think of you as a body part associated with the planet, Uranus. Nonetheless, others admire the fact that you usually manage to get what you want. Aries do well with an outlet for their excess energy. This should be a sport or activity that doesn't involve physical harm to others, no matter how satisfying that may be.

If you have an Aries Moon by progression it will last approximately two and a half years, which is usually long enough to really accomplish something while you have all that energy and optimism. If there is something you'd really like to do with your life, this is a good time to get to it, but don't waste any time. When your Moon slips into Taurus your entire attitude is going to relax and while you'll be very interested in your bank balance at that time, your drive to do something dramatic is going to diminish substantially.

So take advantage of it while it lasts, realizing it's not permanent, which may actually be very good news to those around you who wonder what's gotten into you lately.

Ω Ω Ω

♉ Taurus Moon

Your Moon Sign drives your emotions and how you react to them. Thus, a Taurus Moon will give you the emotional qualities associated with the sign, Taurus. You'll be patient and take your time deciding how you feel about something, which is not always a good thing. Not everyone is on your time table and kingdoms may rise and fall in the time it takes you to figure out whether you're going to ask someone out on a second date. Windows of opportunity close from time to time and you may find yourself bumping your nose on the glass more often than not.

On the positive side, you're non-reactive and stable so you operate well in a crisis when everyone else is running in circles wondering what to do. Remember that Taurus is an Earth sign, which imbues practicality and logic. These traits will be reflected in your emotional nature and if you become emotionally involved with a Fire or Water sign they may become frustrated with the fact you approach relationships in a logical way compared to them. In other words, your head will rule your heart, which can cause problems. You are likely to think they're emotional and should get a grip and they're likely to think that you're cold and unfeeling.

Further clues to what to expect can be found in the Compatibility section for the specific signs or the section that describes Figurative Elemental Reactions. The one saving grace is that Taurus is ruled by Venus and therefore has a certain inherent inclination toward being romantic. You like (possibly even live for) good food and drink. Thus, whether you're a male or female, a romantic dinner is likely to be one of your favorite dates. However, you may have a tendency to really do the comfort food thing and as a result you may have to watch your weight.

You also like a pleasant, aesthetic environment. You value nice things and in spite of your patience, appreciate peace, quiet and order. Comfort is important to you and you like soft fabrics and comfortable shoes. Whether or not they're stylish or not is irrelevant. You'll buy quality items, most likely on sale, and then wear them until they're worn out. The same goes for furniture. Comfort and a nice appearance mean a lot, even though your frugal side may not have a problem getting through college in a studio apartment furnished with floor pillows and shelving units from IKEA or even the local thrift shop, as long as none of it is actual junk. Most likely those pillows will wind up in your summer home someday and those shelves will be in your garage until you die.

Taurus is a Fixed Sign and doesn't like change. Once you make up your mind, that's it and you don't want to revisit the issue. This is a nice theory, but in reality not the most practical. Situations change whether you like it or not so make sure you learn to recognize when it's time to do something a little differently. Along these same lines of not changing your mind, if someone upsets you in any way you'll bear a grudge forever, long after you've forgotten what happened. This is another relationship *faux pas* that will cause significant problems. With a Taurus Moon you don't necessarily avail yourself to all those logical Earth Sign traits found in the Sun Sign, but you need to muster all the logic you can in these situations and decide whether the benefits are worth the cost.

Remember also that Taurus is the Zodiacal Second House of possessions, which includes your values and body, by the way. As such, you will tend to be very possessive of people as well as things. You need to be careful that you don't impose your will on those around you as you would a pet. Taurus is known for its tendency to be stubborn and this can be a significant problem with emotional issues where you may well cut off your nose to spite your face before giving in to something you don't agree with. Learning to listen and being willing to work toward a compromise will do much toward maintaining that peaceful environment you like so well. No matter how comfortable that couch may be, you probably won't particularly enjoy sleeping on it.

When your Moon Sign enters Taurus by Progression it will be noticeable to you as well as everyone else. This is because the previous sign is Aries and there are obvious differences. Generally, everyone will be pleasantly surprised that all of a sudden you've calmed down significantly. However, that Mars energy and enthusiasm will also wane, making laziness and procrastination more likely. But don't worry, a few years down the road when you slip into Gemini all that energy will return with a vengeance.

Ω Ω Ω

♊ Gemini Moon

A Gemini Moon will endow a person with an emotional makeup similar to a fox terrier. They bark and jump around a lot, but the bulk of it is largely air. This doesn't mean they won't bite, only that they'll distract easily and move on to something else once they get bored. They're loyal, enthusiastic and generally optimistic. While they can get depressed like anyone else, their natural demeanor doesn't show it.

As a Mutable Sign, change comes easily and emotions and feelings are no exception. A person with a Gemini Moon can be caught in an emotional maelstrom that would make *Romeo and Juliet* look like a comedy yet pack it all up and make a professional presentation to a boardroom full of humorless investors without batting an eye. Air Signs employ logic in their feeling as well as thinking and have a remarkable ability to use reason to control their emotions when the necessity arises. This does not mean to say that they don't have or acknowledge them. Since they like to talk (and I mean *talk*), you are likely to get a very detailed description of how and what they feel, even though their demeanor and expression will be roughly the same as if they were describing the weather.

Oddly enough, Gemini Moon people often display more overt emotion over a sad song, movie or news story than their own life. They'll react, sometimes strongly, to these stimuli, yet often display little visible emotion when dealing with a personal crisis. They appear very unemotional and compared to others, especially Water Signs, they are. They are likewise uncomfortable if someone has a meltdown or other dramatic display of emotion without substantial provocation. This is not to say they don't feel anything, because they do, but it is an order of magnitude less intense that more emotional signs. They have a remarkable ability to talk to themselves, reason things out and rationalize their reaction so as to control their response, at least visibly. If someone is having an emotional crisis they're very likely to respond with a simple *"Get over it."*

These folks require a lot of intellectual stimulation and are likely to be most attracted to those that can provide it. If they're with a partner who is more interested in smelling the flowers along the path of life they're likely to become bored and unless they can get sufficient mental orgasms elsewhere are very likely to move on to someone they find more interesting.

The Gemini duality of personality applies as well. They have multiple personas and it's often difficult for others to adjust to them. You just never known whom you might be dealing with today, which can be very frustrating to just about anyone unless they have strong Gemini in their own chart and understand the concept. We're not necessarily talking moods here, like you might see in a Cancer, but actual different personalities. They are often most comfortable with two "different lives" whether they're defined by work or distance, i.e. traveling a lot for the job or a weekend home that defines an entirely different life style.

Someone with a natal Gemini Moon is going to be rather appalled by Sign changes in their Sun and Moon Signs relative to their Progressed Chart. As they move through the Water signs in particular and find themselves in a sea of emotion they will be utterly astounded by the feelings that come upon them and wonder why they can't subrogate them with logic as they did before. This will be particularly uncomfortable and the cause of much frustration as they realize that others actually cannot control their feelings as well as they thought they could. Those progressing into a

43

Gemini Moon, especially those who are natives to a Water Sign moon, will enjoy the sense of control they now have and their newfound ability to analyze situations more objectively which they hadn't enjoyed before.

Ω Ω Ω

♋ Cancer Moon

A Cancer Moon brings a double whammy since Cancer is actually ruled by the Moon. Since the Moon chugs through the entire Zodiac every single month, moods are a natural result as it traverses each Sign and conjuncts virtually every planet on a person's chart in the process. While this happens to everyone, for those with a Cancer Moon, they will feel as if they are being yanked hither and yon much more than others because there is a direct link to their emotions. For those that must be around these people, the term "hormonal" has multiple daily applications.

Cancer is a Water Sign and thus ruled by emotion as opposed to logic. They will go with their heart versus their head every time and marvel that anyone else could see things differently. These folks feel things with an intensity that is an order of magnitude beyond Air or Earth Signs. Fire Signs are likewise emotional, but in a different way. Their emotions are more likely to be expressed dramatically and with an overtone of anger and indignation whereas Water Signs are much more empathic and sympathetic with the females very prone to tears, whether they're happy or sad. Males tend to show their emotions differently, often by being visibly more sensitive, animated, and sometimes whiney, grumpy and prone to considerable complaints if someone hurts their feelings. On the downside, these folks like all others with their Moon in a Water Sign, have no problem getting what they want by guilting you out or using various other forms of emotional manipulation.

Cancer is the Zodiacal Fourth House which rules the home environment. Thus, a Cancer Moon creates a very strong emotional bond with one's family. That umbilical just didn't get severed and they like it that way. There is no going for days much less weeks or months without talking to family members for these folks. They feel a strong connection and obligation to family, whether or not they actually like them. Their identity is heavily tied to their roots and their loyalty is exceptionally deep. Try to separate a Crab from his or her family and you'll get a whole new appreciation for those claws. They'll also be very wrapped up in their home itself. Time, effort and creative energy will largely be directed toward the home and making it more comfortable.

A Cancer Moon will also provide an inclination to bond with others whom are essentially "invited" into their family circle. This happens particularly at work, which is somewhat like family anyway. Think about it. There are numerous similarities. You cannot choose your family or your coworkers (unless you're the boss or own the company), you need to pull together to be successful and you spend a lot of time together whether you like it or not.

Having a boss with a Cancer Moon is probably a good thing. They are very likely to care about you as a person as well as an employee plus protect and defend you more fiercely than your Earth or Air Sign mother. On the negative side, they may tend to get a bit too involved in your personal life and be much more intrusive in that area than you'd like. They also may expect you to feel as attached to them as they do to you. Furthermore, not everyone treats their family fairly and sometimes the expectations are a little high because of the loyalty and dedication they expect in return. Your Cancer Sun or Moon Sign coworkers are those sympathetic listeners who give lots of hugs and will do anything to help you feel better when you're upset or stressed.

This is a difficult place to be by Progression for those with Natal Moons in the Earth or Air Signs. The sudden overwhelming emotional assault is frustrating and mystifying. They are likely to wonder what is wrong with them and why they suddenly seem to be crying all the time. They may even go see a shrink or their family doctor. The interest in fixing up the home environment and other traits noted above will also be apparent.

On a personal note, when my Progressed Moon was in Cancer I spent most my time and money purchasing and fixing up my home. I didn't buy any clothes during this time other than casual clothes that I picked up at Sam's Wholesale Club. I never went to the Mall. As soon as my Moon slid into Leo, I went out and bought a bunch of clothes and dug out jewelry I hadn't worn in a couple of years. That is when I did the math and realized I hadn't done so the entire time I had a Cancer moon! If you wonder where your Sun, Moon and other planets are by progression, check out our Progressed Report.

It's important for everyone to know that when they or someone close to them suddenly shows behavioral differences that it's very likely due to a planetary progression of some sort. They need to know that they're not losing their mind or sanity but that often they can blame it all on a Moon Sign change. It's a good lesson in human relations and helps build empathy for those that are more sensitive by nature/Natal Chart influences.

Ω Ω Ω

♌ *Leo* Moon

A Leo Moon will greatly enhance the emotional elements of the Zodiacal Fifth House *i.e.*, the ego, creativity, originality, romantic inclinations and interest in children. As a Fire Sign emotions rule, but in a different manner than Water Signs. While a Water Sign probably reacts to problems with a *"Why me!"* attitude accompanied by tears for the females and complaints by the males, Leos are more likely to roar with righteous indignation because they believe they deserve better.

Leos tend to be caring and affectionate, plus they also believe in themselves more than anyone else. They thrive on attention and are thus very comfortable in the limelight; they love to perform. However, if they make a mistake they're likely to agonize about tarnishing their image far more than necessary and retreat into their den to lick their wounds. This will be especially noticeable if their Leo Moon is in their 1st House. In the 3rd they'll have a somewhat regal outlook in their attitudes and when they were a child probably demonstrated noticeable leadership amongst their peers. Since their creativity is strong, they often are very talented in art, music or especially dance. A Leo Moon will enhance these elements since involvement of the emotions are so important to artistic expression. It will be even stronger if placed in the 5th House.

Leos like nice things and a Leo Moon is likely to incline a person toward impulse buying when they're depressed or upset, particularly if it's Natal placement is in the 1st or 2nd House. They have no problem justifying something they think they need, whether they can afford it or not. Remember that Leos have a touch of royalty that is not conducive to self-denial. They like to look nice and adorn themselves with jewelry and nice clothes. Thus, they love to shop and will know where all the sales are. In the 10th House, they're likely to have a career that involves selling the things that the love , a high degree of creativity or perhaps even children. In the 6th, they'll be proud and a natural leader in the workplace and in the 4th, their home will contain only the best.

A Leo moon will probably provide a great love of children and involvement with them is likely to bring a lot of emotional satisfaction. The children may be their own or others. With placement in the 9th House they are likely to be involved in teaching or organizations that benefit children in some way. In the 11th they're likely to be involved with groups or organizations that promote creativity or perhaps fundraising activities that benefit children.

Leo emanates strong sexuality. They are sensual, attractive and self-confident, plus usually have a natural grace about them that is noticeable when they participate in sports or particularly dance. If you've ever seen a runner, skater, dancer, or swimmer who looked like poetry in motion it's a sound bet they have some strong Leo in their chart. Many love affairs are likely, especially if the Moon is in the 7th or 8th House, and it's best that they not rush into marriage too early in life.

All of the above are likely to manifest as described when the Moon progresses into Leo as well, but the effects will be only for the duration of the progression. When a person's Moon Sign changes from Cancer to Leo there will be noticeable differences. The person will become more extroverted, more interested in their appearance, and have a stronger desire or at least be more comfortable with attention. If they've ever been interested in learning to paint, write, dance, or play a musical instrument, this is a great time to pursue it because the Leo Moon will lend additional abilities and confidence to the effort. Leadership abilities and interest will also be enhanced as well as the inclination to buy expensive items such as a BMW or Mercedes Benz.

$$\Omega \, \Omega \, \Omega$$

♍ Virgo Moon

A Virgo Moon instills a huge dose of perfectionism that needs to be properly managed. Virgo tends to worry a lot, be very critical, look for someone to blame and, being ruled by Mercury, does not hesitate to communicate any noted imperfections. Needless to say, this does not

47

necessarily endear them to others. However, when the Moon is placed in Virgo, a lot of this criticism is turned inward, making them too self-critical and unforgiving of their own faults, especially if on the Ascendant or in the 1st House. Since we all make any number of mistakes daily, if someone obsesses on them (such as a person whose Virgo Moon aspects Pluto) they're going to have significant self-esteem problems.

Along these lines, Virgos tend to be what are commonly called "private" persons. This undoubtedly also relates to their undeserved self-consciousness regarding their own imperfections. Virgo needs to realize that in most cases their most mediocre efforts are far superior to others' best and should give themselves credit where credit is due. Mental acuity will be enhanced if the Moon is in the 3rd House and their memory will be outstanding to the point of being annoying since they'll remember in vast detail everything you ever did to hurt their feelings.

Animals are likely to be a significant part of life and bring great emotional satisfaction to someone with a Virgo Moon. Part of this is because animals are not only cute and interesting but are also very accepting and best of all don't talk or criticize. The closest to criticism you might get from a dog is a disappointed look upon sniffing their food bowl. Cats are a bit more discriminating and if they don't like their dinner and could talk, they'd sound a lot like a Virgo. However, most Virgos can take it from a cat better than a human being.

Virgo rules the zodiacal 6th House of work which includes handwork and crafts of all kinds. Someone with a Virgo Moon will find great personal satisfaction in such thing because these contain the potential for perfection where other areas of life aren't quite as cooperative. Eye-hand coordination and spatial perception is also very acute. This makes them outstanding artists and musicians as well. Since they tend to be a bit restrained on the emotional side, these are all areas in which they can express themselves emotionally in a safe manner. A caution in this area lies in the fact that artistic expression is very subjective so perfection in the eye of the Virgo may not match perfection in someone else's eye, which will qualify that person as "stupid" for the remainder of their association which is likely to be short.

Due to that 6th House link, Virgo has a strong work ethic. With a Virgo Moon, especially in the 10th House, job satisfaction is going to rank high in their requirements for happiness and emotional well-being. If they're unhappy in their job or career it's going to cause significant stress and make them rather difficult to live with, even more so than usual. Ironically, their tendency toward self-effacement will keep them from recognizing success even when they're already there. Things are just never quite good enough for a Virgo.

Since Virgo likes order if they're forced to live in a chaotic environment either on the job or at home it is going to make them either depressed, grumpy, nervous or possibly all three. This will be particularly keen for 4th House Moon placement. If in the 2nd House they'll take exceptionally good care of their possessions and have a complete hissie-fit if anyone harms any of their belongings in any way.

A concern for health goes along with their other efforts toward perfection. Eating properly, the use of vitamins, minerals, herbs and natural remedies as well as staying fit will be of interest. With a Virgo Moon, the possibility to be obsessed in this area, either as a health food nut or hypochondriac is also possible, particularly for afflicted 6th House placement.

I don't even want to talk about a Virgo Moon in the 7th or 8th House since these relate to relationships and sex respectively. Needless to say perfection is not likely in either of these areas and is likely to bring considerable frustration to all concerned if sought for. In the 11th House they're likely to be drawn to participation with groups and organizations, yet be continually frustrated with their lack of perfection. In the 12th, they'll more than likely believe very strongly that spirituality means continually striving for perfection, and may be drawn to spiritual or occult subjects for that reason, though, again, they're likely to be disappointed when the various flaws appear.

With a Progressed Moon in Virgo, perfectionism, impatience, and attention to detail will increase and become much more pervasive. Criticism comes more frequently with worrying an ongoing pursuit. Fretting over how something will be accomplished and planning that goes beyond meticulous to obsessive are forms of worrying; it will be easy to slip into what others see as textbook whining whereas the Virgo Moon person simple feels as if s/he is reciting the truth and the facts, which indeed they are, but to an excessive degree.

An interest in pets of some sort is also likely to arise or an increased interest in health and fitness. Likewise the need for order and job satisfaction as well as all the other traits mentioned above. A Virgo Moon progression is a good time to go to school, certify in a profession, build or remodel a house, direct a cleaning frenzy toward your current home, or organize your finances or files, *i.e.* anything that benefits from organization and attention to detail. These activities will also occupy the person and give them fewer opportunities to criticize, nag, and complain.

Ω Ω Ω

♎ Libra Moon

Libra is the ruler of the Zodiacal 7th House which deals primarily with relationships. Moon Sign placement deals with our emotions, so do the math on that one. In other words, someone with a Libra Moon is NOT going to be a loner. The need for a relationship will be very strong and without one the person will most likely feel lost. However, since these folks tend to be very "nice", albeit charming, they usually don't have much trouble gathering a circle of friends, especially if the Moon is also their 11th House. (Remember that Libra is ruled by Venus.)

Libra is very understanding and has the innate ability to walk the proverbial mile in someone else's moccasins. They listen well and always strive for balance and equality. For those that *want* them to take sides this can be annoying because Libra is very likely to point out the other side of the story, whether they want to hear it or not. Their sense of understanding can also make them indecisive since they want to be fair to everyone. Nonetheless, they generally have a calming effect on others and are very handy to have around in an emergency. As a Cardinal Sign they will take charge and do everything they can to make sure everyone is looked after. They'll be first on the scene of a disaster to help out in any way that they can.

They are naturally more defined than most and have a great affinity for the fine arts. They'll derive much emotional satisfaction from beauty in general, whether it's great literature, fine art, symphonic music, drama in it's various forms and so forth. Without being in touch with some form of the more civilized elements of life they'll experience a void that relationships alone cannot satisfy. If given a matter of minutes to escape a nuclear blast, flash flood, or tornado, after family members, these folks would grab their favorite painting, leaded crystal wine glasses or perhaps their first printing copy of *Gone with the Wind*.

It was the Libras of the world who hauled their china and lace tablecloths across the Atlantic on the *Mayflower* or across the plains in a covered wagon, even if it meant leaving that extra barrel of flour behind. Forgetting that everyone doesn't have the same sense of fairness that they do, they would naturally assume that surely their fellow travelers wouldn't let them starve or, at worst, they could barter one of their finer possessions for whatever they might need. (This would possibly work if they found a Pisces with a well-stocked larder, but in many respects that's a contradiction of terms.)

For all their need for a relationship and ability to see all sides of a story their classic weakness is discussing their own feelings. As an Air Sign they like to talk and they're generally pretty strong in the logic department, but when it comes to their own emotions it's another story. I've never been able to entirely figure this out other than to postulate that in their supreme crusade for fairness they find it difficult to defend themselves because it entails taking sides.

Through the Houses, a Libra Moon is likely to provide exceptional balance to that particular venue. For example, in the 1st House, their very nature will be fair and refined; in the 2nd House, their possessions will especially reflect exceptionally fine taste; in the 3rd, they will be very open-minded and non-judgmental. If placed in the 4th House, they'll do all in their power to keep their home environment as harmonious as possible and will also make regular use of those lace tablecloths and fine china. In the 5th, they'll be very romantic and perhaps creative in one of the fine arts. If found in the 6th House, they'll be the resident peacemaker in the workplace and in the 7th their entire existence is going to thrive or wilt based on the status of their relationships.

In the 8th, which governs intimate relationships and shared resources, they may have a tendency to let others take advantage of them. A placement in the 9th House will predispose them to a love of foreign travel and cultures and in the 10th could motivate a career as a diplomat of some variety. As noted earlier, in the 11th they'll have a wide circle of friends in which they'll be the resident mediator and in the 12th, they're likely to be deeply moved at a spiritual level by beauty of just about any variety, whether it's a beautiful sunset or simply listening to Beethoven's 5th.

When someone's Progressed Moon enters Libra, there will be a noticeable softening of the personality as the Virgo Moon fades into the cosmos. The criticism will fade away with the ability to listen and desire to be fair usually a welcome change. There will be substantially less nervousness and a much calmer demeanor. This is a progression to look forward to with relief as opposed to others where all you can do is be grateful that a progressed Moon Sign usually only lasts from 2 to 2 1/2 years.

Ω Ω Ω

♏ Scorpio Moon

Those with a Scorpio Moon have an intensity about them that emanates like an electric field. They may not be the most attractive person in the room, but you can tell there is something about them that is different and draws attention. The term *"animal magnetism"* was probably invented just for them. Remember that Scorpio is the Zodiacal 8th House which comprises sex, death and other people's money. They're a Water Sign and thus ruled by emotion. Since your Moon Sign rules your emotions, having a Scorpio Moon will be a handful. Emotional reactions are immediate and visceral, often beyond complete control without significant practice.

Scorpio and its polar sign, Taurus, are among the strongest in the Zodiac. They are not to be trifled with. Those with this Moon placement will be strongly affected regardless of what their Sun Sign may be. They will feel things with a depth and power unknown to more benign signs. In emotionally laden situation, their reaction may be exceptionally strong and unexpected, depending on their Sun Sign. Scorpio is ruled by Pluto which bestows instincts and talents in the occult, including psychic ability, particularly when aspected with Neptune. A fascination with death is possible, a strong sexual nature likely.

As far as money is concerned, they'll have no problem borrowing it and possibly taking their sweet time paying it back. Like other Water Signs, Scorpio Moon people have a sense of entitlement than leaves Earth and Air Signs reeling. Earth Signs have both feet on the ground and know intuitively that there is no free lunch and you have to work and subsequently pay for what you get. Air Signs are likewise driven by logic and easily do the math. For example, an Air Sign would recognize that the Lottery is a tax on people who are bad at math; a Water Sign would ignore that, knowing that *someone* is going to win and it may as well be them since they want it so very badly.

While Scorpios are very loyal to those they care about, they are not always very nice to others, kinda like *The Godfather*. They can be ruthless and even cruel, particularly when defending what is theirs. This placement can also instill a tremendous amount of ambition and anyone in their way is advised strongly to move. A large amount of physical energy is also likely. They will expect others to work just as hard and not tolerate laziness in coworkers, spouses or children. A jealous streak is very common with a Scorpio Moon and it can be very easily activated. They need to be aware of this tendency and work with those close to them to keep it within bounds. They should avoid situations and substances that could diminish conscious control and lead them into trouble of one sort or another. While they can display a temper if adequately provoked they generally can keep it controlled. Scorpios will generally believe, *"Don't get mad, get even*" And trust me, get even they will.

Progressing into a Scorpio Moon Sign from Libra can be a significant shock if unexpected. For no apparent reason, all that mellow, fair and well-balanced nature has vanished. The sudden volatility will not only surprise the person but anyone close to them and they'll often wonder, wide-eyed, *"Where did THAT come from?"* This Progression is a good time to engage in activities that require ambition and energy. Go back to school, start a business, remodel your house, build a new one, take some giant steps up that career ladder. Whatever you do, channel it in a positive way and use it to build up, not destroy, both of which are functions of Pluto.

Ω Ω Ω

♐ Sagittarius Moon

A Sagittarius Moon will often predispose a person to a considerable desire for extensive travel. They will dream of it, plan for it, spend lots of money they don't have on it, and cherish every moment of it. They'll take lots of pictures and when they get home get enlargements of their favorites, buy cheap frames and put them everywhere so they can relive their experience multiple times. Being an exchange student is very likely and a fascination with other cultures may drive their entire mission in life. These are the folks that spend their life savings or more on that brief trip to the International Space Station. To these folks such an experience is beyond price!

Academia will feel SO good to these folks and learning will be a pleasure. What other more "normal" folks find boring, Sag Moon people will thrive upon. They'll even read the encyclopedia for pleasure, I kid you not. Intellectually they'll be a notch or two above average and know it. Their dreams and aspirations will be larger than life and they'll achieve them an amazing percentage of the time simply because they don't realize that what they want is impossible. If they're stuck in a mundane, heaven forbid, "normal" life, they'll be tremendously unhappy. They were made for bigger and better things and they know it.

They'll be fascinated by foreign and ancient cultures as well as world religions and what makes them tick. Their dream job may be archeology, Egyptology or some other exotic discipline. They may absolutely thrive on a career in the military and being stationed abroad or perhaps as a foreign missionary. In today's world, a desirable career could also be something like Space Law. After all, who has claim to the Moon? Or Mars? Does whoever gets there first have the right to put a military base there? Why or why not? What do you mean they can't build the *Deathstar*? Who owns outerspace or has the right to legislate its use? Oh, yes, these are the things these folks love.

Being a professional student has tremendous appeal. None of this *"let me out of this place as soon as I've achieved the minimum credits"* business for them. Learning is an adventure, albeit escape, that brings tremendous satisfaction. More than likely they'll take longer than usual to get through college and have credits to spare in a wide array of disciplines. Multiple majors or minors are also likely.

Depending on the Moon's House placement variations could occur. In the 1st, especially on the Ascendant, it will most likely incorporate all of the above and be the prime focus of their life. In the 2nd House, maybe they'll simply furnish their home or collect exotic pieces from around the world. In the 3rd, maybe learning a new language and becoming a specialist in a specific culture is enough. In the 4th, living abroad might be the dream of a lifetime; in the 5th, maybe they'll adopt children from a foreign land or be attracted to someone from a different culture or collect exotic art.

In the 6th, they're likely to seek a job involving foreign travel, such as an import/export business; in the 7th, cross-cultural marriage or other partnership. In the 8th, again expect romantic attraction to those from abroad, an interest in extinct civilizations or foreign investments. In the 9th, which is Sag's native Zodiacal domain, again, all of the above; in the 10th, a career addressing these areas or possibly as a preacher or missionary; in the 11th, extensive association with foreigners, academia or the law. In the 12th, well this gets a bit weird, but more than likely all the Sagittarian affinities, whether foreign travel or visiting a law library or someplace like Washington, D.C., could result in a very profound, déjà-vu or spiritual experience to which the person would feel exceptionally drawn without knowing why.

Sagittarius is a Fire Sign and thus never boring. They're dynamic, slightly ADHD, and very bright. Regardless of their Sun Sign or Rising, they'll have interesting dreams, aspirations, and heart's desires that may never be fulfilled if they don't have a tremendous amount of courage, self-confidence and self-esteem to make them happen. They'll be different and most people will not relate to them at all. They may feel lonely, but never inferior, only that everyone else is out of step and missing a lot.

When your Moon Progresses into Sagittarius an interest in all the above is likely. Someone who has never had any desire whatsoever to leave their home town may go on an excursion abroad, perhaps for months. The study of law may become a fetish or they may go back to school. Whatever the effect, depending on the House placement, they should enjoy and exploit it because it will only last two to two and a half years, and not return for as long as two decades. And this is the stuff that memories and dreams are made of.

As Goethe so profoundly stated (though no one has ever been able to document it, it sounds like something he would say), "Until one is committed, there is hesitancy, the chance to draw back, always ineffectiveness. Concerning all acts of initiative and creation, there is one elementary truth, the ignorance of which kills countless ideas and splendid plans: that the moment one definitely commits oneself, then providence moves too. All sorts of things occur to help one that would never otherwise have occurred. A whole stream of events issues from the decision, raising in one's favor all manner of unforeseen incidents and meetings and material assistance, which no man could have dreamed would have come his way. Whatever you do, or dream you can, begin it. Boldness has genius, power and magic in it. Begin it now!"

55

Ω Ω Ω

♑ Capricorn Moon

A Capricorn Moon will instill a large measure of practicality and logic to the emotional nature. Reactions will be controlled, even stifled, and tremendously understated. For instance, if someone with a Capricorn Moon (or Sun Sign) were to win a $20 million lottery, they'd probably simply smile and say something like, *"Cool. This will bode well for my retirement."* They are usually quiet and reserved and believe that maintaining proper control and dignity is essential. They simply will not lower themselves to emotional displays or give others the satisfaction of knowing they got to them in any way.

Of course in close relationships, whether involving a lover or family members, this undemonstrative demeanor can send a very inaccurate message. Unless the other party is likewise heavily influenced by Earth Signs they are likely to think that Mr. or Ms. Capricorn simply doesn't give a damn when this is really not true at all. These traits can be influenced further by the placement of Venus and Mars in their individual Natal or Progressed Charts.

Would the truth be known, Capricorns feel a lot more than they let on. As an Earth Sign they don't feel emotions with the intensity of the Water Signs by any means, but they are far from uncaring. There are few signs more dedicated to family than a Capricorn except possibly their Polar Sign, Cancer. They have an extremely strong sense of responsibility and will sacrifice just about anything, including their personal happiness, to fulfill their obligations. While they don't seek public accolades and attention like the Fire Signs, they nonetheless have a tremendous need for appreciation. If they don't get any acknowledgement or gratitude they are likely to be very hurt, even bitter, and can even become quite depressed. Saturn is famous for causing discouragement and depression. They need to feel important and needed and that their efforts are recognized.

When in the 1st House or on the Ascendant these elements will be a strong influence on the personality as a whole. In the 2nd House, great practicality will be reflected in their possessions. Their purchases will reflect quality but at the best price and they will often do without if they can't justify the need strongly enough. In the 3rd House, they'll be very logical in their thought patterns and able to easily identify practical solutions to problems. In the 4th, they'll be especially close to their family and devote nearly all their free time toward making it as secure as possible. They will want a home in a respectable, stable neighborhood and most likely have it paid off a lot sooner than the mortgage requires.

In the 5th House, children will be a strong focus. Their creativity will be colored with practicality. There probably won't be too many love affairs as compared to other signs since they tend to be quite selective and have better emotional control. They'll generally fare somewhat better by themselves than other Signs as well, e.g. Libra. 6th House placement will put even more emphasis on the importance of their work and may also spur an interest in health and fitness. In the 7th and 8th House it could particularly stifle relationships by further inhibiting their emotional expression in these areas.

In the 9th House they may be particularly drawn to academia or the study of law as these are quite compatible with the Capricorn tendency toward social climbing. The 10th House is home base and will further spur them toward career success, which will be terrifically important to them emotionally. In the 11th House their group interaction will be quite reserved or possibly nonexistent, and in the 12th they'll have a strong inclination to rationalize and control their subconscious. They'll be able to do quite well using self-help books to "fix" their various hang-ups.

When your Progressed Moon is in Capricorn it's a good time to work on advancing your career or improving your financial security. Taking care of your family is likely to be quite important, noticeably so after coming out of Sagittarius. Any practical endeavor will be enhanced and some of those tedious albeit boring tasks like putting your investment portfolio or will in order will be much more interesting at this time.

Ω Ω Ω

♒ Aquarius Moon

An Aquarius Moon will give a person an unconventional spin that can be quite incongruent with certain Sun Signs. For example, if their Sun is in an Earth Element they can appear to be very practical and conservative, yet have a surprisingly liberal social view. This placement will instill a microcosm of The Age of Aquarius on the individual that will show up in how they dress, the friends they have and what they do in their spare time. It is likely that they won't even understand this themselves. They tend to be attractive and enigmatic, making them difficult to really know because what you see if usually not what you're going to get.

Remember that Aquarius is ruled by Uranus, planet of surprises and the unexpected. You never know what will happen when this planet is active, either in a person's Natal or Progressed Chart much less current Transits. Since the Moon affects our emotional nature, this will instill an unpredictable nature which can confuse the hell out of anyone associated with this person. Cancers are known for being moody, which results from being ruled by the Moon, but an Aquarius Moon affects more than simply moods that come and go as the tides.

Creativity, innovation and unconventional thinking will be solidly linked to their emotional nature. Aquarius is an Air Sign which likes to talk so they will most likely have no problem expressing their feelings. They are also ruled by logic as opposed to emotion, and thus are very good in a crisis. On a global level they care for people perhaps more than individuals and will often pitch in and help, even organize, major humanitarian or relief efforts when required. Their problem solving ability is strong and thinking outside the box comes naturally.

An Aquarius Moon in the 1st House or especially on the Ascendant will have a strong influence on the personality generally. It could even dominate the Sun Sign, depending on its placement. In the 2nd House, depending on other planetary aspects, it could make them extremely disinterested in material things perhaps to the point of giving things away whenever someone seemingly likes or needs it more than they do. In the 3rd House it will enhance innovative thinking. In the 4th the home environment is likely to be unconventional either in the home itself (like those houses you see entirely covered with hubcaps or made from bottles) or in the family structure.

In the 5th, their humanitarian streak is likely to be directed toward children's organizations and their creativity will also be strong. Love affairs are likely to be quite numerous and colorful or different in some way. These folks could really be inclined toward shipboard romances and similar flings. In the 6th, their work could be heavily directed toward charitable activities, healthcare or possibly veterinary pursuits. In the 7th, relationships will definitely be different and likely to evolve from group activities. Eighth House placement could make for an interesting sex life, an interest in death-related activities such as Hospice and could also make for some unconventional entrepreneurial activities.

In the 9th they could become heavily involved in large scale social change either at home or abroad. Tenth House placement could make for some fascinating career choices from which they would need to obtain a lot of emotional satisfaction or be very frustrated. The 11th House is homebase for Aquarius and would make group interaction and acceptance an inherent element in their life. In the 12th House, they would be very likely to come up with some interesting and unconventional ideas relative to psychological issues.

A Progressed Moon in Aquarius will more than likely incline the person toward more group involvement and social interaction than before. They'll be more interested in helping others, charitable activities, and world events, depending on other chart elements. The emotions will be slightly less aloof than Capricorn, but will still be controlled and driven by logic. This is a good time to get involved in group activities, expand your circle of friends and interests, network in your career field, and exercise your individuality.

Ω Ω Ω

♓ Pisces Moon

Here's another one of those double-whammy Moons, since Pisces is a Water Sign and already significantly emotional. Feelings will be deep and sometimes visceral, moving the person in ways unknown to Earth, Fire and Air Signs. They are very likely to be moved to tears by such things as a sentimental song or even a tragic news story. In the case of the latter, they are very likely to want to help in some way to relieve any human suffering. No thanks to Neptune, they can be easily duped so must be careful not to fall too quickly for "hard luck" stories or the pleadings of televangelists.

Since this placement magnifies the emotions, it also can predispose a person to escapism if life becomes too painful. They should be careful to avoid drugs and alcohol, particularly when under stress, and realize they could suffer adverse side effects to medically necessary drugs as well. Other coping mechanisms should be sought as well as healthy outlets for stress. Pisces seek transcendence in one form or another and some are healthier than others. Yoga, tai chi, or other sports as physical capabilities allow are often ways in which to zone out in a positive way.

Since these individuals are so sensitive to emotional pain themselves, they will generally do everything possible to spare others from being hurt. Unfortunately, this makes it easy for them to justify lying which they can do very easily with fabrications and untruths generated effortlessly and convincingly. They can also deceive themselves in an effort to avoid unpleasant and/or painful situations.

It is important to find suitable outlets for all this emotional energy. Creative efforts can serve well in this area, since they are usually enhanced when imbued with emotion. The most moving music, artwork and writing, whether prose or poetry, always has a strong emotional element which these folks can certainly provide. The excursion provided by the imagination in such endeavors is another acceptable means for escape, provided they are able to discern between their fantasies and reality.

Individuals with Water Sign Moons need to be especially cautious in relationships. Due to their empathic and caring nature, they are easily taken advantage of and the scars of such can run deep. They need to be certain that they know what they are getting into and that they can trust anyone they're involved in, whether in a personal or business sense. Their instincts are generally quite strong and they need to be able to read them and when required separate them from what is purely an emotional reaction. That pitiful looking beggar may well deserve his sorry situation and not be helped by an easy way out.

Conversely, since their entire existence is afloat in a sea of emotion, they also know how to use others' feelings to their own advantage by using guilt, pity or other ploys to get what they want. A sense of entitlement is commonly found with Pisceans and they have no problem asking for a favor. Remember as well that the Grand Canyon was formed by water and in a similar manner Water Signs have quite the knack for wearing down people and their resistance until they get what they want.

When you acquire a Pisces Moon by progression, you may find yourself being manipulative when you never did so, or possibly even abhorred such practices, before. Moving into that territory from Aquarius, which is a logical Air Sign and inclined to be a bit detached, can be a bit of a shock. One thing to remember is that if and when you find yourself reacting entirely differently emotionally for an extended period of time from the way you did in the past, the chances are good that you have not lost your mind but have simply changed Moon Signs.

THE PLANETS

I've always been fascinated by the heavens so it's not surprising that clear back when I was a kid I learned the mnemonic to help remember the planets in order from the Sun...

I've encountered quite a few people who know this same one or with slight variations, but I'm always surprised by how many people don't know it at all. In the interest of sharing for those who are less enlightened and in the interest of humor for those who do, here it is, along with an experience I had passing it on to the next generation.

Many Very Early Men Just Sat Up Nights Playing

You don't have to be a rocket scientist to figure out the first letters stand for the first letters of the respective planets. However, a few years back when I was a Merit Badge Counselor teaching this to a roomful of about 30 church-sponsored Boy Scouts as part of the Space Exploration Merit Badge *(No, it wasn't Astrology--not yet!)* they didn't seem to catch on. So, in response to a roomful of deer in the headlight looks, I proceeded to go through it, letter by letter to illustrate. So go with me here: *"Many - Mercury; Very - Venus; Early - Earth; Men - Mars; Just - Jupiter; Sat - Saturn; Up - Uranus....."*

Ah, yes, our friend, Uranus, whose name makes it far too easy to inadvertently make a very bad pun, no matter how you pronounce it. Amid laughter that exploded like a water balloon hitting the sidewalk, my mind raced with how I could possibly recover from such an incredible *faux pas,* the entire time all too conscious of the fact I was in a church gymnasium surrounded by Scout leaders of all varieties. When the last of the laughter had subsided, I somehow stammered out something like, "Well you get the idea..." and managed to carry on with some modicum of dignity, though I couldn't help but notice that the scoutmaster was facing the wall, shoulders shaking, apparently having more trouble gaining control than his young charges. While my mortification managed to keep me under control at the time, I must admit I laughed myself silly all the way home. Since then I've found that the most common pronunciation in astrological circles is *yur-ONN'-us,* which helps a little, at least.

At that time, however, I figured I'd hopelessly marred my reputation as a serious merit badge counselor, even though I somehow knew that everyone in that room would remember that little mnemonic for the rest of their lives. As it turned out, they must not have held me in too low of regard, however, because years later I was still receiving announcements when those boys went on to earn their Eagle Scout Awards. And I'll bet there's not a one of them who can't name the planets in order from the Sun. How about you?

Personal Planets

The term "personal planet" or "personalized planet" is often confusing. How do you get personal with a planet, anyway? Actually, it's more like they get personal with you.

Simply put, *your* planets are those that are most applicable to your Natal, Progressed, Solar Return or other specific charts. The Sun and Moon belong to everyone and are thus always personalized. Other planets that have particular meaning to you would be the planetary rulers of your Ascendant (also considered the chart ruler), the ruler of your Sun Sign, and the ruler of your Moon Sign.

These "personalized" planets will have a stronger influence on you than the others. Thus, when looking at any of your chart aspects as well as transits/horoscopes you should concentrate on the influences that involve "your" planets.

For example, if your Sun Sign or Ascendant is Gemini or Virgo, which are ruled by Mercury, you would feel Mercury's retrograde periods on a more personal level than everyone else who would simply be inconvenienced by the global influences such as all the breakdowns in communications, appliances, etc. Those individuals with heavy Mercury in their charts would probably have numerous difficulties getting others to understand what they're trying to say, have a hard time concentrating, or not be able to grasp ideas and situations as easily as usual. In other words, if Mercury is one of your personal planets you should make every effort to avoid mental challenges such as entrance exams or professional certification testing when it's retrograde.

If you've ever had a personal horoscope done, such as those available in our reports section, there may be days where you have seemingly conflicting influences. For example, you could have a Mars Square Venus that would indicate conflicts in male-female relationships while at the same time have Neptune Trine Venus which would tend to make you feel more dreamy and romantic than usual. *(If you have an exceptionally dysfunctional relationship this could actually work, but I digress.)*

If Mars is one of your personal planets, the inclination to be irritable or combative would probably overrule the other. *(Since this indicates an Aries Ascendant, Sun or Moon you're probably that way most the time anyway.)* If Venus were personalized, you'd most likely feel amorous, but might find your significant other less than cooperative and possibly argumentative *(especially if they've got heavy Aries influences.)* If Neptune were personalized, you'd be more inclined toward daydreaming, fantasizing, or being too idealistic and you probably wouldn't be interested in any serious or realistic conversations, which could be particularly annoying to those around you. *(Neptune personalized means heavy Pisces influences so this is likewise somewhat typical.)*

Of course House placements will also drive the area of your life where the influences show up, *i.e.*, your work interactions (6th House) could be a wreck while your personal relationships (7th House) are going well or vice versa. Any planet transiting your Ascendant or other angles on your Chart will be felt, but even more so if personalized.

Sign Rulership

Each of the planets (which include the Sun and the Moon for Astrological purposes) has a specific influence. Nearly everyone has heard reference to Mars as the God of War and Venus as the Goddess of Love. These references are not out of synch with their astrological influences and each of the other planets has a specific character as well, which is usually in harmony with mythological references. These characteristics will manifest themselves within the astrological sign and house in which the planet resides. This applies whether the chart is a Natal, Progressed, Solar Return or any other kind of chart. The character and personality of the planets do not change. Naming an object has a strong and even mystical influence.

The signs all reflect the predominant trait of its ruling planet. For example, Aries, like Mars, will be aggressive and energetic; Taurus, like

Venus, will love beauty and comfort even as Libra will be uncomfortable without a relationship. Their association with the Signs of the Zodiac are in the following table. Note that Scorpio, Aquarius and Pisces had different rulers prior to the discovery of the modern planets. In my experience, I can see how both have a bearing and thus always look at both.

Sign	Symbol	Ruler
Aries	♈	Mars
Taurus	♉	Venus
Gemini	♊	Mercury
Cancer	♋	Moon
Leo	♌	Sun
Virgo	♍	Mercury
Libra	♎	Venus
Scorpio	♏	Pluto (Mars prior to the discovery of Pluto)
Sagittarius	♐	Jupiter
Capricorn	♑	Saturn
Aquarius	♒	Uranus (Saturn prior to the discovery of Uranus)
Pisces	♓	Neptune (Jupiter prior to the discovery of Neptune)

Table 1 Sign Symbols and Rulers

For each of the Sun Signs, the ruling planet largely defines the overall theme or focus of those born under that sign. There are exceptions, of course, particularly when a person has very strong influences such as a stellium, *i.e.* three or more planets in a single sign, which can counter-balance the Sun Sign. However, even as the Sun is a major influence in our lives generally, the placement of the Sun will usually define our basic character, which will be further defined by the ruling planet. Other planets besides your Sign Ruler are considered Personal Planets as well.

Each planet has an elliptical orbit, which carries it around the sun in a specific period of time as noted above. Mercury makes a trip around the Sun quite quickly (approximately 88 days) while Pluto will not make a complete circuit in your lifetime (248 years). Thus the slower moving planets that remain in a sign for several years are said to have a "generational effect" since all the people born during a given period will have those planets in the same sign, giving them similar characteristics.

65

When planet returns to the position it holds on your Natal Chart, you experience what is called a Planetary Return, which starts a new cycle related to whatever that particular planet rules. More detailed information is contained in the section below on Planetary Returns.

Here are the basics for each planet, including the Sun and Moon which are referred to as "planets" or simplicity sake even though technically astrologers are well aware that they're not.

Planet	Rules *(Ancient)*	Influences	Orbital Period	Time in Each Sign**
☿ Mercury	Gemini, Virgo	Communications, precision, information, logic, speech, writing, conscious thought, movement	88 days	~1 month
♀ Venus	Taurus, Libra	Love relationships, affection, beauty, comfort, the arts, harmony, possessions, wealth, needs, pleasures	225 days	~1 month
♂ Mars	Aries *(Scorpio)*	Aggression, energy, drive, assertiveness, impulsiveness	687 days	Variable month
♃ Jupiter	Sagittarius *(Pisces)*	Expansion, intellectual pursuits, travel, luck, extravagance, flamboyance, confidence, jovial	12 years	~1 year
♄ Saturn	Capricorn *(Aquarius)*	Responsibility, wisdom, discipline, structure, authority, conservatism, ambition	29.5 years	~2.4 years
♅ Uranus	Aquarius	Surprises, instability, spontaneous, innovative, freedom	84 years	~7 years

		loving, rebellion, break-throughs, undisciplined		
♆ Neptune	Pisces	Fantasy, dreams, imagination, deception, intuition, spirituality, transcendence	165 years	~14 years
♇ Pluto	Scorpio	Obsession, compulsion, fanaticism, passion, death, elimination, transformation	248 years	~21 years
☉ Sun	Leo	Basic self, appearance, identity, father or husband, ego	365 days	~1 month
☽ Moon	Cancer	Moods, domestic nature, nurturing, home, mother or wife, memories, emotional center	N/A	~ 2.3 days/month

**It's important to remember that astrological placement of the planets is with respect to the Earth, or a geocentric view. Thus, planets that are between Earth and the Sun, i.e. Mercury and Venus, always appear fairly close to the Sun, such as when they are visible as the evening or morning star. Due to this placement, Mercury and Venus actually take as long as the Sun and sometimes longer to go through all the signs of the Zodiac.

Table 2 Planets, Signs, Influence & Timing

THE PLANETS THROUGH THE SIGNS

☿ Mercury

Mercury is the planet closest to the Sun and has an orbital period of only 88 days. As such, you will always find these two in fairly close proximity to one another with Mercury no more than one Sign away, 28 degrees to be exact. It rules both Gemini and Virgo and affects how we think and communicate with one another in all media from spoken words to email. Whether we are logical, intuitive, pessimistic or optimistic can largely be determined by Mercury's placement. While a person's Natal 3rd House will indicate a lot about their thought processes, Mercury's Sign placement will also heavily influence communication style and skills.

When Mercury goes retrograde it bogs down communications of all sorts, whether it's between individuals, electronics, or mechanical devices. Gemini's and Virgo's are particularly affected since it's their ruling planet. People have a hard time understanding one another, computers crash, traffic signals don't operate properly, mail gets lost, mistakes of all sorts are more common, cars break down, and anything purchased during this time of a mechanical or electronic nature will usually not work properly. If your car is a lemon it was probably either purchased or manufactured during Mercury Retrograde. Avoid such purchases as much as possible during this time and if you absolutely MUST do so buying that extended warranty is probably a good idea. If it's an appliance or something that requires installation, make sure it is done properly. If you're not an expert, pay someone to do it for you.

If you buy a computer, new software or any kind of peripheral device such as a printer, read all directions before hooking it up, though it's best not to buy such items at this time. In fact, it's better still to wait until Mercury has exited from the "shadow period" and reaches the position where it originally went retrograde because things will still not progress properly until that time. If you're waiting on a business deal, job interview, home purchase, delivery of something they ordered or just about anything else, it's likely to be delayed until Mercury goes direct if it ever materializes at all.

1st House/Aries: Decisions will be quick and made with a direct approach. They'll generally be optimistic, to the point, and applied quickly. Slow or foolish types will not be tolerated. Details, however, are boring, so someone's assistance should be used to assure completion. These folks are also the ones who cram all night the day before an exam. Recreational fighting in the form of debates and arguments are likely. Impulsiveness is greatly increased if in negative aspect to Mars.

2nd House/Taurus: These natives may learn rather slowly, but once they have a grasp on something, it's there to stay. Flexibility should be developed as well as the ability to entertain fresh ideas to avoid being unduly or inappropriately stubborn. Nonetheless, these folks have a lot of common sense and can express themselves with considerable charm. This is enhanced further with aspects to Venus.

3rd House/Gemini: Since Mercury rules Gemini, it will further strengthen the ability and need to exchange ideas and opinions. These folks like to talk, and I mean TALK. They're the ones that will strike up a conversation in the line at the bank or McDonald's. Their thought process is quick and as expected, mercurial, meaning they also change their mind a lot. Since they get bored easily, they often don't have all their facts in order unless they have aspects that provide more stability. Nonetheless, the love to gather information.

4th House/Cancer: Mercury in Cancer predisposes folks to an outstanding memory, which tends to make them favor the past over the present or future; they are often serious history or genealogy buffs. They also have good imaginations, which enhance their creativity, but their thoughts and opinions will be heavily influenced by their emotions rather than logic.

5th House/Leo: These folks are enthusiastic, optimistic and creative. They express themselves well, but sometimes ego-centric, which they are usually oblivious to but should try to overcome. They can "think outside the box" but are often stubborn about changing or modifying their ideas.

6th House/Virgo: Mercury also rules Virgo, so its influence here is particularly strong. Furthermore, it is not only in dignity but exalted as well. The ability to plan and analyze situations and problems down to the most minute detail is outstanding. However, these folks can get so hung up on details that they don't comprehend the big picture or get so hung up on perfection that they never finish revising. They also tend to worry a lot and like to know exactly what is expected of them. Changes are often troublesome as they may be perceived as criticism and taken personally. These folks should cultivate the ability to accept constructive criticism and realize that often "the best laid plans of mice and men" fail.

7th House/Libra: Mercury in Libra will slow down the thought processes somewhat because these folks will be preoccupied with identifying and understanding all sides of an issue. This can incline them toward indecisiveness as they strive to be fair, not take sides, or be controversial. They are usually very charming, sympathetic and understanding and enjoy talking to friends and family. They don't particularly like to study but will often look for the path of least resistance.

8th House/Scorpio: This placement will provide a tremendous amount of intuition, Scorpio intensity and an interest in finding every possible aspect of a situation. Ferreting out hidden details and remembering them all makes these folks great researchers, detectives or any other occupation that requires the ability to synthesize data and unearth secrets. Nonetheless, they tend to be introspective, possibly secretive and in some cases obsessive.

9th House/Sagittarius: A wide interest range of interests but perhaps limited attention span characterize this placement. These folks pick up ideas very quickly, often giving them the appearance of being much more intelligent than they really are. They are likely to have a strong flair for languages and often love to travel, not necessarily physically but via reading or studying. They need to develop perseverance and not change their interests too often or they'll be lacking in satisfaction and/or long-term accomplishments.

10th House/Capricorn: Cool and objective assessment of every subject or situation will be the norm, though a tendency toward pessimism is likely. Planning abilities are strong as well as determination and decisiveness. Conservative viewpoints, traditional attitudes and strong ambition will also be apparent. This person means what they say and will not be interested in gossip or trivial matters.

11th House/Aquarius: Originality and unconventional opinions and ideas are likely. The mind is quick, but these folks are also likely to be easily victimized by nervous tension or find it hard to relax. They can be stubborn in maintaining their ideas, which generally evolve in a logical manner. They are usually very friendly and often do well in charitable or social work. There is often an interest in the distant past or future as well as unusual hobbies.

12th House/Pisces: Mercury's energy does not blend well in Pisces, sign of its debility as well as fall. Thoughts will tend to be disorganized with decisions usually reached in an intuitive way. There is considerable empathy for others, but a practical approach to problems seldom arises. Worry is quite likely and these folks have a vivid imagination that often makes it worse. They'll usually take the path of least resistance and can be deceitful, though this is sometimes only to avoid facing an uncomfortable truth.

♀ ♈enus

Venus rules both Taurus and Libra and is universally associated with love with its symbol often used to designate women. Its influence is broader than that, but is generally positive with Venus considered a benefic planet. Other areas affected besides relationships include comforts of all kinds, *e.g.* food, clothes or your home and work environments as well as work itself. Venus also influences your appearance and how you feel about yourself. Transits of Venus through the Houses on your chart will bring a soft touch and desire to improve these areas in much the same manner as its placement natally. It also tells something about a person's love nature, which will be expressed through that sign.

As the second planet from the Sun, Venus' orbit lies between Earth and Mercury. It will thus always appear relatively close to the Sun and is often seen as what we identify as the morning or evening star. If you look at Venus with a telescope or binoculars frequently you'll see that is has phases similar to the Moon. It's often the brightest object in the sky short of the Sun and Moon, particularly when it's at maximum elongation. At that time, when it's extremely bright, it gets reported occasionally as a UFO! Anciently Venus as the evening star was considered the love goddess but as the morning star, which occurs when she's retrograde, she was considered the goddess of war. You can read more about Venus retrograde below.

Venus signifies the woman in a relationship while the Moon signifies the mother or wife when a couple marries. Conversely, Mars represents the man in a relationship and the father or husband in a family. Venus' placement in a man's chart will indicate the Sign or Ascendant of the type of woman he's attracted to, whether or not his Sign is compatible with it. Mars will yield similar information on a woman's chart.

Venus in the different Houses can provide the following influences. Aspects with other planets, either natal or transiting, will also have an effect, as always. The Sign of the Natural Houses is included since the effect will be similar in either placement.

1st House/Aries: Venus on the Ascendant will give the native a classic beauty that others will be drawn to and find very attractive. This will be permanent if this occurs in your Natal chart and transient if on your Progressed chart or from Transits. If present in the 1st House it will have a similar though less dramatic effect. Those with this placement are aware of their appearance and maintain it well, according to the actual Sign involved. In Aries there will be a direct and possibly impulsive approach to love. Venus is in a condition known as "debility" in Aries since her energy isn't naturally compatible with the nature of that sign.

2nd House/Taurus: As Taurus' ruling planet, placement here will be strong and considered "dignified." The person will be attracted to beauty and items of high quality. They'll like soft, comfortable clothing and will manage their money and finances well, though they may also have a bit of an entitlement attitude, expecting others to provide these things if they can't do so for themselves. The love nature will be very sensual and there may also be a tendency to consider loved ones as belongings.

3rd House/Gemini: Venus in the 3rd House will provide a general consideration of others that makes them very sympathetic listeners. Their decisions will be made with an awareness of their affect on others and they'll want to preserve relationships though their approach will be driven more by logic than emotion. They'll find learning a pleasant experience and be particularly attracted to colorful and informative coffee table books.

4th House/Cancer: The aesthetics and emotional climate of the home environment will be important. They'll want to be surrounded with high quality items and will take good care of them, regardless of how modest the actual home happens to be. Harmonious relationships will also be very important with demonstrative expressions of affection such as hugs and kisses likely.

5th House/Leo: There will be a strong appreciation of the arts and all creative efforts and any talents in these areas will be enhanced. These folks are flirtatious by nature and enjoy the company of others of the opposite sex. They will love luxury and dressing nicely will mean a lot to them. Children will be very important and most likely slightly spoiled. The 5th house is also the house of speculation, making Venus' presence fortuitous since she also rules wealth and money.

6th House/Virgo: These folks will be inclined to derive emotional satisfaction from their work and will dislike dirty or unpleasant work environments. They are also likely to be drawn to rich foods and may consequently have a weight problem. If they don't like their job it will affect them more deeply than others. They are also likely to be fond of animals and may be inclined to take in strays of all kinds or volunteer at animal shelters. Venus is in a condition known as "fall" in Virgo because the sign's critical, detail-oriented nature does not combine well with the concept of unconditional love.

7th House/Libra: Like Taurus, this is a natural home for Venus. In this location it will strengthen one's tendency to need involvement with others. These will definitely not be the loners of the world. They will genuinely care about others and consider their needs and feelings, sometimes to the point of allowing others to take advantage of them. Others will be drawn to them, which bodes well for those in a business that depends upon patronage.

8th House/Scorpio: Those with this placement are likely to have a tremendous amount of charisma and be especially intense emotionally. They will have a natural sex appeal and have a satisfying sex life, provided Venus is not afflicted by Saturn or Pluto. There is a possibility for an inheritance and/or these individuals often make successful investors. Venus is also in "fall" in Scorpio where her love nature can become overly passionate, sex-oriented, or obsessive. As the house of shared resources Venus in the 8th may also provide the native with an exaggerated sense of entitlement.

9th House/Sagittarius: There will be a particular love for travel, academia, other cultures, politics, religion, philosophy and the laws which govern society. They will identify strongly with other lands and are likely to marry someone from one of them. They enjoy learning and philosophical discussions and the college experience is likely to be pleasant and rewarding.

10th House/Capricorn: Status and recognition will come easily to those with this placement because they will project themselves favorably such that others will naturally like them and want them to succeed. They'll receive a lot of outside help and mentoring, which they'll accept graciously. Career will be an important element of their life as well as financial security. If they don't have a profession of their own, they can easily become deeply involved and supportive of their partner's.

11th House/Aquarius: Venus in the 11th House will predispose a person to an active social life with numerous friends. Others will be drawn to them and they're likely to be the center of attention. They'll make superb organizers and know how to put on an outstanding party. Charitable activities are likely with fundraising efforts highly successful.

12th House/Pisces: There may be a tendency to be shy and inhibited about love relationships and possibly fantasize about them more than they actually participate. Religious faith may become a replacement for romance or solace found in eating or drinking to excess. A creative interest which can draw from the inspiration inherent in this placement, particularly one that produces a tangible result such as painting, is a good outlet. There is also a tendency to attach extreme sentimental value to any possessions with special or symbolic meaning. Venus thus situated can instill great compassion and empathy but the native must take care that they don't mistake such feelings for love and get romantically involved with someone they want to "save" or "rescue." Nonetheless, Venus is exalted in Pisces where their respective energies combine nicely, allowing the planets energies to be uninhibited or restricted.

♂ Mars

As most people know, Mars is the God of War and the ruler of Aries. Astrologically it signifies aggression and energy. The planetary symbol is identical to that used for the male gender. (Look at it carefully and see if you can figure that one out.) In a woman's chart, Mars' placement indicates the Sun or Ascendant sign of the men she'll find more attractive. This does not mean that she'll be compatible with men with this Sign, only that she'll be drawn to them, which usually explains a lot.

The House and Sign placement of Mars will indicate an area where a lot of energy will be directed. It can especially become aggressive if negatively aspected, *i.e.* Squares or Oppositions. Mars transits will have a similar effect as it goes through a Sign or House.

Recall that the basic Aries philosophy of life, particularly the males, is to shoot them all and let God sort them out. They're natural warriors and have nothing but disdain for those they consider weak, whiney, cowardly or stupid. Mars does not inspire patience or benevolence and is generally considered malefic unless the energy is consciously directed in a positive way. Mars is often involved in aspects related to violence and accidents, especially when Pluto or Saturn is involved via hard aspects. When Retrograde, the native's response will generally manifest as passive aggression in the areas ruled by the resident house. Its placement or transits in the Signs/Houses will carry the following or similar influences:

1st House/Aries: This is Mars' native environment and will generate a lot of energy, drive and aggression. A person could easily be their own worst enemy with Mars on their Ascendant. As someone with this placement, I know this to be true. They'll be perceived as aggressive by others and are often unaware of this projection themselves. On the positive side it can provide a lot of impetus and motivation for pursuing goals since they will want to be the best or first in their field. They'll always be pursuing something and will have little patience for those who are less active.

2nd House/Taurus: This placement is not particularly comfortable with Mars considered "debilitated" based on its ancient rulership of Scorpio, Taurus' polar sign. The person may to be a bit too tied-in with their possessions and constantly pushing themselves to attain more. They may be inclined to impulsive spending or have a strong sense of ownership; it's unlikely they would take kindly to loaning anything to someone, even their mother. Nonetheless, they may not maintain these overly valued possessions as much as they should.

3rd House/Gemini: The thought process will be greatly quickened, especially if aspected with Mercury, and the attitude will be noticeably aggressive; we're talking ADHD on espresso. If they disagree with someone or something a calm discussion to resolve the dispute is unlikely. These folks will have a quick temper and tend to overreact to anything they perceive as opposition. Recreational fighting in the form of animated arguments are likely. However, they're also likely to be very successful because they'll have the strength and ambition to go the distance determined by their mental prowess. These are the kind of people who can wind up in high places and you'd do well to be considered their friend. However, all that energy may have an impulsive flavor such that they don't necessarily stick to one thing for very long, depending on where Mercury lies in their chart.

4th House/Cancer: This placement will direct a lot of Mars energy into building, improving and redecorating the home or other related activities. The Mars restlessness could also be expressed by moving to another house on a fairly frequent basis, perhaps by purchasing "fixer uppers" and then selling them for profit. On the negative side there is a possibility for abuse, perhaps in their past. If Mars is retrograde, it could indicate an inclination to be passive aggressive with respect to one's family.   Mars is in "fall" in Cancer's emotional environment where all that energy can result in emotional outbursts such as temper tantrums.

5th House/Leo: An active and rewarding love life is likely and they'll appreciate a responsive partner, if you know what I mean. Much enjoyment will be found in parenthood, but if negatively aspected, this placement could incline the person to view children as possessions and be fairly dictatorial as a parent. (You know the type.) Pursuits and hobbies of a creative nature are likely to be rather physical or involve weaponry, e.g. martial arts or fencing and collecting guns or knives. With speculations also in the 5th house, these natives may be inclined to be aggressive investors. With this also the house of ego, it's also likely to be expressed in an assertive or aggressive way.

6th House/Virgo: Mars is aggression and Virgo is meticulous and critical. Put them together and you have someone who can really create a morale problem at work (another 6th House domain) or, in other words, a real pain in the wazoo. In other Signs the aggression will be expressed more in synch with the character of the resident sign, but definitely will throw a lot of energy toward work ambitions. Health is also a 6th House issue. There could be a tendency toward skin problems in the form of rashes or allergies, particularly when the individual is stressed. This placement also implies a career in a Mars-ruled career such as a surgeon.

7th House/Libra: A lot of energy will be invested in relationships and there will be a lot of desire to make them work. It is likely that to be successful a relationship will involve a lot of talking and other activities that keep it from getting stale, *e.g.* joint hobbies or interests. If afflicted, Mars' impatience can be a problem, possibly even abusive (either verbal or physical), but the drive for success can be used to overcome it. Mars is in debility in this sign. His action-oriented nature is inhibited, often by the need for the approval of others before taking action.

8th House/Scorpio: This is the House of primal instincts, death, transformation, and other people's money. Throw Mars aggression and energy into that environment and anything could happen. There is likely to be a very strong sex drive that requires satisfaction in order for the person to function properly in other areas. They're likely to be very intuitive, especially with regard to their partners, and be ruthless when investing. There's a fascination with anything hidden or potentially exciting, making this a likely aspect for detectives or even surgeons. Mars is the ancient ruler of Scorpio so has a lot of energy in that sign. An 8th house Mars can also predispose the native to exciting and possibly dangerous experiences.

9th House/Sagittarius: The domains of this house include long distance travel, academia, beliefs and expectations, religion, politics, other cultures, and legal matters. The Mars influence will direct a lot of enthusiasm toward these areas. Impulsive excursions abroad on minimal funds are likely, which will bring a tremendous amount of pleasure. Higher education pursuits are also likely to be satisfying, particularly when colored by the Mars love of competition. However, Mars impatience could be a hindrance and means to deal with this should be pursued, perhaps by participating in sports to dissipate excess energy.

10th House/Capricorn: This has the potential to be a very fortuitous combination since it might lend some energy and optimism to a sign ruled by Saturn, which tends to slow down and inhibit. Mars is exalted in Capricorn, giving its energy discipline and ambition. However, in the 10th house of community status and reputation, any aggressive tendencies need to be tempered properly or it could cause some significant reversals. Burning bridges with Mars temper tantrums and sarcasm can definitely be counter productive to success.

11th House/Aquarius: Mars in this locale can provide the impetus for significant group activities and perhaps even activism. Its the stuff civil disobedience and, with Uranus aspects, general social reform. Strong views that may or may not have any substantiation are likely, but leadership with lots of energy and the ability to spread that enthusiasm to others is likely. The 11th is also the house of goals, providing energy and drive to pursue them, possibly in an aggressive manner.

12th House/Pisces: On the positive side, this could yield a high degree of compassion for others and the desire to help share their burdens. However, this house which comprises compassion and the collective consciousness is a somewhat contradictory placement for the God of War. Numerous dissatisfactions of a vague nature are possible and this person could easily be on a first-name basis with their psychiatrist. This has the potential to be *War of the Worlds* turned inward unless tempered with positive aspects to the Sun, Venus, Jupiter or possibly the Moon. Any aspect to Pluto or Saturn could make this quite a dark influence.

♃ *Jupiter*

Jupiter rules Sagittarius and the natural 9th House of long distance travel, academia, your beliefs and expectations, politics, religion, and legal matters as well as anything associated with them, such as ethical, societal and cultural issues. Jupiter is the largest planet in the solar system, which is also indicative of its astrological influence of expansion; he is primarily known for bringing good luck and considered one of the benefic planets in classical astrology. Jupiter expands and magnifies anything he touches, *generally* in a positive way. Thus, his presence in a sign will exaggerate its expression.

In transits to your Natal or Progressed chart, he will lend his influence to those areas affected by the resident House. For example, while transiting your 2nd House of income and possessions you could get a financial windfall or in the 10th House you could get a promotion.

In aspect with other planets, either natally or by transit, the results will be further colored by the other planets involved. If the Sun, expect attention to be drawn to you or your accomplishments; the Moon, emotional issues; Mercury, communications will be expanded; Venus, comfort, beauty and affection; Mars, increased energy; Saturn, bureaucratic issues, responsibility or reputation; Uranus, unexpected events; Neptune, inspiration, intuition, fantasy; Pluto, introspections or obsessions.

Again, house placements will further indicate which area of your life will be affected. For example, in aspect to Venus with one or the other in the 7th House of relationships should bode well for your love life. Naturally the Sign comes into play, also. An aspect to Saturn in Cancer in the 5th House could indicate a change to a larger residence to accommodate a significant hobby/avocation or possibly the arrival of another child.

When Jupiter goes retrograde it draws attention to any need for reassessment regarding the Jovian issues previously mentioned and often focuses on ethics issues. Are the precepts still valid or is it time for some adjustments? This will start at the global transit level and work down to you as an individual. By transiting your own Natal or Progressed houses, Jupiter retrograde could stimulate them in the following ways:

1st House/Aries: Is your personal integrity and value system in place? Do you live by it? Over-confidence or exaggeration is possible along with considerable personal growth.

2nd House/Taurus: Are your finances and possessions in order? How important are they? More so than people? Are you honest in attaining your income or a snake oil salesman who epitomizes "let the buyer beware?" Jupiter's luck can bring wealth but exaggerated wants or needs can likewise spend it too liberally.

3rd House/Gemini: Are your current thoughts and decisions in synch with your belief system? Do you treat your siblings and neighbors with integrity or with less regard than the others in your life? A philosophical approach to learning is likely. Jupiter is in debility in Gemini, however, where he may generate too much information which can become overwhelming. Too many interests are also possible.

4th House/Cancer: Is your neighborhood and home a true reflection of your deepest desires? Does it represent you well? Are you proud or embarrassed to live there? Are you treating your family properly? Jupiter is exalted in Cancer where his expansive nature can ebb and flow. His presence may also indicate a large family, either by birth or as a parent, or even living in numerous places. Preference for a large, spacious home or environment is likely.

5th House/Leo: Are you keeping to the same standards you teach your kids or are you a "Do as I say, not as I do" type? How do you behave in romantic relationships? What about speculations? Bearing in mind that Jupiter tends to inflate what he touches, is your ego healthy or a bit over-indulged?

6th House/Virgo: Are you honest in your work? Are you comfortable with your employer, its standards and policies? Are you a good example who represents your company or business well? What about volunteer work? Do you perform it as diligently as you would if you were getting paid? In Virgo that signs characteristics could appear excessive, such as being critical or perfectionistic.

7th House/Libra: Are your relationships as they should be? Are you honest with others and yourself? Jupiter in the 7th implies generosity with regard to others while Libra's environment brings fairness to any philosophical issues.

8th House/Scorpio: How self-serving are you when it comes to sex? Are you self-sufficient in your finances or do you depend on credit cards or exploit your friends or family members? How respectful are you of life? Do you suck up to older relatives hoping they'll remember you in their will? Generosity to the point of extravagance and going into debt is possible. Transformation as a result of adopting a belief system is possible. Jupiter exaggerates and inflates and this is the house where issues are suppressed which could manifest as obsession.

9th House/Sagittarius: Legal matters or property disputes could arise. Will you handle them properly or exploit others? Did you obtain your education honestly or make your way through school by cheating? Are your beliefs reflected in your actions or are you a hypocrite? Are your *a priori* assumptions valid? Jupiter rules Sagittarius and is thus in dignity in that sign or accidentally dignified in the 9th house. A philosophical attitude is likely, an interest in other cultures, a love of foreign travel and learning are also likely.

10th House/Capricorn: Are you comfortable with your reputation and community standing? Do you care how you're viewed by others? Will you do anything, moral or otherwise, to advance your career? Is everything on your resumé true? Capricorn tends to be restrictive and is the sign of Jupiter's fall.

11th House/Aquarius: Do you exploit others in your work environment or within any of your social circles? Are your aspirations honorable? To what lengths will you go to attain your goals? Do you tend toward having lots of friends to avoid intimacy? Do you need the company of others to feel complete?

12th House/Pisces: What are your spiritual values? Who are you at the core? Do you try to undermine those around you to advance your own interests? Are you deceiving yourself in any way? Are you a productive member of society or a drone? Jupiter is the ancient ruler of Pisces so retains dignity in this sign. In most cases he will contribute to a charitable attitude but dreams and illusions could be prone to exaggeration.

♄ Saturn

Saturn rules the 10th House/Capricorn and is know for its restrictions and general soul-testing properties. This is not a real obvious tie-in to 10th House matters of reputation and community standing though it does reflect the innate ambition Capricorns exhibit so clearly and the traditional nature of establishments such as corporations and the government which move slowly according to regulations and law, respectively. Saturn can also be well represented by the simple warning that if you have a Capricorn working for you, take heed because they're probably after your job. Saturn ruled individuals are hardworking, dependable, responsible and practical to say nothing of ambitious. In traditional astrology Saturn also ruled Aquarius with many still considering Saturn its rightful ruler instead of Uranus.

Saturn is the proverbial wet blanket, a planet so encumbered by rules, tradition, authority and pessimism disguised as wisdom that everyone groans at its mention. It spells delays (especially when retrograde), speedbumps, bureaucratic hassles and the depression all these ultimately precipitate. It does not spell F-U-N but rather W-O-R-K and F-R-U-S-T-R-A-T-I-O-N, all in the hope of future rewards that hopefully you'll live long enough to claim.

Saturn takes approximately 29 years to make one circuit around your Natal Chart. Its return to its natal position is called a Saturn Return (duh) and holds a lot of significance as a major life milestone. If you're around 29 or 58 years old and wonder what's going on with your life, more than likely it has something to do with Saturn and this report will explain a lot. As someone who's been through two Saturn Returns I have definitely felt their impact. Of course as a Capricorn Saturn is my Sign Ruler so it probably hit me a bit harder, but it's always significant and maps out much of what to expect for the next 29 years.

Saturn's placement on the Natal and Progressed charts or during transits will result in the following or similar effects:

1st House/Aries: If someone has Saturn on their Ascendant or in the 1st house they are probably so responsible that they lie awake nights wondering who's going to win the next presidential election and how their economic policies will affect their 401K. If in Aries, Saturn is in its fall, meaning it isn't comfortable and doesn't operate very well in that sign. Saturn in Aries is similar to a stuffy old professor going to a party at the local fraternity house. Since the sign sets the environment in which the planet must operate, Saturn's usual restraint will be less apparent with its tendency toward hard work and responsibility compromised by Aries' impulsive nature. This is the sign of Saturn's fall due to the fact he cannot express his true nature there.

2nd House/Taurus: Saturn in the 2nd house will provide a tremendous sense of responsibility toward one's possessions. They will not only take good care of them but pay cash for most everything. Their investments will be conservative and if they use credit at all it will be the lowest possible rate. These are the folks who play credit card roulette, moving any balance about from card to card to keep that introductory low rate. They may also use coupons so effectively that their grocery bill looks like they stocked up on food ten years ago, which is also possible. They'll also manage to get a surprising number of items for free or a remarkable price. If you want to know where the really good sales are, this is the person to ask.

3rd House/Gemini: Saturn in the 3rd house or in Gemini will slow down the thought process but will add depth to the comprehension. The synthesis of data will improve and sound principles and common sense will abound. An eye for truth and an uncanny research ability are also possible, especially with aspects to Pluto or when the 3rd house is placed in Scorpio.

4th House/Cancer: This is the house of home environment and Saturn will be quite at home here. Saturn is dedicated to tradition, responsibility, authority and family, so its influence will greatly strengthen the home. Solid values will be taught, debt avoided, the children taught respect for their elders and authority, and the home itself kept in good repair. College funds will probably be started for each child within a year of their birth and everyone will know their genealogy back at least six generations. However, it can sometimes be too strict or demanding and have a difficult time conveying the usual nurturing found in Cancer. This is the modern and traditional sign of Saturn's debility since its cool nature isn't particularly comfortable here.

5th House/Leo: Areas covered by the 5th house include love affairs, creative efforts, entertainment, speculation, ego expression and children. Saturn will imbue a heavy dose of common sense in these areas, particularly love affairs. Saturn is definitely not known for being overly affectionate in spite of its attachment and loyalty to family and tradition. Common sense will prevail and those with this placement are more likely to pair with someone because they have a good future, income or reputation as opposed to mad, passionate love. Children will be welcomed and loved but will have more memories of doing chores at a young age than romps through the park. Hobbies and interests will have a serious nature such as genealogy or have the potential to pay off financially, such as painting or possibly writing. Ego expression can be inhibited as well. Traditionally this was a sign of Saturn's debility along with Cancer.

6th House/Virgo: Saturn is another way to spell "work ethic" so placement in the 6th house of work, health and pets will be another one that predisposes a person to possible success. There will be great pride in one's work, dependability, respect for one's superiors, a willingness to assume responsibility and all the ambition required to move forward in life and progress in a career. The person will probably like animals and take the responsibilities associated with pet ownership quite seriously. They won't necessarily take in every stray cat and dog that wanders by, but you can bet they'll call the pound and criticize those who do not get their animals appropriately neutered. They'll be conscious of healthy food and probably have a cabinet full of vitamins and herbal remedies. A strict fitness regimen is also possible.

7th House/Libra: The 7th house covers relationships and partnerships and Saturn will lend a serious sense of obligation to these areas. They will be honest and trustworthy in their relationships and expect the same in return. They tend to be quite private about their own feelings and lives and will respect the privacy of others as well, unlike others who will be researching every potential partner on the internet. Business partnerships will also be honored and a handshake deal will mean as much as a contract to these folks. They'll work hard and expect the same of others. The fair and balanced nature of Libra works well with Saturn's discipline and responsibility. Libra is the sign of Saturn's exaltation where his structured and responsible nature finds fairness and balance.

8th House/Scorpio: This is the house of sex, death and other people's money implying that Saturn's placement here would have interesting effects. Saturn types are not known for their wild and kinky sexual exploits, so chances are this will instill conservative approaches to sex. There's a possibility that this aspect could indicate a future need to care for a loved one who has a long-term illness or perhaps is elderly. Saturn usually imparts very practical financial behavior, so there's a strong possibility for sound and lucrative investments. They would do well in a profession where they handle or invest money for others such as the insurance, finance or banking industries.

9th House/Sagittarius: Saturn is well placed in the 9th house of long distance travel, higher education and legal matters. There is a strong respect for tradition so trips to ancestral homes or countries are likely to bring a lot of pleasure. Pursuit of a higher education is extremely likely, particularly with the Saturnine drive for success. There will be few frat parties for these folks. Rather, they'll be home alone in the dorm, even during spring break, studying their little hearts out and will probably graduate cum laude at the least. Their natural respect for authority could also direct them to a career in law or government.

10th House/Capricorn: This is Saturn's homebase so its influence will be particularly strong. The drive to be successful will be unstoppable and noticeable at an early age. Even as a child, this person is likely to be class president due to their strong sense of responsibility (unlike those that would be such simply for attention) and most certainly the teacher's pet for their serious dedication to their studies and proper behavior. They'll be somewhat shy and quiet, but don't mistake it for disinterest or slowness. They're busy taking everything in and planning their next move which is always in the direction of the top.

11th House/Aquarius: This house influences group interactions, hopes and wishes. Saturn located here will result in a strong dedication to organizing and running groups or organizations. While saturnine individuals tend to be loners and dislike crowds, their leadership abilities also seek an outlet and with this placement, it will probably be through this means, whether it be a church, scouting, professional organizations, community service or other similar means. Saturn ruled Aquarius anciently which further enhances his functionality in this sign.

12th House/Pisces: Saturn's placement in the 12th house of the subconscious is likely to really bring out the tendency to be a loner. Even if this person has an active career, they'll be most comfortable in their own home, albeit their own little world, and be hard-pressed to leave. They should pursue hobbies of a creative nature and develop any talents they may have in areas such as writing, art or music. Exercise is essential but it should be of a creative nature such as dance or get them outside in the fresh air, even if they prefer not to interact with others on a large scale. Natives with Saturn in the 12th may take spiritual matters very seriously or seek its expression in areas which require considerable discipline such as transcendental meditation.

♅ *Uranus*

Uranus is the modern ruler of Aquarius and is the planet of change, disruptions, unexpected events, rebellion, and surprises. It also influences innovation and invention plus it can contribute to nervousness and dissatisfaction. On the positive side it is also the planet of breaking away from previous restrictions and pathfinders or pioneers of all types. It's the seventh planet from the Sun and spends about seven years in each sign. As such, it will lend its affects in a given sign to all people born during that period, giving them all similar traits and resulting in what is known as a generational effect. Nonetheless it will be located in different Houses, since that placement depends on the time of birth.

Uranus is seldom visible without a telescope and the history of its discovery goes along with its astrological character. It was first discovered in 1690 by Astronomer Royal John Flamsteed, but he thought it was a star and added it to the catalog accordingly. Sometime after that, astronomer P. Le Monier observed it, but it was stationing (*i.e.*, when a planet goes retrograde or posigrade and appears from Earth not to be moving) so it was not identified as a planet then, either. In 1781 William Hershel discovered it but he thought it was a comet. A few months later they realized it wasn't, and it finally was recognized as a planet.

It was eventually assigned astrologically to rule Aquarius. Previous to that time, Saturn had the honor and many astrologers still consider Saturn the true ruler. It's name was chosen for continuity with the other planets which had been named for mythological characters with the Greek spelling "Ouranos." Uranus had a somewhat sordid experience in mythology that we won't go into here. In modern times just about everyone cringes at its pronunciation, particularly when pronounced with a long "a". Somehow the fact it has an awkward name fits in with everything else about it. If you want to say it correctly and without embarrassment, try pronouncing it *yur-on-us*, like "you're on us."

Naturally, changes and such can be good or bad and that will depend on the Aspects, *i.e.* whether they are positive or negative and in which Signs and Houses they occur. When retrograde Uranus is even more unstable and is extremely unpredictable; whatever you expect is not going to be what occurs.

1st House/Aries: Uranus is very compatible with Aries energy and will provide a spontaneous and unique mode of expression along with plenty of original ideas. In other Signs, he will still imbue a lot of originality and perhaps eccentricity or unpredictability, depending on how it's aspected. It is likely that when the Ascendant progresses to the point that it conjoins Uranus that a significant event will occur in the person's life. Isaac Newton had this placement.

2nd House/Taurus: This placement is likely to provide a somewhat unconventional attitude toward money and investing. In Taurus, it can attach an element of eccentricity to otherwise stable Taurean traits. For example, since Uranus tends to make a person strong willed, it could contribute to further strengthening the tendency to be stubborn to the point of being inflexible to a fault.

3rd House/Gemini: It is very likely that this person will have extremely brilliant and original ideas, but if negatively aspected may possess other traits that will prevent them from executing them properly and seeing them through to fruition. From childhood on they may be bored with school or too much structure in their environment and/or be so ornery that others find them downright annoying. A classic example of someone with this placement is Albert Einstein.

4th House/Cancer: Uranus in Cancer can exacerbate the natural moodiness of this sign and accentuate the generally unpredictable nature. In the fourth house it could create a conflict between the need for freedom and the stimulation of change versus the need for a stable home, depending on what other Signs are predominant in the Natal or Progressed Chart.

5th House/Leo: In this House Uranus could be particularly beneficial to any creative tendencies, unless aspected in a negative way. Any creations will be original, innovative and most likely very distinctive. In the love life department, they'll be inclined to be very enthusiastic and optimistic but perhaps a bit too oblivious to emotional risks. They should cultivate a conscious awareness of this and throw some calculated logic toward their relationships before becoming too involved. The person's children are likely to be very intelligent and innovative as well. In Leo, it adds additional dazzle to the leonine nature and could possible add a bit of a power trip coupled with an unconventional attitude. It can also exacerbate the Leo temper, leading to explosive outbursts. Uranus is in debility in Leo where his egalitarian nature clashes with the sign's tendency to be self-centered.

6th House/Virgo: The innovative and brilliance factor will be apparent here in the house of work, but there may be a definite problem dealing with a regular work routine. If it's boring or tedious in any way, the person is very likely to become very frustrated. Nervousness is likely as well as a tendency to eat erratically. These are the people who'll try to subsist on fast or snack food rather than maintain a healthy diet though there is also the possibility that such a placement could lead to incredible breakthroughs in the healthcare professions.

7th House/Libra: While Uranus will throw its creativity and sparkle to the initiation of relationships, in the long haul the need for independence can preclude long-term stability. There could be significant inner conflict in the person if their Ascendant, Sun and Moon signs incline them in the opposite direction, *i.e.* toward the need for stability. This will be particularly true of Libras, who have a fundamental need of people in their life. Any partners will require a strong understanding of this need and be secure enough to allow adequate freedom to the individual so as not to stifle the relationship out of existence.

8th House/Scorpio: Uranus is exalted in Scorpio, primarily since both are related to power. The originality and innovative propensities of Uranus combine well with Scorpio's passion and ability to uncover secrets, providing fertile ground for a unique or inventive approach, particularly to investments or shared resources. The 8th includes death and regeneration, which combined with Uranus would bring about unique experiences or attitudes in that regard. I don't want to freak anyone out, but Uranus also rules explosions, which has interesting implications. Transformation is also an element of this house which goes well with Uranus' influence toward rapid or sudden change. Attitudes toward sex could tend to be unique at best and perverted at worst.

9th House/Sagittarius: This placement can be especially beneficial when it imparts Uranian brilliance and innovation to the intellect, making higher education a significant experience. This can offer the opportunity to really shine and utilize those inventive and creative abilities as never before. They will also benefit significantly from travel, particularly abroad, and true to the Uranus character, surprises are likely to occur. Care should be taken that positive aspects are in force with planetary transits during travel or they may have a little more excitement than even they would prefer.

10th House/Capricorn: The effects of Uranus are somewhat contrary to Capricorn, which inclines toward traditional methods and conservative behaviors. Nonetheless, when in the 10th house, particularly if very close to the cusp, it's likely that their career will involve an area with heavy Uranus influence. These include airlines and the space industry, science, astronomy and other innovative areas or perhaps those in the social sciences with an emphasis on reform. They are likely to make numerous career changes during their lifetime and need to make sure they don't throw the baby out with the bathwater when doing so, but retain their previous experience in such a way that they're not entirely starting over each time. These individuals will also require a career where they have a lot of personal freedom as being micromanaged will not be tolerated. It's also very likely they'll find themselves in "pathfinder" jobs which lack precedent and require new methods or techniques.

11th House/Aquarius: Since this is the sign and natural house that Uranus rules, at least in modern astrology, it will have a very strong influence here. The individual will have a strong affinity for groups of one kind or another, most likely one related in some way to the resident sign. Their social life will be active and they'll be friendly and well-liked. However, they are also likely to not have that many close friends compared to their many acquaintances and maintain a strong sense of personal freedom. Their behavior can be erratic, sometimes breaking ties abruptly with a particular group or perhaps making a big scene in order to accomplish a needed change when the rest of the group has disintegrated into group-think.

12th House/Pisces: While there are significant differences between the general character of Uranus and Pisces or the 12th House, nonetheless this placement tends to work out quite well. Pisces is generally empathic and caring and the 12th House represents our subconscious and our need to help others. Uranus is very humanitarian, but often on a larger scale and thus detached on the one to one human level. When this sign or house and Uranus get together, it can result in some very significant social interactions. However, sometimes these individuals will also entirely dedicate themselves to some kind of charitable activity and never get involved in a close, permanent relationship of their own. They may also seek enlightenment or spiritual fulfillment in an unusual way or perhaps display extreme psychic abilities.

♆ *N*eptune

Neptune was discovered September 23, 1846 at the Berlin Observatory by astronomer Johann Gottfried Galle. This discovery was unique in that it was not the result of visual observations, but rather the direct result of mathematical predictions made by Urbain Le Verrier based on Newton's Laws of Gravitation. Perturbations in Uranus' orbit indicated that another planet was there somewhere, and based on those perturbations, Verrier calculated Neptune's location, which Galle confirmed. The discovery was made almost simultaneously by Astronomer Royal George Airy with the assistant of similar calculations provided by British mathematician, John Couch Adams.

Neptune, which rules Pisces, takes 146 years to complete a circuit through the Zodiac, staying in each sign for approximately 14 years. This is another planet that has a generational influence since everyone born during that 14 year period will have Neptune in the same sign. However, since House placements depend on the time of birth, it will affect different areas of the individuals' lives, even though collectively they're in the same sign. If that's clear as mud just keep reading. I think the meaning will become apparent when you read the influences in the different houses. Remember that in spite of which Sign a planet is in, the house placement will depend on the time a person is born.

Thus, Neptune (or any other planet for that matter) could show up in any of the houses even though the Sign will be consistent for individuals born during certain times. In other words, one person may have Neptune in Libra in their 2nd house while another may have Neptune in Libra in their 8th house or wherever, where Neptune will influence those things included in that house and thus be different for the people involved. Signs are associated with the house they rule zodiacally. For example, Aries, the first Sign of the zodiac, displays characteristics of the 1st house; Taurus, the second Sign of the zodiac, displays characteristics of the 2nd house, and so forth. However, on an actual horoscope, the signs typically do NOT line up with the houses in that fashion except for those with an Aries ascendant.

If you look at the periods when Neptune was transiting the different signs over the past century or so you can see predominant themes emerge. These will be covered below for the relevant signs, *i.e.* Cancer (1901/2-1915), Leo (1915-1928/29), Virgo (1928/29-1942/43), Libra (1942/43-1956/7), Scorpio (1956/7-1970/71), Sagittarius (1970/1-1984/85), and Capricorn (1984/5-1998). Children born from 1998-2010 will have Neptune in Aquarius and it's too soon to determine how that influence will play out. No one living can have Neptune in Pisces, Aries or Taurus and very few remain with it in Gemini, which covered birthdates from approximately 1886-1901.

Neptune's influence tends toward inspiration and introspection on the one hand but clouds and confuses to the point of deception on the other. When Neptune is retrograde intuition is strengthened and, depending on its house and transit placement, will tend to dismiss logical arguments in favor of gut feelings.

1st House/Aries: If Neptune is within approximately 8 degrees of the Ascendant it will have a strong influence and tend to cloud the characteristics of the sign itself with Neptunian traits. Those who have it in the 1st House will generally have difficulty getting organized and tend to make excuses for any lack of success. Taking the easy way out and letting others handle any problems is likely. This person is likely to be a dreamer on steroids, i.e. delusional, or in a more positive vein, possess incredible psychic or intuitive abilities.

(Thank heavens Neptune will not enter Aries until 2025. This propensity to be unrealistic will have an interesting effect on Aries' impulsive behavior.)

2nd House/Taurus: Attitudes toward money and possessions will tend to be quite magnanimous. These individuals will be a soft touch for hard luck stories and be perhaps too generous and quick to help others financially, sometimes to their own detriment, unless countered by heavy Earth influences. Those with this placement need to make a concerted effort to hang on to their resources and have someone they trust who is more practical help them make financial decisions. *(P.S. I have Neptune in my 2nd house, which is in Libra, and it took my children and various others about one nanosecond to figure out this is true, even though I have a Virgo ascendant and Capricorn Sun. Taurus tends to hang onto* *its possessions rather firmly so it will be interesting to see how willing they are to share under this influence, though there is a significant wait until we find out. Financial astrologer, Christeen Skinner, presents an interesting case that Neptune is the planet that brings true wealth, which makes it even more interesting. For a transcript of Christeen's talk on the subject go to the Breaking Down the Borders conference recordings in the shopping area of www.astrocollege.org.)*

(Neptune will not transit Taurus for approximately another thirty-five years.)

3rd House/Gemini: This is the House of the mind and thought processes and Neptune's presence here will tend to cloud and confuse logical thought while enhancing the imagination. Imaginary friends and lack of attention coupled with difficulty in school are likely for children with this placement. Artistic talent is likely, but finding the discipline to direct and develop it may be difficult, depending on other chart elements such as a strong Saturn. Some astrologers believe that this placement enhances the voice so the individual may have a talent for singing. Strong psychic and intuitive abilities are also possible.

(Neptune will not transit Gemini for approximately another fifty years.)

4th House/Cancer: Neptune in the 4th House often relates to childhood experiences, perhaps growing up in a home that stimulated the imagination, either due to an unusual environment or perhaps as an escape from domestic problems. In adulthood it can tend to make the person want to create an ideal home or environment that is not in synch with reality.

(Those born from 1901/2-1915 had Neptune in Cancer. There was a tremendous amount of disruption and confusion among families and homes during this time due to men being killed during World War I as well as illness including a flu pandemic (flu is ruled by Neptune.) There was also little support for society as a whole for keeping families together. Between 1905 - 1911 Uranus in Capricorn was opposite Neptune, compounding these unfortunate effects. My mother was born during this time and suffered tremendously from the death of her mother when she was 6 and death of her father at 12 at which time she and her three siblings were separated with my mother going to live with an aunt on the other side of the

91

country. With the death of her aunt, with whom she'd be sent to live at 14, she was left to fend for herself. Along these lines, the Titanic sank in 1912, under similar aspects. Remember also that Neptune rules water.)

5th House/Leo: Neptune will definitely turbo charge any creativity associated with this house, which will also be colored by its sign placement. The caution here lies in the tendency to fall in love too easily and then maintain unrealistic and/or idealistic expectations for the relationship. The heart will rule the head and much foolishness in the name of love can result, ultimately causing a lot of hurt. This same attitude can be expressed toward their children, *i.e.* having unrealistic expectations for them or trying to live out their own dreams through their offspring.

(Neptune was in Leo for those born from 1915-1928/9. During this time the movie industry (ruled by Neptune) was in its infancy with the silent film era. Tough times were still afoot with WWI and the Great Depression in 1929 and people welcomed this escape into a fantasy world.)

6th House/Virgo: The Neptunian imagination could have a detrimental effect on the person's health, predisposing them to hypochondria, allergies and various vague ailments which most likely will not respond to conventional medical treatment. In the workplace there will be numerous challenges such as a persistent tendency to daydream, lack of discipline, perhaps absenteeism (due to the previously mentioned physical ailments or simple lack of motivation) and missed deadlines. Attaining an education in a creative profession so they can find suitable employment later is advised.

(Neptune was in Virgo from 1928/29 - 1942/43. The movie industry continued to progress with sound being added at this time, showing the strong influence of Mercury-ruled Virgo's communication enhancements. Inventions such as radio also improved communications and provided entertainment via dramatic presentations that also provided escape into a fantasy world, if only for a few minutes each day. The Great Depression also occurred during this time period, a time when work, resources and assets disappeared, another Neptunian function.)

7th House/Libra: This placement, depending on the Sign, can predispose the person to preconceived notions about relationships that are entirely out of synch with reality. They'll have a fairytale view of romance and, while they'll do a good job creating a romantic and imaginative environment for their partner, they're also likely to be very disappointed when real life doesn't match their idealistic expectations. They're also unlikely to share responsibilities involved in running a household so their partner will be forced to handle more than their share, which could strain the relationship. Similar characteristics could afflict a business partnership.

(From 1942/3 - 1956/7 Neptune was in Libra. This was the post-WWII era and everyone was ready for peace. These folks grew up and became the "flower children" of the late 60s and early 70s. They sought for an easier life style, smoked a bunch of pot and thought that everyone ought to get along. Conversely, this was also about the time that divorce rates began to increase as expectations of the institution of marriage became more idealistic.)

8th House/Scorpio: This placement will add considerable intensity to the sexual nature, possibly because it dissolves conventional moral boundaries. The individual is likely to have a tremendous amount of mystery and allure (possibly to both sexes) but the possibility also exists for Neptunian confusion in this area coupled with increased imagination and fantasies. In the financial arena, they will tend toward the same generosity as with 2nd house placement, but this time it might be someone else's money they're giving away. Either that or they're the person with the "hard luck" story who is vying for assistance from anyone they can convince to help, perhaps using some of those talents of seduction previously mentioned.

(Neptune was in Scorpio from 1956/57 - 1970/71. This was when hard rock music, often with dark, Scorpionic undertones, came into its own and a new aggressive and sexual theme pervaded society in general. With it came the advent of easy and reliable birth control and the abortion issue. Many in the forefront of gay rights issues were born during this time. The inability to cope with life and thus use drugs and alcohol to escape also increased during this era as well as an increase of individuals who could not support themselves and turned to 8th house tax-funded government, a.k.a. other people's money, i.e. welfare, for support.)

9th House/Sagittarius: Neptune has the potential to have a positive influence in this house. It will lend inspiration and idealism to the

93

person's intellectual pursuits and may even provoke interest in mystical or spiritual subjects as its influence pervades organized religion. It is likely that any travel abroad will be tremendously inspiring and may also provide for some strange or even weird experiences. Very vivid dreams and strong recall are also likely.

(Neptune was in Sagittarius from 1970/71 - 1984/85 so this generation is just now coming into its own. Themes toward idealism and Neptunian views toward society seem to be emerging, though on the negative side these can be seen as an attitude of entitlement that lacks practicality. This generation seems to be living at home dependent on their parents much longer than previous ones and shows a general resistance to accepting responsibility of their own. Neptune's influence on 9th house politics ranges from idealism to deception which is certainly more and more apparent as this generation enters that arena.)

10th House/Capricorn: In the 10th House of status and reputation, particularly if conjoining the Midheaven, Neptune could indicate a very charismatic individual who makes all the right moves to achieve high standing in a field related to the resident sign. They are likely to be imaginative or perhaps inspired and thus inspirational to others. These could be visionaries with high aspirations, though it is possible that they may lack a true sense of direction and may change their paths numerous times during their lifetime. On the negative side, they could also be masters of deception.

(Neptune was in Capricorn from 1984/1985 - 1998 so the jury is still out as far as the accomplishments of those born during this timeframe. Historically, however, we had numerous events that are somewhat telling. Environmental issues, especially related to Neptune-ruled oil, have definitely come to the forefront (Capricorn is an Earth sign). On the political side, deception has been on the increase worldwide and the quest for status on the part of individuals, countries and organizations has been apparent.)

11th House/Aquarius: An individual with Neptune in the 11th House of group interaction will probably interact socially with individuals of an unusual or creative nature. They will use their social circle and activities to escape the humdrum nature of their lives and find at least temporary relief from their looming responsibilities. However, they need to make sure that they see these people as they really are and not expect too much from them in time of need. They should also exercise caution that they not be used by others. These folks may also find great satisfaction in charitable work. An historical figure with this placement is Wolfgang Amadeus Mozart. Considering that the 11th house also comprises goals, this could tend to make them either too idealistic or perhaps too nebulous to attain.

(Neptune entered Aquarius in 1998 and left for good in 2012. While Aquarius lends humanitarian inclinations, the Neptune influence could infuse more sensitivity and genuine caring. With the numerous natural disasters that have been occurring worldwide the past several years, there will be ongoing opportunities to exercise these activities; note that floods and tsunamis are Neptune-ruled. However, I can also see more of that Neptunian entitlement attitude emerging within groups of people which implies that society bears total responsibility for taking care of the individual instead of vice versa.)

12th House/Pisces: Since Neptune rules Pisces, this is its home base. Time for introspection and spiritual renewal will be important to this individual. It is a good placement for those that work in public service professions since it enhances intuition and caring which will assist in providing genuine help to their constituents, whoever they might be. However, socialism also resides in this realm which comprises elements of both idealism and deception. With negative aspects, there is also the unfortunate possibility of self-deception or an escapist attitude which the person will need to keep close tabs on, possibly thru a very realistic friend or confidant. The 12th house also comprises hidden enemies, institutions, seclusion, confinement and self-undoing, all of which can be affected with the full spectrum of Neptunian influences, from inspired visions to the dissolution of boundaries and illusions.

(Neptune entered Pisces in 2011, returned to Aquarius a few times due to retrograde motion, then arrived to stay in 2012. Thus, we are just beginning to see its effects on the mundane level and still have several years to wait to see how it affects individuals. I suspect that what we'll see is a lot of genuine good work being done on the humanitarian level but that we'll also see a tremendous amount of confusion and idealism. We've already seen a new high in deceptive practices, whether at the individual, government or corporate level, and all those blood suckers looking for a free ride are making more noise than ever before.)

♇ 𝓟luto

Pluto, the pokey little puppy of the Solar System, takes 246 years to go around the Sun and thus the Zodiac. His trip through the signs is not equally divided, however, because of the eccentricity of its orbit; it may "zip" through one sign in 13 years and then take 32 years to limp through another. Thus, its influence is also considered generational like Neptune. Pluto was in Sagittarius until late November 2008, when he moved into Capricorn until 2024, except for a brief gig back in Sagittarius due to retrograde motion. There is no one alive with Pluto in Aries or Taurus.

Of course there's been a lot of flap over Pluto being "demoted" from a full-fledged planet to the minor leagues. Let me tell you that Pluto doesn't care. His power is the same, regardless. In fact, from what I've seen, I think that the planets are one of those areas where size definitely doesn't matter. Since no one knows for sure why astrology works, it's hard to say, but possibly the smaller planets, minor planets or whatever, have a frequency to which humans are more receptive.

If you know anything about modern physics, you know that sometimes a particle acts like a particle and sometimes it acts like a wave. Obviously the planets are mighty big particles, but the principle's the same, so maybe smaller planets affect us more because their wavelength is more influential. The asteroids, which are similar in size to Pluto, certainly have a very strong impact, both on a person's Natal Chart and in transits. In fact, there are astrological entities out there that aren't even a physical body, just a point in space with some mathematical significance, that also have a strong influence, so go figure. Good examples of this include the lunar nodes and Dark Moon Lilith; check it out.

Pluto, god of the Underworld, rules Scorpio and was discovered at the Lowell Observatory in Flagstaff, Arizona on February 18, 1930 by Clyde Tombaugh based on calculations that oddly enough later turned out to be in error. Note that around the time of its discovery, when the archetype of the god of the Underworld was unleashed, we saw fascism reach new proportions through such men as Stalin, Mussolini and Hitler. Prior to that Mars was considered Scorpio's ruler.

Pluto transits are known for their dark influences that sometimes manifest as obsessions related to the House in transit. Progress is sporadic at best during a transit and any that results is usually heavy and soul-testing. The end result is often compared to death and regeneration where some personality element related to the house in transit figuratively dies and comes back in a new form. In other words, it facilitates deep and sometimes painful change, but the purging effect generally is positive in the long run; it's often overlooked that Pluto is also involved with healing. On a more mundane level, Pluto also rules all things hidden, including plumbing. This includes your home as well as your own, *i.e.* your bowels.

I had a particularly Plutonian experience a while back when my vacuum cleaner broke a belt. Of course I hadn't looked at the underside for quite a while and as you'd expect it was clogged with all sorts of lovely things, which I proceeded to clean out. I installed a new belt and *voilà,* it worked like new. This is a very simple example of the rooting out of hidden problems and eventual healing that Pluto accomplishes so well. This particular event occurred when Pluto was opposite Mercury retrograde. During that particular cycle, plumbing and power issues were common right along with all the communication problems that Mercury RX is famous for. It was actually a great time to do home maintenance and repairs. While several things caused problems, their repairs went relatively well with positive results. After all, everyone needs to clean out their garage or basement every now and then, either figuratively or literally.

Of course it's not as easily resolved or as painless when Pluto is grinding on your chart somewhere. Pluto transits are particularly unpleasant in certain areas of you chart. If you know someone who has one problem after another and absolutely nothing seems to go right, there's a good chance that this poor soul is undergoing a Pluto transit of some sort. Yet, no matter how endless or grueling it may seem, when it's over the person will be able to go forward with his or her life and heal from the experience.

When Pluto, Mars and/or Saturn aspect each other negatively the result is often not pretty and is sometimes a harbinger of death. For example, these planets were in cahoots for both space shuttle accidents. My mother's natal chart had Pluto squaring both the Sun and Moon with Saturn in the 4th house; she lost both her parents to death when she was a child. My father had Pluto in the 4th House and lost his father when he was a mere toddler to a freak accident.

1st House/Aries: Pluto in the 1st house by birth or transit will darken the personality and infuse it with passion and intensity. The person will have a penetrating gaze and will project power in a way that others can sense. They are likely to be fascinated by mysteries and secrets and want to explore subjects of interest in considerable depth, making them talented researchers. Obsession is possible as well as a need to dominate others. Negative aspects can further influence these traits, however, and possibly cause psychological problems that emerge as illnesses.

(There is no one alive with Pluto in Aries on their natal chart. This is probably a good thing.)

2nd House/Taurus: Pluto in the 2nd house by birth or transit usually provides a strong business sense. They will have considerable drive to succeed and could become obsessed with building their own "empire" if further strengthened by Earth sign placements in Capricorn or Taurus. There may be a tendency to view their loved ones as possessions. The 2nd house also comprises needs and pleasures, suggesting that Pluto could promote some interesting propensities in this area, perhaps as extreme as sado-masochism.

(There is no one alive with Pluto in Taurus, either. However it's interesting to note that Josef Stalin had this placement.)

3rd House/Gemini: These individuals will have a nearly insatiable curiosity. Their mental powers may be strong but sometimes dark and they won't miss a thing. In certain situations they may put on a classic, Plutonian poker face and look totally bored and oblivious to their surroundings, unless you take a close look at their eyes which will reveal they're taking in every word, which they will use as necessary to the astonishment and possible demise of those around them. They synthesize data exceptionally well and can instinctively ferret out or derive information that others miss. They won't be satisfied with inadequate or superficial explanations but will persist in finding the answers they seek. With this aspect natally, these traits will be lifelong; otherwise, they'll endure for the length of the transit, but remember that Pluto transits can take anywhere from 13-32 years! If we could turn on this trait at will during our college years we'd really have something.

(Pluto was in Gemini from the late 1800s until 1912/13. This era saw great growth industrially and many sweeping social changes. Remember this was the timeframe when the Titanic was built and then sank, where it remained hidden in the deep for

decades before its discovery. Individuals with this placement are inquisitive though skeptical, but have a deep appreciation for learning. On a personal note, my mother was a Virgo who had this placement and when she was in a rest home in her nineties she would have me bring her encyclopedias as reading material! Many people born during this time period were involved in scientific research and inventions that reflect this depth of knowledge. For example, Major General Leslie R. Groves, who headed up the Manhattan Project which developed the first nuclear bomb, had Pluto in Gemini.)

4th House/Cancer: Pluto in the 4th House often signifies a difficult childhood and adolescence. Perhaps their parents were overly controlling or abusive or other frustrations dominated their life. Often they have a highly developed intuition, perhaps because they needed it to survive emotionally. As mentioned in the general description of Pluto at the top of the page, this placement sometimes denotes death of a parent at a child's early age. Considering that the 4th house also comprises memories and endings, this further supports the inclusion of death.

(Pluto was in Cancer from 1912/13 - 1937/38. WWI was underway at this time, which clearly demonstrated fascism, a Plutonian ideology, which left numerous children fatherless or with other substantial hardships related to their homelife. On an individual level, these folks generally have strong intuition and deep emotions. If negatively aspected, they tend to lock up their problems inside and sometimes obsess on them.)

5th House/Leo: Pluto in the 5th house will enhance the person's creativity and provide considerable determination to pursue their potential. They can achieve much satisfaction from these efforts, even if the quality of their work itself is not the best in their field *(sounds like Napoleon Dynamite to me, folks)*. Since this is also the house of love affairs and we're talking about Pluto, as you can imagine they're going to have a very intense and rich love life with many lovers *(then again, maybe not....)*. There may also be a tendency to take risks or pursue endeavors which are driven strictly by passion or obsession.

(Pluto was in Leo from 1937/8 - 1957. During this time WWII broke out. Again power and domination were strong themes. On the positive side, this was also the advent of today's technology with many who developed computer technologies having Pluto in Leo in

the birth charts, though technological breakthroughs are also closely tied to Uranus. On an individual level, it's very possible for Pluto power to combine with the Leo desire to rule and create a real empire builder in one form or another, perhaps an obsessive one. It is very likely that many of the dictators and power-hungry individuals in the world today have this placement with one obvious example Osama bin Laden.)

6th House/Virgo: Those with this house placement natally or during transit will tend to be rather autocratic regarding doing things exactly right, particularly in the work place and especially if the sign is Virgo as well. There may also be a tendency to dominate others. Health problems, particularly of the bowels, are common with this placement as well as the tendency to turn to food for comfort if emotional fulfillment is lacking. If negatively aspected, there is potential for cruelty to animals as well. They may also be critical in a harsh way or obsess on perfection.

(Pluto was in Virgo from 1957 - 1971. During most of the 60s, Uranus was also in Virgo and the combined energy of these two planets was apparent in the social unrest, protests, war activity of a darker nature than WWI or WWII, and even the advent of the computer age which combined Virgo's obsession with detail, Uranus' innovation and Pluto's thirst for unearthing secrets. Individuals born during these years often have obsessive tendencies related to the resident house and if there is a conjunction with Uranus, it could motivate a deep desire to facilitate change or innovation of some type with covert means employed if necessary. One interesting connection to note for this time period is the advances made in modern medicine which relate to discovering the hidden elements of disease.)

7th House/Libra: Relationships will definitely feel the Pluto influence and could tend toward obsession. It is very likely that this individual will need to be the dominant partner in any emotional relationship and if this occurs by transit while in an existing relationship, it could easily cause considerable problems. Besides the power trip angle, Pluto's destructive powers can come into force with the individual compulsively digging through the rubble of old relationships and perhaps recreating it for existing ones. The influence is especially powerful when Pluto transits the 7th house cusp where it is also opposite the Ascendant, and even more so if it grinds away on it for a while due to retrograde motion. Nonetheless, the Pluto passion and emotional depth can lend exceptional intensity that will have its euphoric moments as well.

(Pluto was in Libra from 1971 - 1983/4. It goes without saying that on the mundane level during the 70s there was considerable emphasis on sexual activity and freedom. The "pill" was in its heyday and the abortion controversy was likewise an issue. There was the Vietnam war, rock concerts with heavy metal music and increased drug use thanks to Pluto and the Libran desire for love and harmony evident in the "flower power" and "make love not war" attitudes of the time. For individuals born at this time, the sex life is usually stimulated by this placement, particularly if they have a Libra Sun or Moon. They may also tend toward provoking their partner to prove their affection or lack of it.)

8th House/Scorpio: This is Pluto's homebase, unleashing his power in unprecedented ways. A strong, perhaps insatiable, sex drive is possible as well as a fascination with death. This is also the house of transformations, which could give the native a propensity for intense, perhaps death-defying, experiences. Shared resources and debt also belong to this house, implying the potential for secretive dealings, with the fact that taxes also reside here providing more interesting implications with regard to entitlement. As the zodiacal backhoe, Pluto also excels at unearthing hidden facts and facilitating transformations.

(Pluto was in Scorpio from 1983/84 - 1995, which was fortunately one of his shorter sojourns in a specific sign. When you consider what happened when Pluto entered Scorpio and conjoined natal Neptune for those born from 1956 - 1970 it isn't too hard to figure out why everyone was wearing black and turning punk! It also is evident in the onset of the AIDS epidemic. Major technology-related entrepreneurial efforts also came into their own at this time, such as the Internet. The personal influence of this placement adds intensity and determination, though negative aspects to the Sun or Moon can cause psychological challenges. There is a lot of emotional and physical energy, particularly if the Sun, Moon or Ascendant is in Scorpio making it critical that these individuals find positive releases for this energy.)

9th House/Sagittarius: Pluto in the 9th house often provides a compulsive drive to study and challenge oneself mentally, sometimes beyond the person's ability. They also tend to have a need or even obsession with perfection that they continually try to reach. Needless to say this causes considerable stress and as a result they are likely to eventually become totally disgusted with their "failed" efforts and give

101

up entirely. Wiping the slate clean and starting over is typically Plutonian, but throwing the baby out with the bathwater is usually counterproductive. It is also likely that those with this placement will have a great fascination with foreign travel and they're likely to have numerous weird experiences doing so.

(Pluto was in Sagittarius from 1995 until 2008. In the last decade we have seen numerous Plutonian influences, none more obvious that the terrorist attacks on September 11, 2001. Here we had a covert attack in the Pluto tradition that was perpetrated primarily for philosophical/religious reasons, whether we agree with them or not! Furthermore, Sag's primary traits are openness, independence and a love for freedom, which certainly personify the USA. In addition, the politics of the last several years have been tinged with dark, secret acts versus highly intellectual ideologies. The personal influence will undoubtedly impart a depth and intensity to the upcoming generation, particularly in view of the world events surrounding them as they grow up.)

10th House/Capricorn: Individuals with Pluto in the 10th House will have a passionate and perhaps even obsessive involvement in their career or other compelling goal they wish to achieve. If this is missing from their lives for one reason or another they will be unfulfilled and frustrated. If located where it conjuncts the Midheaven, there can be a considerable thirst for power which can be pursued ruthlessly if there are negative aspects to personal planets. These folks need to keep their goals within reach and make sure their tremendous store of energy is directed in constructive ways or they can bring major problems upon themselves and those close to them.

(Pluto entered Capricorn in January 2008. bounced back and forth a few times due to retrograde motions, then came to stay in November 2008. One signature effect of this transit on the mundane level is vividly illustrated by the eruption of Eyjafjallajokull in March - April 2010 and the BP Oil Spill around the same time. Exposure of corporate and government corruption is also apropos. Capricorn is an Earth Sign which rules structure, thus the Earth herself will be involved as well.)

11th House/Aquarius: Of course this entire Pluto in Aquarius generation won't all be like that anymore than everyone with Pluto in Gemini became a dictator, though the idea was quite popular at the time. With Pluto in the 11th an individual is likely to be too concerned or even obsessed with their friends and group interactions or perhaps have the desire for power and control over them. Considering that goals are also in this house, obsession or willingness to go to extremes for their attainment is also likely. On the mundane level, this placement will probably expose corruption and/or see dictatorial takeovers of or by various groups.

(March 2023 is a long ways away so I'm not going to worry about it just yet.)

12th House/Pisces: Pluto and it's propensity for things hidden can have a strong effect on the subconscious. This could result in exposure of various subconscious matters individually or on the collective level when Pluto reaches this sign, considering that the collective consciousness resides in Pisces. The 12th house is where spirituality, enlightenment, inspiration and transcendence reside, which implies that these individuals may undergo significant transformations in this part of their life. Also residing in the 12th are institutions, seclusion, confinement, hidden enemies and self-undoing. Of course these last two, especially, are going to be challenged by Pluto's inclination to expose such things. Thus, individuals with a 12th house Pluto are likely to discover such things more readily than others.

(It's going to be so long before Pluto goes into Pisces that on the global basis it's the least of my worries.)

RETROGRADE PLANETS

All the planets move around the Sun in the same direction (counterclockwise) but they are in different orbits and traveling at different speeds. Thus, at certain times they "pass" each other, much as you might pass another car on the freeway; the other car isn't really moving backwards, it only appears that way. Thus, there are times when, from the Earth, a planet appears to be in retrograde, *i.e.* moving backwards. Like the slower car on the freeway, this is only an illusion, but astrologically it is considered retrograde and this phenomenon has specific effects, generally to internalize the energy.

Since planetary orbits are predictable, we know when this will occur. And this is a good thing, because there are some things that you probably don't want to do when certain planets are retrograde. For example, Mercury retrograde is nearly famous for the communication problems it causes. Buying anything mechanical or electronic such as a car or a major appliance at this time generally does not go well. I once bought a conventional litter box for my cat during Mercury RX thinking what could possibly go wrong? For starters the lid didn't fit properly and after about ten days one of the plastic hooks holding the door in place broke off. Pardon the expression, but it's almost as if a curse has been placed on them and they are prone to breakdown and malfunction on a regular basis. Phone, cable, internet and computer problems in general are also common.

Each planet has a specific affect when it goes retrograde, which has been compared by astrologer, Christine Shaw, to placing it in Capricorn. Retrograde planets aren't only a nuisance during transits, but they can also have a specific effect if found in your Natal or Progressed Chart. Basically, the energy that planet generally emits will be turned inward. For example, Mars usually lends itself to energy and aggression but in retrograde tends toward passive aggression. Venus affects what we find pleasing in others or aesthetically but when retrograde, we have a hard time expressing our emotions in this area. The chart at the bottom of this page gives a brief summary of the effects of each planet, though books have been written on this subject so it is far from simple in its astrological effects.

Before a planet can move backwards it has to stop and during this period it is referred to as stationing. Once it starts to slow down the retrograde effects will be felt and they won't end until it stations again and resumes posigrade motion. And sadly, retrograde's full effects won't diminish entirely until the planet actually overtakes the position it was in when it decided to go backwards! If the retrograde planet is one of your personal planets, i.e. the Sun, Moon, your Sun Sign ruler and your Ascendant ruler, then the effects for you will be more dramatic than others. Which area of your life will take the brunt of its wayward journey will depend on which House it's transiting and any aspects it may throw along the way. The moment the planet stations institutes a blast of energy that characterizes that particular RX period. Retrograde planets are indicated on astrological charts with an "Rx."

The various retrograde effects of each of the planets (except the Sun and Moon, which have the good graces to keep moving in the proper direction) follow so you can know what to expect and plan accordingly, at least as much as humanly possible. More specific analysis of the effects can be done with your individual chart.

The landmark book on this subject is *"Retrograde Planets"* by Erin Sullivan, to which I refer readers if they're interested in learning just about everything there is to know about them.

Planet: Mercury
Stationary: Hours to days
RX Frequency: 3 times/year
RX Duration: 3 weeks

Transit Effect: Communications of all types, verbal and electronic, are disrupted or misinterpreted on all levels, including personal, business and legal. Paperwork gets lost or messed up, computers crash, appliances go out, cars break down. Anything purchased during this period is likely to never be "quite right."

Natal/Progressed Effect: You are likely to be frequently misunderstood or you may have problems with self-expression. You are likely to be introverted. When Mercury goes posigrade in your progressed chart, you are likely to "come out of your shell."

Planet: Venus
Stationary: 3 - 4 days
RX Frequency: Once every 18 months
RX Duration: 6 weeks

Transit Effect: Forces a good hard look at areas affected by Venus, i.e. romantic relationships and finances. Value system is likely to be questioned and may be redefined. (See following section that addresses Venus RX in detail.)

Natal/Progressed Effect: You may have relationship issues in that you either feel unloved, cannot accept affection comfortably or withdraw from your partner. You could also feel as if you never have enough money. For a woman, especially if Venus RX is in their 1st house or conjunct their ascendant, she is likely to be stronger and more determined than most men and thus demonstrate "Warrior Goddess" traits.

Planet: Mars
Stationary: 5 days
RX Frequency: Once every 24 months
RX Duration: 2 months

Transit Effect: Emotions and energy are turned inward resulting in passive aggression & stress. Competitive nature is likely to be also turned inward, causing a person to compete more with themselves than others. Motivation and enthusiasm for a project can wane.

Natal/Progressed Effect: May have trouble asserting yourself, be overly shy, and unable to stay focused on goals. Allowing others to walk on you or expecting them to fight your battles for you are also possible. If/when Mars goes direct in the progressed chart, these can reverse and vice versa.

Planet: Jupiter
Stationary: 5 - 8 days
RX Frequency: Once a year
RX Duration: 4 months

Transit Effect: Ethics reevaluated, religious beliefs questioned, philosophies revisited, often on a grand scale. Not a good time to travel as plans are likely to be disrupted.

Natal/Progressed Effect: May constantly seek the meaning in life and attempt to find spiritual values that never quite seem right. Can also be enthusiastic about worn-out ideas, but on the positive side may found hidden value or potential in certain situations or businesses. When/if

Jupiter goes direct in the progressed chart, over-confidence can result in over-extending plans or finances.

Planet: Saturn
Stationary: 11 - 12 days
RX Frequency: Once a year
RX Duration: 4.5 months

Transit Effect: Expect delays and the necessity of extra effort. Authority issues could arise. Projects you thought were completed will require rework.

Natal/Progressed Effect: Likely to have frequent conflicts with authority figures or feel persecuted. May fear approaching authority figures in general. If/when Saturn goes Rx in the progressed chart, may acquire a sense of "What's the use?" and sabotage your own achievements. Saturn RX often indicates an absentee father, either physically or emotionally.

Planet: Uranus
Stationary: 2 weeks
RX Frequency: Once a year
RX Duration: 5 months

Transit Effect: Expect the unexpected. Surprises and changes abound in events and behavior. Plans, no matter how firm, are likely to be disrupted. Introverts may become extroverts and vice versa.

Natal/Progressed Effect: Behavior is likely to be unpredictable, especially in areas affected by Uranus' house placement and/or aspects to planets in other houses.

Planet: Neptune
Stationary: 2 weeks
RX Frequency: Once a year
RX Duration: 5 months

Transit Effect: Logic yields to intuition and creativity. As the planet of illusion, there may be more media emphasis on fantasy. More likely to be deceived or misled. Rather than feeling connected with others may feel isolated.

Logic yields to intuition and creativity. As the planet of illusion, there may be more media emphasis on fantasy. More likely to be deceived or misled. Rather than feeling connected with others may feel isolated.

Natal/Progressed Effect: Can be very prone to living in a fantasy world steeped in idealism. May set unrealistic goals and not possess the logic required to meet them. Very intuitive and possibly psychic with a deep understanding of human nature. May be incapable of dealing with harsh realities and try to escape via denial or alcohol or drug abuse. Strong affinity for the arts.

Planet: Pluto
Stationary: 17 days
RX Frequency: Once a year
RX Duration: 5 months

Transit Effect: Fresh starts/dead ends; destruction/ rebuilding. Can be heavy forces outside your control, i.e. war, weapons, government upheaval. May be forced to reevaluate what you value most or trigger intense soul searching and figurative digging through old baggage, especially when opposite or in conjunction with the Ascendant.

Natal/Progressed Effect: Abuse of power is common, either as the one being used and manipulated or the one on a power trip.

♀℞ Venus Retrograde

Venus retrograde cycles operate beneath the surface on issues where there's a conflict between your actions and core beliefs. You may see parts of yourself that you normally keep hidden or make more mistakes than usual. If you're not sure what your values actually are, you may be forced to confront that question once and for all.

If you're wondering how a specific Venus retrograde cycle is going to affect you, the first place to look would be approximately 8 years before that, when she went retrograde in the same sign. This is particularly apropos if you have any unfinished business in that part of your life which has been lying dormant since that time. Aspects other than a conjunction may be felt as well, but not as strongly. The House these degrees fall upon in your Natal Chart will determine which part of your life is affected. Venus goes retrograde roughly every 18 months in a sign approximately seven signs away from the previous one. For example, she went retrograde in Scorpio Fall 2002; Gemini Spring 2004; Aquarius and Capricorn Winter 2005; Leo and Virgo late Summer 2007; mostly Aries Spring 2009 and Libra and Scorpio in October 2010.

One of the most fascinating things about Venus' retrograde cycles is the pattern that the retrograde station positions form over time on the Zodiac (see below). There are numerous associations made with this particular five-pointed star pattern, some of which are related to witchcraft and various other things such as secret societies or devil worship. With Venus the natural ruler of women, relationships, and also material wealth, it's not surprising that such organizations would pick up on this particular symbol, especially when the retrograde cycles bring out Venus' darker side. As a result, the five-pointed star is frequently associated with evil where in reality it is simply a cosmic pattern created by Venus' planetary cycles.

On a more positive note it can also be compared to the Lotus blossom, the symbol for enlightenment, a spiritual condition which requires first and foremost that you know and love yourself before you can extend that sentiment to the world at large. As ruler of the zodiacal 2nd House which

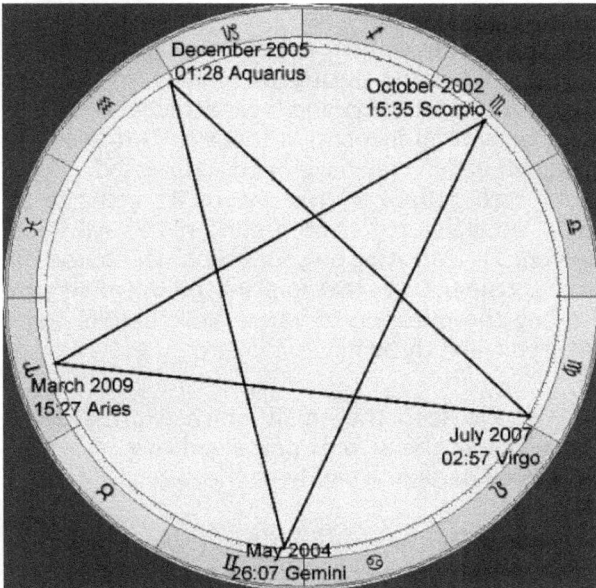

Figure 1 Venus Retrograde Station Positions

comprises those things you value, including yourself, Venus has a strong influence on this part of your life. Thus, during a Venus retrograde cycle you may be seeking enlightenment, even if you're not consciously aware of it until much later. Venus has a dual nature which is reflected in the fact that the ancients considered her not only the Goddess of Love but also the Goddess of War,

109

depending on when she was visible in the sky. When she was the Evening Star, she was the love goddess, when she was the Morning Star, which occurs during her retrograde phase, she was the warrior goddess. Remember that Venus retrograde affects the entire world, collectively and individually. As Erin Sullivan points out in her landmark work, "Retrograde Planets: Traversing the Inner Landscape," this is a time to particularly watch the news with regard to what is going on at the international level as far as diplomatic issues are concerned. The Maya believed that when Venus reached her heliacal rising stage, just prior to when she becomes visible as the Morning Star, that political situations were particularly unstable and leaders insecure and fallible.

Astrologer Bruce Scofield states that this time "often corresponds to a time of failure or resignation on the part of leaders and often coincides with a major accident or storm." Consider that the 2010 U.S. midterm elections occurred during this period. If those congress critters, as some call them, weren't in a very insecure and vulnerable state at that time I don't know when they were. And what was Venus' effect on each individual as they went to the polls? This was truly a time when your social values were up for review and your deepest feelings about them were more likely to surface as opposed to those you learned and accepted at a conscious level; nonetheless, your heart is not as easily fooled.

Ponder Venus' dual nature again for a moment as you consider that Venus defines your love nature as well as its antithesis of how you defend yourself. Both have an element of intuition and logic attached. During a Venus retrograde cycle your natural inclination tends to switch as you deal with some part of yourself which may have been suppressed. If you are out of synch with your core beliefs or true nature it's going to be under review and cause an imbalance. As noted earlier, this will most likely relate to the house Venus is transiting on your chart. Of course you can't do too much about your true nature, that imprint the Universe gave you at birth, but it does beg the question of where your beliefs come from and how you've nurtured them throughout your life.

Along those lines, you may have seen the email which expressed the various ways in which four to eight year olds perceived love. Since I couldn't possibly do it justice by paraphrasing, here they are:

'When my grandmother got arthritis, she couldn't bend over and paint her toenails anymore. So my grandfather does it for her all the time, even when his hands got arthritis too. That's love.'
Rebecca- age 8

♀

'When someone loves you, the way they say your name is different.
You just know that your name is safe in their mouth.'
Billy - age 4

♀

'Love is when a girl puts on perfume and a boy puts on shaving cologne
and they go out and smell each other.'
Karl - age 5

♀

'Love is when you go out to eat and give somebody most of your French
fries without making them give you any of theirs.'
Chrissy - age 6

♀

'Love is what makes you smile when you're tired.'
Terri - age 4

♀

'Love is when my mommy makes coffee for my daddy and she takes a
sip before giving it to him, to make sure the taste is OK.'
Danny - age 7

♀

'Love is when you kiss all the time. Then when you get tired of kissing,
you still want to be together and you talk more.
My Mommy and Daddy are like that. They look gross when they kiss'
Emily - age 8

♀

'Love is what's in the room with you at Christmas if you stop opening
presents and listen.'
Bobby - age 7

♀

'If you want to learn to love better, you should start with a friend who
you hate,'
Nikka - age 6

♀

'Love is when you tell a guy you like his shirt, then he wears it everyday.'
Noelle - age 7

♀

'Love is like a little old woman and a little old man who are still friends even after they know each other so well.'
Tommy - age 6

♀

'During my piano recital, I was on a stage and I was scared. I looked at all the people watching me and saw my daddy waving and smiling. He was the only one doing that. I wasn't scared anymore.'
Cindy - age 8

♀

'My mommy loves me more than anybody
You don't see anyone else kissing me to sleep at night.'
Clare - age 6

♀

'Love is when Mommy gives Daddy the best piece of chicken.'
Elaine-age 5

♀

'Love is when Mommy sees Daddy smelly and sweaty and still says he is handsomer than Robert Redford.'
Chris - age 7

♀

'Love is when your puppy licks your face even after you left him alone all day.'
Mary Ann - age 4

♀

'I know my older sister loves me because she gives me all her old clothes and has to go out and buy new ones.'
Lauren - age 4

♀

'When you love somebody, your eyelashes go up and down and little stars come out of you.' (what an image)
Karen - age 7

♀

'Love is when Mommy sees Daddy on the toilet and she doesn't think it's
gross.'
Mark - age 6

♀

'You really shouldn't say 'I love you' unless you mean it. But if you mean
it, you should say it a lot. People forget.'
Jessica - age 8

♀

The winner was a four year old child whose next door neighbor was an
elderly gentleman who had recently lost his wife.
Upon seeing the man cry, the little boy went into the old gentleman's
yard, climbed onto his lap, and just sat there.
When his Mother asked what he had said to the neighbor, the little boy
said,
'Nothing, I just helped him cry'

♀

Did you notice that every example is based on either the child's own
observation or experience? This clearly illustrates that what children
know about love is what they witness and experience which plant seeds
that germinate into beliefs. These are classic examples of the
development of the love goddess' energy. However, remember that
Venus has two sides. How do you think the darker side develops? No
doubt this darker side develops through experiences related to hate or
lack of love, which surface when you're frightened or threatened in some
way. Both of these energies are stored within you and express
themselves as the occasion warrants. In some cases how you act may be
simply as a result of socialization. For example, if a child is beaten until
he tells his father that he loves him, he is not going to be experiencing
the true essence of love during that declaration. Throughout your
lifetime you may learn similar lessons that ultimately make you dishonest
in your expression of emotion, perhaps even to yourself. This dishonesty
will be a target of Venus retrograde periods until the true essence of love
is reconciled.

Other parts of your life which Venus influences include where you find
beauty and incorporate it into your life, as well as what you value
whether it's your possessions, your self-esteem or beliefs. During a Venus
retrograde period you may see parts of yourself that are normally
hidden. As with all retrograde periods, the planet's energy is

113

internalized, yielding opportunities for introspection, review, and dealing with any issues vying for attention.

Thus, during this Venus retrograde cycle, ponder how you define love, how you express it, and whether there is anything holding you back from its full expression. This applies to how much you value each individual area of your life. Consider your attitude toward your material possessions as well. Do you associate them with your value as a person, requiring only the best, so that you can impress the world? Or are you at the other end of the spectrum and have no regard for them? Similarly, how do you treat the things you have? Are you wasteful or frugal? How do you view the people you interact with every day, whether at home or work? Do those same sentiments extend to the world at large?

Depending on what you find, this may be the time when you declare war on some part of yourself which is out of line and holding you back from achieving your highest ambitions. It is also a time to examine your sense of social responsibility and whether your actions as an individual are contributing to or detracting from the world around you. Retrograde Venus is demanding your attention to these issues and will don her armor as the goddess of war if required to make her point. As always, it's in your best interest to listen when these cosmic tutors speak.

ECLIPSES

Eclipses have been a source of fear and fascination for millennia. You can imagine what reaction a sight like the Sun disappearing at midday or the Moon turning red caused in different cultures when they had no understanding of the astronomical mechanism at work. Today most modern people understand what causes them, but they probably don't know why they happen when they do. . .

As a quick review, a Lunar Eclipse occurs at a Full Moon when the Sun and Moon are in opposition. The Earth gets between them and casts its shadow on the Moon, which is what you see gradually moving across it. Due to "earthshine" or the reflected light of the Sun from the Earth, it's not entirely dark so the Moon looks reddish and doesn't entirely disappear. A Solar Eclipse happens with a New Moon when the Moon's path takes it directly in front of the Sun, blocking it out. This is by far the more dramatic of the two, does not last nearly as long, and is viewed across a much smaller geographical area. Of course the question now is why does this only happen twice a year instead of every month? The answer is simply because they aren't lined up properly with the lunar nodes.

In order for an eclipse to occur, the ecliptic and lunar nodes need to be within approximately 15 degrees or less. The ecliptic is the apparent path of the Sun and the lunar nodes are the points where the Moon's orbit crosses it going from South to North (North Node) and North to South (South Node). The nodes rotate slowly in a counter-clockwise direction around the zodiac and represent important personal points in your horoscope. Typically aspects to the North Node indicate something new is coming into your life or a significant event or change is on the way and aspects to the South Node indicate something is ending or going out of your life. There is karmic meaning to them also where the South Node indicates where you've been and the North Node where you're going.

Not all eclipses are total, according to how close the ecliptic and nodes are aligned. There are three types of Lunar Eclipse including an Appulse, *i.e.* an eclipse where the Moon enters only the penumbra of the Earth, its larger shadow as opposed to the smaller cone at the center of the Earth's shadow. There are also Partial Eclipses where the Moon enters the umbra without being totally immersed in it and of course Total Eclipses where the Moon is entirely consumed by the umbra.

There are six types of Solar Eclipses including a Partial, where the Moon doesn't quite cover the Sun; a Total where the Moon completely covers the Sun as seen from the path of its shadow on the Earth's surface; an Annular Eclipse where the Sun is entirely covered but the Moon is too far away for the apex of its shadow to reach the Earth. Furthermore, it will not entirely hide the Sun so a narrow ring of light will surround the dark New Moon (see picture at left). An Annular-Total eclipse is a Total Eclipse for part of its path and then Annular for the remainder. There are also Annular and Total Eclipses where the central line does not touch the Earth's surface.

Needless to say both the Sun and Moon have a strong influence on our horoscopes so when they pair up with the nodes it's normally going to facilitate a significant effect. Nonetheless, some are noticeable in our lives or even in the world at large while others come and go largely unnoticed. One place to look for their affect is in the astrological Houses in which they fall on your Natal Chart as that is the area of your life that is most likely to be affected. The Houses represent polarities with the 1st/7th axis the Axis of Identity which relates to our self and those close to us; 2nd/8th, the Axis of Desire (including both love and money); 3rd/9th the Axis of Thoughts and Beliefs as well as our surroundings; 4th/10th, that ongoing struggle between home and career or our private and public persona; the 5th/11th, Axis of Love and Creative Power where we develop our love of self and then extend it to others; the 6th/12th, the Axis of Work and Service to self and others.

Eclipses come in pairs and sometimes trios that will influence one of these axes with the effects lasting as long as 18 months. Their effects are sometimes noticeable up to three months before they occur; time is not necessarily linear in space. Others have theorized that it's actually the nodes that bring the effects and as they line up previous to the actual eclipse, which acts as the climax, they trigger events. The House influence will rotate counter-clockwise around the horoscope according to the placement of the lunar nodes. You can find out when and in which astrological sign they will occur in an ephemeris.

Eclipses have been observed in a scientific manner for millennia. As far back as 747 B.C. the Babylonians could accurately predict the timing of eclipses and also noticed that lunar eclipses only occurred when there was a solar eclipse but that a solar eclipse could occur without an accompanying lunar eclipse. Sometimes solar eclipses even came with two lunar eclipses, each one about two weeks either before or after the solar. By the 4th Century B.C. they even noticed that eclipses were not isolated events, but occurred in series which the Greek lexicographer Suidas named the Saros Series in the 10th Century A.D.

Each series begins as a tiny partial eclipse at either the North or South Pole and produces an eclipse every 18 years plus 9 to 11 days, depending on how many leap years there are in the 18 years span. Each one advances approximately 120 degrees of longitude from the last and each one will move a little further north or south, depending on which pole it began. As it closes in on the lunar nodes, the partial eclipses will become total, then become partial again as it moves beyond them again. Each series contains approximately 71 - 73 solar eclipses and runs for approximately 1300 years after which it will end at the opposite pole from where it began.

Each series is named according to its "birth pole" and are also given a number based on the actual years that series will produce an eclipse. Thus, they are not numbered based on when they originated, but when they'll occur. Their names will thus be such things as 15 North, 16 South, etc. Each year will have two eclipse "seasons" with one from the North series and one from the South. It's also interesting to note that each series makes the rounds of the Zodiac and thus when they progress from partial to total, they will be around the same zodiacal longitude as when they were born and will eventually fade away in that same general area.

The truly interesting part as far as their astrological influence is concerned is that each series has its own characteristics, which will be expressed in some way by each eclipse within that family. Even as family members have certain traits in common, yet maintain their individuality, eclipses will do the same. Thus, when an eclipse occurs, think back approximately 18 years to what was happening at that time and you may find a clue on how the current one will affect your life.

Typically the difference between a Solar and Lunar eclipse as far as its astrological influence is concerned relates to whether it's external or internal. In other words, Solar Eclipses tend to stimulate events around you whereas Lunar Eclipses work more on your thoughts and feelings, though these, in turn, are likely to motivate you to act and perhaps facilitate various events. They tend to highlight a certain area of your life and if you've been ignoring anything, it will be brought to your attention in a way that is hard to miss.

If you were born during a Solar or Lunar Eclipse, the theme of that particular Saros Series is going to be reflected in your life. For famous individuals born during an eclipse, astrologer, Bill Meridian, has identified a correlation between the location of the events that brought them fame and the path of visibility of the eclipse. For example, Karl Marx was born during a solar eclipse on May 5, 1818 and the path extends across geographical areas most affected by his idea. The Confederate army leader, Robert E. Lee, was also born during an eclipse and the path slices the USA in half.

For more information on the personality of a particular Saros Series and when they occur I recommend the book *Predictive Astrology: The Eagle and the Lark* by Bernadette Brady. Another excellent book on eclipses is *The Predictive Power of Eclipse Paths* by Bill Meridian. NASA has maps available of eclipse paths at:

http://eclipse.gsfc.nasa.gov/eclipse.html

ASPECTS

Aspects refer to the different angular configurations that planets form with each other in a horoscope or those which transiting planets form with a specific chart. Those most often referred to are the **Conjunction, Square, Opposition, Trine** and **Sextile** which are often referred to as Ptolomaic aspects. The others, which include but are not limited to the **Semi-sextile, Quincunx, Semi-square** and **Sesquiquadrate**, are included below but are used primarily when more detail is required to understand a given chart. This isn't to say that they're not as important, only that the more common aspects are usually sufficient.

Any major character trait or event usually has several indicators, making them hard to miss, and usually going to this level of detail isn't required. Nonetheless, the less common aspects are very handy at explaining such things as the personality differences between twins and other traits that are not obvious or explained otherwise.

The **Orb** refers to the allowable degrees on either side of exactness where an influence is still felt. There is a range indicated since astrologers weigh other factors besides simply the amount of degrees including whether the aspect is applying (just starting toward exactness) or separating (ending). Which planets are involved, whether they are personal planets, which house they rule and other forms of planetary dignity are also considered. For personal transits, the typical orb is a mere one degree with the Sun a possible exception.

Aspects represent an energy exchange between the planets and other celestial bodies such as the Sun and Moon, which are frequently referred to planets in astrology for simplicity sake, even though astrologers are fully aware they are not technically a "planet."

Astrologers tend to have different opinions with regard to "out of sign" aspects. For example, a planet at 2 degrees Taurus and a planet at 29 degrees Leo are 116 degrees apart, which is within orb of a trine, which is 120 degrees. However, both Taurus and Leo are Fixed signs, which makes their energy exchange significantly different than for Taurus and Virgo, another Earth sign. I tend to look at out of sign aspects as similar to a quincunx, which occurs when the two signs involved have nothing in common, either through element or modality.

Aspect: Conjunction
Symbol: ☌
Angle: 0 degrees
Orb: 5 - 8 degrees up to 10 degrees for Sun and Moon

Description: This aspect occurs when two planets conjoin. Its affect is a basic blending of the energies of the respective planets. When a Full Moon or New Moon conjoins with a planet it can activate aspects tied to it in the Natal, Progressed or Return Charts that were previously dormant. Its effect can be either positive or negative, depending on which planet and other existing aspects it encounters.

Aspect: Square
Symbol: ☐
Angle: 90 degrees
Orb: 5 - 8 degrees

Description: The square occurs when two planets are 90 degrees (or 3 signs) apart. It precipitates a need for action, a struggle or something to be overcome and/or changed. It is considered a harsh or negative aspect, but the final outcome depends on the motivation of the person and how they handle the challenge. If handled properly, personal growth will result of a positive nature.

Aspect: Opposition
Symbol: ☍
Angle: 180 degrees
Orb: 5 - 8 degrees up to 10 degrees for Sun and Moon

Description: This aspect occurs, as it name implies, when two planets are 180 degrees (or 6 signs) apart. A polarity is implied and often other people are involved. Some sort of tension or tug-o-war is likely. This aspect is considered negative. When you're at Solar Opposition, i.e. six months from your birthday, be especially careful. You're likely to encounter some sort of issue at this time.

Aspect: Trine
Symbol: △
Angle: 120 degrees
Orb: 6 - 8 degrees

Description: A trine occurs when two planets are 120 degrees apart, which usually amounts to 4 signs. It is generally interpreted as a soft or easy aspect with harmony implied. However, if a person has nothing but trines in his chart, he could be inclined to be lazy or expect an easy life. They would be lacking the motivation to overcome anything, which tends to result in character development.

Aspect: Sextile
Symbol: ✶
Angle: 60 degrees
Orb: 3 - 6 degrees

Description: This aspect occurs when planets are 60 degrees (or 2 signs) apart. Its affect is similar but not as strong as a trine. It's generally considered positive and in transits frequently signifies an opportunity. Some astrologers believe sextiles give talents in the areas indicated by the planet and house placements involved.

Aspect: Semi-square
Symbol: ∠
Angle: 45 degrees
Orb: 2 degrees

Description: Similar to a square but with more internal struggle. It is also considered negative, but not as strong. It will often represent an irritation, tension or some sort of friction between the planets and houses involved.

Aspect: Quincunx or Inconjunct
Symbol: ⚻
Angle: 150 degrees
Orb: 2 degrees; 3 degrees with Sun or Moon

Description: Somewhat negative, a quincunx generally indicates an awkward situation that requires readjustment, a Catch-22, or one in which the person will have to change course or defend their position on an issue. The planets would be approximately 5 signs apart.

Aspect: Sesquiquadrate
Symbol: ⬕
Angle: 135 degrees
Orb: 2 degrees

Description: Generally considered similar to a square and thus a negative aspect, but may be easier to release and express.

Aspect: Semi-sextile
Symbol: ⋁
Angle: 30 degrees
Orb: 2 degrees

Description: Generally regarded as being a slightly negative aspect that can represent an annoyance or nuisance of some type. It can also represent an opportunity that will require significant work to attain like a cloud with silver lining or a blessing in disguise.

There are various other aspects often referred to as harmonics which simply divide the 360 degrees by additional numbers but these are the ones most commonly used.

Aspect Patterns

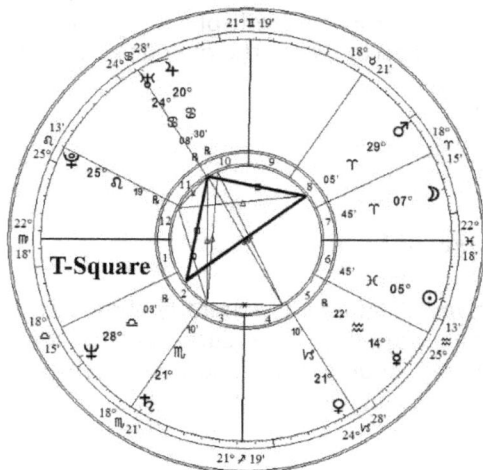

Figure 2 T-Square Aspect Pattern

While most charts look like little more than a system of random lines, occasionally you can see a definite pattern. One of the most common is called a **T-Square** (left) which looks like a involving three planets with one at the apex and the other two at the base. Two planets will be in Opposition to one another with the third squared off with the other two. While all these aspects are considered negative, it nonetheless seems to give strength to the individual as they overcome the tension and conflicts imposed. Some charts have more than one.

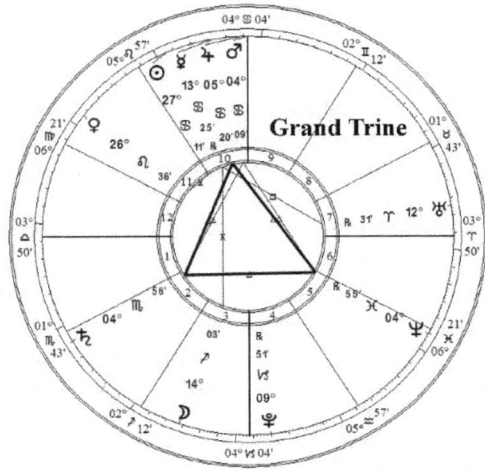

Another pattern that is easy to see in a chart is a **Grand Trine**, (right) which shows up as an equilateral triangle centered on the chart. In most cases the points of the triangle will be in signs with a common Element, *i.e.* Air, Water, Earth or Fire signs, thus making it a Grand Air Trine, Grand Water Trine, etc. While it would seem

Figure 3 Grand Trine Aspect Pattern

that having three trines joined together would be very positive, this is sometimes not the case as the person may lack balance in their life and thus understanding of others, making them perhaps lazy or judgmental, particularly if things come too easily for them, sparing them of taking on challenges that refine and strengthen the character. They will not have as much incentive to broaden their reach or overcome the adversity indicated by T-squares.

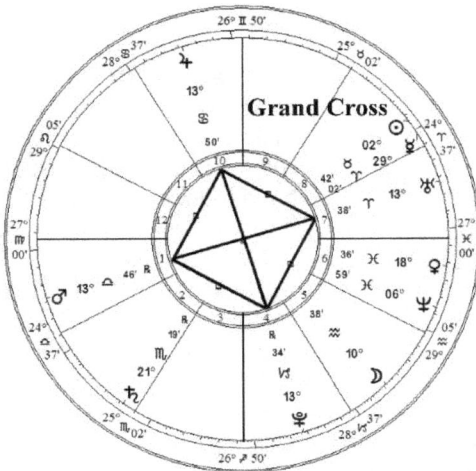

Figure 4 Grand Cross Aspect Pattern

If there are two T-squares joined at the base, they then form what is known as a **Grand Cross** (left). This shows up on the chart as an obvious red square with an "X" connecting the opposite corners. This is a powerful influence, particularly because the planets will be located in the same modality, i.e. cardinal, fixed or mutable signs. In other words, a Cardinal Grand Cross would involve planets in Aries, Cancer,

Libra and Capricorn; a Fixed Grand Cross would involve planets in Aquarius, Taurus, Leo and Scorpio; and a Mutable Grand Cross would involve Gemini, Virgo, Sagittarius and Pisces.

Thus, there are a lot of similar characteristics being conveyed, yet there is still the square and opposition influence that introduces numerous conflicts. Grand Crosses are somewhat rare and generally denote a person who has numerous challenges and contradictions to deal with in their life. The strength and degree of opposition will naturally also depend on which planets and houses are involved.

Business consultant, Steven Gaffney, has described the challenges of this aspect perfectly when he said, "Most people will say that in retrospect their most difficult and challenging experiences were some of their most valuable ones. In fact, most people say that hard times generally produce much growth because responding to such times demands ingenuity. We all know that even when we are not responsible for our challenging circumstances, we are 100 percent responsible for our response to the challenge."

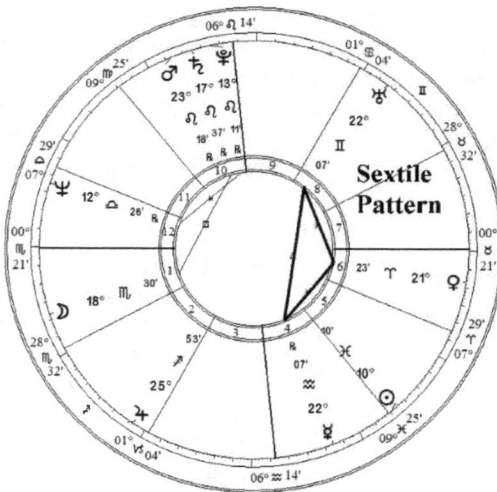

Figure 5 Sextile Pattern

A fairly common pattern is a simple **Sextile Pattern**, (next page) a small triangle that combines two sextiles with a trine, tying three planets together in a fairly tight aspect with generally good implications, though these folks sometimes seem inclined to fall into a rut. Sextile people usually have inborn abilities in the Houses affected by the pattern and are willing to work at developing these talents and skills.

Another pattern that comes up occasionally is known as the **Mystic Rectangle** (below). This pattern, as it name implies, creates a rectangle with a set of parallel sextiles linked to a set of parallel trines, tying four planets together. Two modalities and two elements will be involved, linked in positive aspect. However, if you look more closely you can see there are also two or more Oppositions involved from each of the diagonal corners.

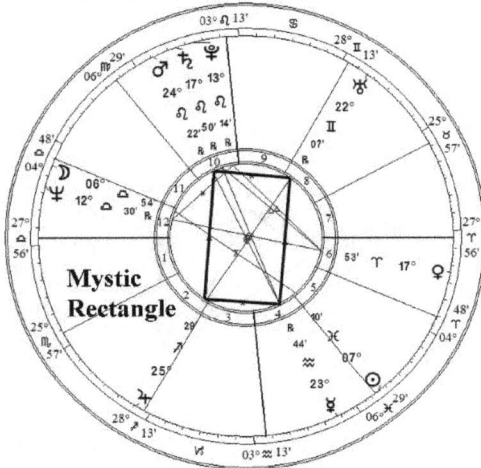

Figure 6 Mystic Rectangle

This results in a blending of positive and negative effects that will depend on the planets and houses involved, but could also indicate a choice or decision is involved. Both choices may be positive, but mutually exclusive. Another possibility would be that either choice will have a price that somewhat counters its benefits. For example, you may find your dream home, but the mortgage will be slightly out of your comfort range or you are given an opportunity to take a much-wanted trip but don't have enough vacation time.

A **Triangle of Potential** (right) is another fairly common pattern that comprises a trine, sextile and opposition, in other words two soft aspects and one hard aspect. In this case, the planet at the apex of the trine and sextile is the key to solving the opposition. The person will experience struggles, but by utilizing the energy of the trine and sextile will be able to make them work, so to speak. In many respects the hard aspects are what

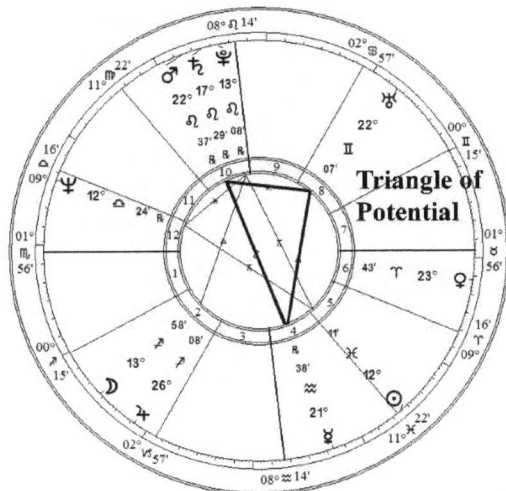

Figure 7 Triangle of Potential

motivate us. If life was always easy we'd have a lot less incentive to grow. A Triangle of Potential will give a person just enough friction to utilize latent talents and abilities that otherwise might lie dormant.

A **Yod** (right) is formed by two quincunx aspects to a single planet which are joined at the base by a sextile, making it look like a pointer. The term originated with the engraved silver hand with the index finger pointing which is used in the Torah to mark where the last reading ended and the subsequent one is to take place. It is also called the finger of God or the hand of fate. Frequently these are seen where a person has a very specific and perhaps fated ambition in life.

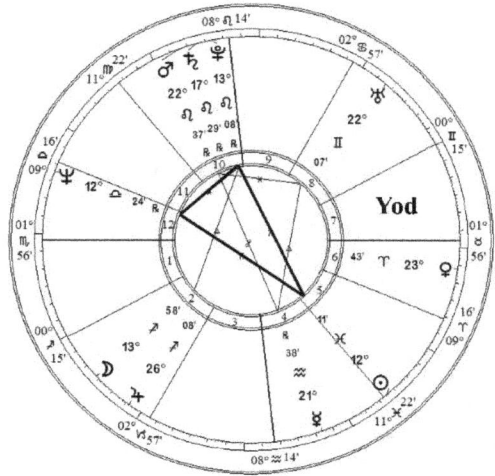

Figure 8 Yod

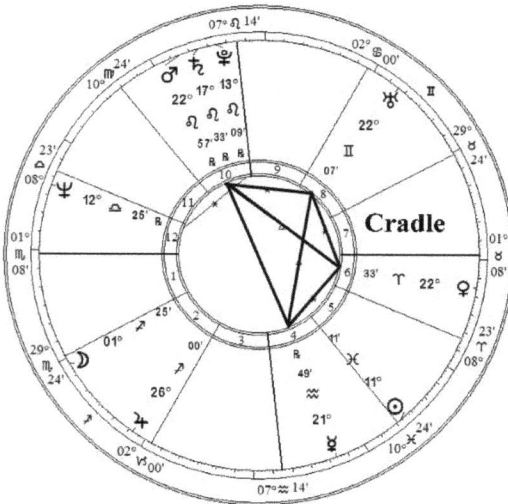

Figure 9 Cradle

There are various other patterns as well such as the **Cradle** (left), which is similar to a sextile pattern and sometimes has yet another sextile which makes it a **Hooded Cradle** (not shown). Another way to look at it is two Triangles of Potential. This would imply that the two planets at the apex of the two Triangles of Potential, which sextile one another, would be the driving force to overcome the opposition between Mars and

Mercury, which suggests the person may be perceived as verbally aggressive.

The **Kite** (below) combines a Grand Trine with a Sextile Pattern. While these two patterns are usually favorable, the combination introduces an opposition, in this case between Uranus in the 8th house and Jupiter in the 2nd. If you look closely at this chart you can also see a yod, the triangle of potential and a cradle. In fact, this same chart was loaded and used for several of the above example though at slightly different times.

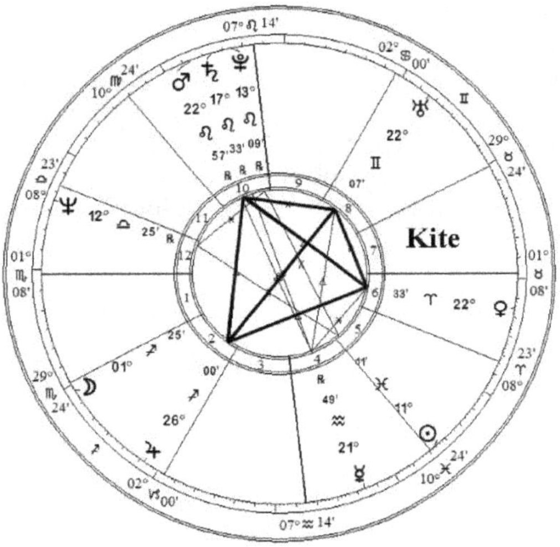

Figure 10 Kite

HOUSES

If there's anything that astrology tends to do it's give you too much information, which can easily boggle your mind. However, it is this richness and complexity that makes it so valuable. The ability to understand each of the elements and its effect is essential to building the instinct necessary to integrate all the information into a meaningful whole. For example, it's not uncommon to have numerous bits of conflicting information in a chart, its interpretation or a horoscope. You could have a Neptune Trine Venus that would ordinarily put you in a very tolerant and easy-going frame of mind simultaneously with Mars squaring your Ascendant, which would normally make you aggressive and probably less than pleasant to be around. Which one will be more strongly manifested can depend on numerous other factors, including the House in which they fall.

The chart below shows house placement, the House numbers running counterclockwise in the inner-most circle. You can also see them in the charts in the previous section.

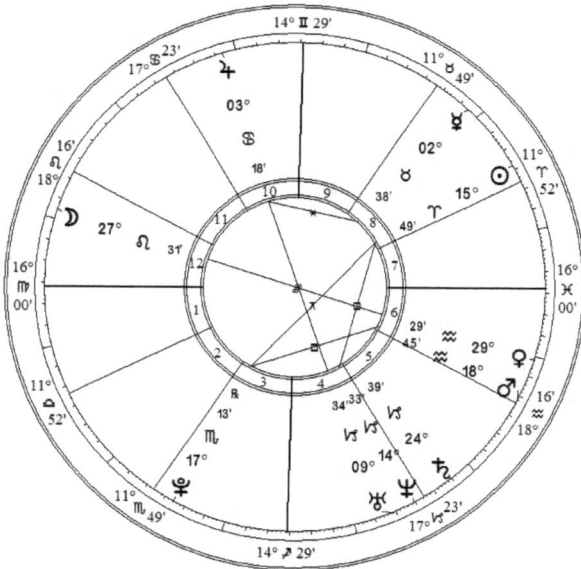

Figure 11 Houses Begin at the Ascendant

128

One of the most difficult things for someone new to astrology to understand is the concept of the twelve Houses. Each House covers a specific area of your life, which can be very generally summarized as follows:

1st House - The Ascendant; influences the person's appearance to the world, their general attitude toward life, outward personality and how they assert themselves.

2nd House - Influences a person's values, how they handle money, and feel about their possessions. It includes their belongings, finances, values, ethics and their physical body. Peace, pleasures, comforts, needs, and liberty are also influenced.

3rd House - Defines the thought process and intellect. It affects a person's understanding, learning ability and style. It also covers brothers, sisters, relatives, neighbors, early education, short journeys, manuscripts, and letters; anything you get in writing other than the legal implications of a contract, which are covered by the 9th.

4th House - Relates to the home and family environment, past and present, including past lives, and what makes you feel comfortable. It also includes inherited tendencies and subconscious as well as our mother and relationship with her.

5th House - Colors the expression of personal creativity, sports, love affairs and relationships with children. It also includes entertainment media, speculations, and games. Your ego is also in the 5th House domain.

6th House - Affects work and other practical efforts, such as anything you do or produce. Health and pets are also included as well as servants, inferiors, service, dress and hygiene. I also suspect that time falls in this house.

7th House - Drives close relationships, partnerships, open enemies, and patronage. Whereas the 1st house describes who we are within, the 7th house affects who we are with those closest to us and how we relate to them.

8th House - Governs other people's money and shared resources, attitudes toward sex, death, healing and regeneration. It likewise covers inheritances, legacies and secrets. Also affects endings and new beginnings. This is the house of transformations, where events and/or experiences occur that have a major impact on who and what we are, after which we are never the same.

9th House - Relates to higher education, long distance travel, relocation, and legal matters. Also our core beliefs, expectations, ethics, philosophy, religion, teaching, politics, and other cultures.

10th House - Relates to reputation and standing before the community and your attitude toward authority figures. Influences honor, worldly power, fame, promotion, calling, and position. Some believe it represents the person's father as the 4th represents the mother, though some astrologers reverse them, depending on which parent held the authoritarian role. "Status" is included in this house as well. This rather vague term relates to such things as titles and labels, if you will. For example, when you graduate from high school or college, get married, become a parent, earn a promotion (or conversely get fired), win an election or other contest, (heaven forbid) go to jail (also 12th House) and so forth, your "status in the community" has changed and will be reflected in this House.

11th House - Influences importance and interaction with friends, acquaintances, organizations, and groups including coworkers. Hopes and wishes are also included as well as the person's attitude toward humanity in general. I've often wondered why goals, hopes and wishes are in this particular house and the primary reason I come up with is that these are those things that are dependent on acceptance or help from others. There are some accomplishments that we achieve entirely on our own, but if we require any help, including kudos or other support from others such as accepting and purchasing a product we develop, then those "others" in the 11th House are going to come into the picture somewhere for us to succeed. As has been said for decades, "No man is an island," a statement that summarizes the essence of the 11th House quite nicely.

12th House - Includes spirituality, inspiration, enlightenment, dreams, hidden enemies, martyrs, insanity, institutions and the collective consciousness. This is the house of inner struggles, self-undoing, confinement, anxiety, care and limitations. It is also related to prisons, convents, and hospitals, which imply seclusion and limitation.

ZODIACAL HOUSES					
1st House	2nd House	3rd House	4th House	5th House	6th House
Aries	Taurus	Gemini	Cancer	Leo	Virgo
7th House	8th House	9th House	10th House	11th House	12th House
Libra	Scorpio	Sagittarius	Capricorn	Aquarius	Pisces

Table 3 Zodiacal Sign and House Assignment

An individual's 1st House cusp is delineated by their Ascendant and the other Houses follow from there in a counter-clockwise direction around the Natal Chart. Since each sign has its own character and personality, this will reflect on the House. For example, if a person's 3rd House, which rules the thought process and intellect, is placed in Scorpio, it's very likely that this person will be very interested in subjects of a mysterious nature or the occult. If their 6th House of Work, Health and Pets is in Aquarius, they're likely to do well working for a large company of someplace where they'll be interacting with groups of people as opposed to a more isolated career. Planets placed in the Houses natally as well as current transits also affect these areas of your life.

If you're familiar with the general characteristics of the Sun Signs you probably noticed a strong similarity between them and the twelve houses described above. Not surprisingly, Zodiacal House placement coincides with these signs as noted in the table above. Some astrologers also consider the placement of the Sun Sign as defining the first house, especially when the exact time of birth is unknown or when casting a mass horoscope.

So, in summary, there are:

- Your Natal Houses, which are for you personally, based on your birth information, including your time and place of birth which determines your Ascendant.
- The Zodiacal Houses which are noted above and based on Aries being the first House.
- The Natural Houses for each sign such as those used in Sun Sign astrology, where the 1st House is denoted by the placement of the Sun. In other words, if your Sun Sign is Leo, then Leo is your first natural house.

CUSPS

Cusps are borders between either Houses or Signs. For Signs, the Sun will typically cross the cusp in the middle of the day or night, not at a nice clean cutoff at midnight. The Houses also may extend over more than one Sign, but the one with the most influence will be the one where the cusp lies.

Four of the House cusps are significant energy points and more influential. These are called the **Angles** and for most house systems occur at the **1st, 4th, 7th and 10th Houses.** These are defined by a system of "Great Circles" which are specific to your location. One is the horizon (whether or not you can see it); the Ecliptic (apparent path of the Sun); and the Meridian (parallel to the lines of longitude and passing directly over your head).

The Ascendant (1st house cusp) is the intersection of the horizon and the ecliptic in the east, or where the Sun rises. The *Imum Coeli* or IC or 4th house cusp, is defined by the intersection of the Meridian and Ecliptic (where the Sun is at Midnight). The Descendant or 7th house cusp, opposes the Ascendant and is the intersection of the Ecliptic and Horizon in the west, where the Sun sets. The Midheaven or *Medum Coeli*, a.k.a. 10th house cusp, is the intersection of the Ecliptic and Meridian, or where the Sun is located at Noon, local time. On your Natal Chart it represents which degree and sign of the zodiac was directly overhead when you were born. Thus, these house cusps derive from your actual geographical location.

There are various House division systems, but for Placidus and most others, the 1st is your Ascendant. Your Ascendant has strong bearing on your appearance before the world; the IC relates to your home environment, memories, and cultural roots; the Descendant has significant bearing on the close relationships you maintain in your life; and the Midheaven or MC relates to your public image and community standing. When natal or transiting planets form aspects to these cusps they will influence these respective areas of your life. If the planets are personalized, their influence will be particularly influential.

MODES AND ELEMENTS

Modes and *Elements* refer to certain inherent traits of a similar nature to be found in the various Signs. Depending on what a person's Natal Chart indicates, there may be more influences in a particular Mode or Element than others, giving that individual stronger tendencies in one direction than another. For example, someone with most of the planets resident is Earth Signs would be very practical and probably have a strong need for security. If a person had a bit of each, *i.e.* a chart with the planets evenly spread across the Zodiac, it could make them either more balanced on the positive side or unpredictable on the negative side. Like all character traits, there's a positive and negative manifestation for each of the modes and elements as well, both of which will be demonstrated at one time or another.

Modes

Each sign is one of three modalities, *i.e.* Fixed, Mutable or Cardinal. These signs square one another and often do not get along too well because they tend to be too much alike.

Cardinal

Cardinal signs like to make their own decisions and thus tend to be leaders. On the positive side they are just that, leaders, and on the negative side they're bossy and opinionated. Cardinal signs include **Aries, Cancer, Libra** and **Capricorn**.

Fixed

Fixed signs tend to be just that—fixed—and do not like change. On the positive side they are stable, on the negative side they are stubborn. If you think they're ever going to change, think again. They are what they are; *love 'em or leave 'em*. Fixed signs include **Taurus, Leo, Scorpio** and **Aquarius**.

Mutable

Mutable signs tend to be more flexible and adapt well to change. On the positive side they are flexible, on the negative side they are so busy examining all the options that they tend to be indecisive *(though the real champion of indecision is often Libra because they try so hard to be fair)*. Mutable signs include **Gemini, Virgo, Sagittarius** and **Pisces**.

Ω Ω Ω

£lements

The elements in ancient times were considered Fire, Water, Air and Earth. Zodiac signs are associated with these elements as well, the traits of which also tie in to the characteristics and tendencies of their associated signs.

Fire

Fire signs tend to be bubbly and enthusiastic, enjoy the public eye and like attention. They include **Aries, Leo** and **Sagittarius**. Fire signs tend to have tempers and discernable attitudes of aggression, royalty, and academia/snootiness, respectively. They typically make decisions based more on their emotional needs than logic, especially if and when their head and heart disagree. These emotions usually run true to what you'd expect from a Fire Sign, *i.e.* a bit of fiery temper and hot verbal expression.

Air

Air signs are good communicators and like to talk. And talk and talk and talk. They include **Aquarius, Gemini** and **Libra**. They like to learn as much as possible about any given subject, particularly those associated with their individual signs, *i.e.* unique/ nonconformist ideals, general learning and relationships, respectively. Aquarius and Gemini tend to be more logical than emotional and Libra tries to be a little of both. Generally, however, if their head and heart don't agree, they'll go with their head, *i.e.* logic. (Thus, these are not the classic "air heads.")

Water

Water signs tend to be emotional and will react to situations and make their decisions based on what they *feel* more than what they *think*. They are often prone to allergies and vague diseases, which are usually physical manifestations of unresolved emotional issues. Please note, however, that when I say "emotional" that I do not mean to imply that men and women manifest emotion in the same way. This should be intuitively obvious, but I want to make sure everyone understands.

Everyone pretty-well knows what it means when a woman gets emotional--it will probably mean tears and various other female-specific mood swings. You know, like going from zero to bitch in 7 seconds.... Men will manifest emotions in a different way, most commonly by being grumpy, perhaps a bit whiney or, depending on their other elements, maybe just sullen and quiet. However, just because a guy is ruled by emotion rather than logic doesn't mean he's a wuss. These folks often have highly developed intuitive powers, sometimes to the point of being psychic. Water signs include **Cancer, Scorpio** and **Pisces**. As being a Water Sign implies, the women are likely to cry when emotionally affected, which is often, though Scorpios are likely to swing that scorpion's tail around while they're at it.

Earth

Earth signs tend to be well-grounded, practical and stable and will use logic in their decisions more than emotion. If their head and heart don't agree, they'll go with their head. They are good with money and usually have assets accumulated in land interests, collectibles of all sorts, and stocks and bonds respectively. If you need advice on your finances, investments or how to handle a situation in the most sensible way, these are the ones to ask. They are dependable, almost to a fault, and will rarely, if ever, let you down, even if they gripe about doing so. They include **Taurus, Virgo** and **Capricorn**.

Element/Mode	Cardinal	Fixed	Mutable	Driver
Fire	Aries	Leo	Sagittarius	Excitement
Earth	Capricorn	Taurus	Virgo	Security
Air	Libra	Aquarius	Gemini	Communications/ Data
Water	Cancer	Scorpio	Pisces	Emotions
Reaction to Change	Initiates	Resists	Adapts	

The above table shows how the modes and elements line up and which sign is the epitome of a particular mix. For example, if a person has planets in their Natal chart that reside in several Air and Fixed signs they will probably show many of the same traits as an Aquarius, regardless of where the Sun is located. Likewise, if they have several Fire and Cardinal signs, they will act very similar to an Aries, and so forth.

Table 4 Mode & Element Relationships

Elemental Interactions

Given the analogies to fire, earth, air and water it's hard not to use them as a further analogy to how the different signs interact. If nothing else it demonstrates even further how apropos these designations are besides helping you get a better feel for how these different signs relate to one another.

Air - Air

In a relationship between Air signs (Gemini, Libra, Aquarius), the winds are definitely going to blow. Both of these people like to talk and are good at it. Since there is a strong element of compatibility, they will generally get along quite well, much like fluffy white clouds skimming across the blue sky on a spring day. Air signs generally approach the world logically and make most their decisions based on facts rather than emotion. This does not mean they don't have emotions, only that they will favor logical arguments over emotional ones. When both parties agree on the same approach, this can help make true disagreements infrequent, but at the same time they might be missing an element that would improve the solution and enrich their lives.

Thus, it would behoove these folks to make a conscious effort, in their own logical way, to factor their feelings into relevant decisions. For example, say they can get a really good vacation deal going to North Dakota in February instead of *Mardi Gras*, but is that where they really want to go? Giving into their sense of adventure and their actual feelings could offer an experience that would have far more value in the years to come. They would do well to solicit how their partner *feels* about something, which will help them learn to incorporate this new dimension into their decisions. It can also serve as a tie-breaker if it ever becomes necessary. When two logic-driven Air sign people have opposing viewpoints you're going to have some serious wind forces which could easily evolve into a tornado. This could possibly be prevented if both parties will go to the next level and consider what their intuition and heart is telling them and not just the cold, hard facts.

Earth - Air

Both Earth (Taurus, Virgo, Capricorn) and Air (Gemini, Libra, Aquarius) signs are driven primarily by logic, meaning that the emotional side of any argument is likely to be ignored. While this sounds, well, logical, this is not always a good thing. The parties will probably be able to conduct nice, factual arguments, which in most cases will result in sound decisions, but there are two possible problems.

First, not all problems should be solved logically and second, since Air tends to talk a lot more than Earth, all sides may not be presented, factual or not. Furthermore, Earth tends to be judgmental and jump to conclusions. Best case, these two should be like a windmill, using both the foundation of solid Earth and the moving Air to create energy. Earth's practical nature and Air's communication skills should generally make for a balanced relationship.

However, they may need to make a conscious effort to talk about the emotional side, albeit in a logical way, and acknowledge the fact that sometimes our heart knows more than our head. Both will generally know what they really want, even if they're trying to set it aside for the sake of logic. They may have to strive a bit harder for balance than signs with both the logical and emotional sides represented. At worst, arguments could assume the power of a dreaded dust storm, particularly since Air is more inclined toward verbal communication and could overwhelm Earth, creating a very unpleasant event.

Earth - Earth

A relationship between two Earth (Taurus, Virgo, Capricorn) signs is generally stable and relatively quiet. It can achieve the peace and tranquility of a Cavern, deep and solid beneath the ground and filled with inner beauty unlike anywhere above. But what both parties need to realize is how dark it is when the lights go out. Earth signs are driven by logic as opposed to emotion. While this is what contributes to all that peace and tranquility, life is not only about logic and facts. Many of the richest moments in life have little to do with anything but emotion. Earth signs have emotions, they just tend to keep them buried and seldom talk about them. They try to pretend that they either don't count or are below consideration. Furthermore, they tend to be judgmental and jump to conclusions, which is always dangerous when dealing with something that isn't logical, like emotions.

However, after they're ignored for too long, the result can be an Earthquake that scores eight on the Emotional Scale. As part of their use of logic, these folks need to make a specific effort to recognize their emotional needs. They should not stuff them underground but need to

137

learn to develop a sense for when they should allow their heart to lead instead of their head. Since Earth signs don't like to talk about their feelings, they'll need to help each other learn to do so. Being similar in nature, these two should recognize the other's discomfort and make it easier for their partner by soliciting what they feel as part of the discussion. By learning to recognize the value of the emotions and needs associated with them, they will assure that pleasant cavern doesn't get torn asunder by forces even further beneath the surface that they chose to ignore. It's not a good idea to build a relationship or anything else on top of a fault line.

Earth - Water

These two elements blend well. Earth needs Water in order to be fruitful and Water can accomplish much more in a medium like Earth than by itself. Water (Cancer, Scorpio, Pisces) is driven largely by emotion and if they're struggling with a decision that involves both logical and emotional elements, they will side with what their intuition and hearts tell them to do regardless of the facts. Earth (Taurus, Virgo, Capricorn), on the other hand, will go with logic and what their heads tell them to do, even if their heart is screaming at them to do otherwise. Thus, when in proper balance, these two can provide two sides of the issue and help the two of them arrive at the most appropriate solution.

At best, these two are like a Flower Garden, the Earth a proper balance of sand, clay and organic matter that can hold the appropriate amount of moisture to keep the plants healthy. Anyone who has ever tended a garden knows that too much water can be as harmful as too little and needs to be balanced according to what you're trying to grow. Thus, depending on what the decision is about, Earth or Water should perhaps give a bit more weight to the other. For example, if the issue involves finances, it might be wise to allow Earth to prevail, while if it involves people or relationships an element of emotion is usually wise, which would be best handled by Water's sensitivity to others. Worst case can result in a total mudslide if Earth becomes too saturated with Water and loses its grip on solid ground.

Fire - Fire

These relationships will never be dull. Fire signs (Aries, Leo, Sagittarius) are flamboyant, thrive on attention and need their egos fed. Naturally, getting their way is going to factor into the equation so a tremendous amount of caution and restraint needs to be exercised when these two disagree. Not only can the argument quickly evolve into a Forest Fire of massive proportions, but there will be hurt feelings all around and a long recovery period. Fire signs are ruled by emotion as opposed to logic and tend to be impulsive and somewhat reactionary. This doesn't mean that they can't think in a logical way, it only means that the feel before they think and if their mind and heart disagree on an issue, they will side with their heart and its intuition rather than beat themselves to death with the facts.

Since both parties have many traits in common, there is a fundamental understanding between them. There is much potential in their everyday interactions to be like Twin Flames, each supporting the other and basking in the reflected light. Nonetheless, both need to realize their natural tendency is to dispense with logic and recognize that when they disagree perhaps the best solution is to introduce some logic. Both will excel at spitting fire like a dragon, but the burning and scorching this can achieve on the relationship landscape over time can take a long time to recover.

Fire - Air

Fire and Air signs are a good mix since Fire needs Air to burn. More specifically, Fire signs (Aries, Leo, Sagittarius) thrive on attention and do not do well if their egos are not fed on a regular basis. When Fire is struggling, it tends to get quite cranky and will demand attention in some form or another, consciously or subconsciously, pleasantly or unpleasantly. If Air (Gemini, Libra, Aquarius) lets the flame go out, it's going to have to employ quite a set of bellows to revive that flame. When these two are interacting in a healthy, well-balanced manner, they operate like a hot air balloon, the inner flame lifting the balloon to heights it could never reach alone and providing an idyllic view of the ground below. Everyone looks better from a few thousand feet, *n'est-ce pas?*

Fire - Earth

Fire and Earth signs can interact in a variety of ways. Earth signs (Taurus, Virgo, Capricorn) tend to be very stable, practical and logical to the point they can be considered stuffy, picky and cold, respectively. When these folks pair with a Fire sign (Aries, Leo, Sagittarius) it brings a certain level of balance to the relationship since these individuals will emanate energy, dash and sparkle, respectively. In the ideal state, the combination will be like the warmth of a campfire on a cool evening in the mountains. Earth provides a nice, solid base while Fire radiates light and warmth in all directions. However, if these two disagree, the worst case can be similar to a volcanic eruption, either spewing molten lava far and wide or simply creeping toward the village below in a stealthy, lethal floe that is only visible in the dark or with night vision goggles.

Earth signs don't like to talk that much about problems that are emotional in nature. If they can't solve it with logic, then they either internalize the issue for further processing or ignore it, neither of which is going to resolve anything. Fire signs, on the other hand, are basically emotional in nature and they're going to want to talk about it. What point it reaches between the campfire and volcanic eruption is going to depend on how much Earth goes underground to avoid discussion versus engagement of Fire's temper. If Fire decides to throw a hand grenade into Earth's burrow, it's going to get messy. Fire thrives on adventure. It may vary a bit in flavor between the three Signs, but it will be there is some form. If life gets too boring, Fire might turn tail and run. Earth may be perfectly happy sitting home before the fire, figuratively and literally, but this will eventually drive Fire to drink, also figuratively and literally. Balance between stability and some form of newness or excitement are essential and will do you both good, even if it's no more than a stimulating hobby or sport you both enjoy.

Fire - Water

Fire and Water signs, while they sound tremendously different, are alike in the respect that they are both driven more by emotion than logic. This means that when they're making a decision they will most often go with their heart or gut feeling rather than logical facts. It doesn't mean they can't or don't use logic, only that when they have to choose between logic and emotion that the latter will win. This gives Fire and Water something in common, but also makes for some pretty emotional discussions. When in equilibrium, the interaction will be similar to the soothing warmth of a hot tub that offers an environment where you can relax and forget the harsher parts of life. However, if the thermostat goes out and that water heats up, that comfort zone can dissipate and fast.

Fire (Aries, Leo, Sagittarius), particularly if their temper is aroused, is likely to throw a fair amount of heat while Water (Cancer, Scorpio, Pisces), especially the females, is very likely to literally throw water on the issue in the form of tears. When neither party is coming from a logical, controlled standpoint, the emotional energy can build up until the result is similar to a Boiler Explosion where people get burned and hit with flying debris to say nothing of the noise and damage it creates.

These couples need to make sure that they address issues early, long before they get so far out of hand that few if any facts are being incorporated into the argument.

Water - Air

Water (Cancer, Scorpio, Pisces) and Air (Gemini, Libra, Aquarius) signs should be naturally compatible, largely because they are simply different forms of the same elements. The combination should also bring balance to a relationship in that Water tends to base its decisions on what their heart and intuition tells them while Air leans more toward logic. At best, these two should achieve a happy balance similar to Windsurfing, exploiting their best possible characteristics to glide through life while they explore both approaches to problems and agree on the best solution. Nonetheless, if a serious disagreement arises, this couple has the potential to create a regular, emotional Hurricane. If neither will budge from their view of the world, *i.e.* Water is stuck on the emotional side and Air on the logical, the water level and wind speed will start to rise.

If Water is too tangled up in emotion to speak clearly, or perhaps at all, the Air element's strong verbal skills are likely to overwhelm the argument by sheer gale-force winds. Remember, however, that the most destructive force in a hurricane derives from the storm surge and wall of water delivered on the coastlines as well as the many inches of rain delivered over a short period of time. Once the wind dies down, there can be a tremendous amount of water damage to deal with, so Air needs to make sure they know when to introduce the ultimate in logic by making the suggestion that discussion be deferred until they both calm down.

Water - Water

A relationship between Water signs (Cancer, Scorpio, Pisces) is likely to get quite wet from time to time. Both parties are driven by emotion and can be easily overwhelmed by them. While most of the time they will appear as a Peaceful Lake with a few sailboats skimming along the water while fisherman enjoy the challenge of catching some fish, they need to be aware of the potential for a Tsunami in the event the two of them ever absolutely don't agree on something and totally lose control. The depth of feeling between these individuals will be deep and they will go places that others cannot even conceive. That fundamental understanding is a bonding agent in and of itself. Furthermore, Water signs tend to be masters of emotional manipulation, which can turn into quite a tidal wave when each person tries to out-manipulate the other.

These folks need to realize that there are many things in the world that require a strong dose of logic. It is also rather useful when opposing emotional arguments fail to reach resolution. Thus, they should consciously strive to incorporate logical thought into their decisions. It's not that this couple is incapable of being logical, only that when a decision arises that has both a logical and emotional element, they will go with the latter, *i.e.* their intuitive, heartfelt solution, over the facts. This is not to say that most of their decisions aren't correct, but particularly in certain areas such as finance, logic should generally prevail. Developing the ability to approach a problem from a logical, black and white perspective will help prevent either from getting lost on the sea of life or winding up as a massive wall of water that has few rivals as a destructive force.

TRANSITS

Transits refer to the continual movement of the Sun, Moon and Planets and how their current positions relate to an individual's Chart. The aspects formed are used to determine what is commonly known as your Horoscope. Those that appear online, in magazines, or in the newspaper are cast largely against the presumed Natal Sun position for each Sun Sign. Since the Sun is generally the strongest influence on our Chart, these predictions can often be reasonably accurate. However, to have a clearer picture of what influences are active for you as an individual, your Horoscope needs to include not only the exact position of the Sun but the Moon and other planets as well as correct house positions.

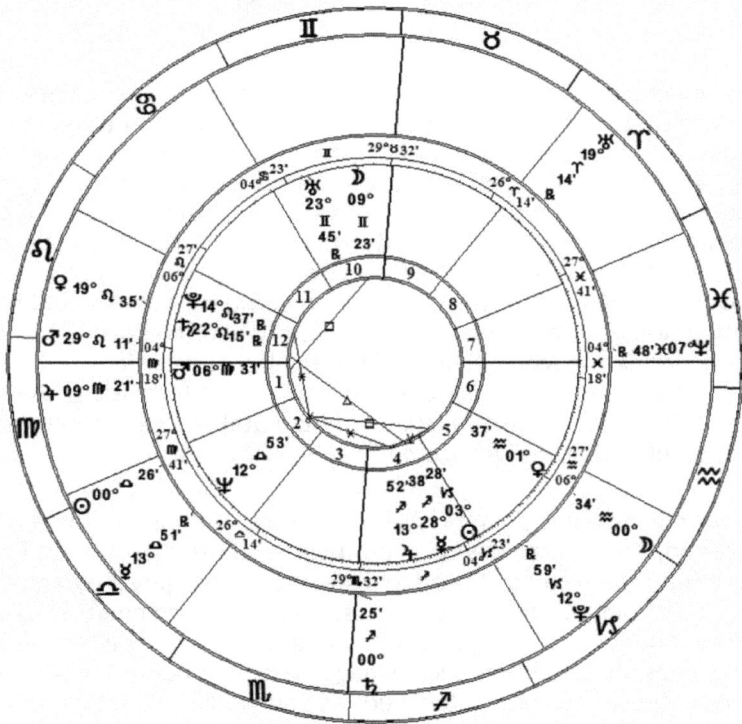

Figure 12 Transit Biwheel

For example, if the position of the planet Mars forms a conjunction with your ascendant, you may feel more aggressive than usual for the time that aspect is in effect. If it squared or was in opposition to your ascendant it would probably have a similar effect. If it formed a trine or sextile that aggression is more likely to be expressed in a positive way than with a square or opposition. Another example would be if Mercury formed a trine aspect to your natal Saturn, you may be inclined to tackle serious matters such as financial planning. Retrograde planets also have an effect.

One way to get a clear view of these aspects is to combine a person's chart with the transit chart in question, such as that shown to the previous page where the person's birth chart is in the inner circle and the position of the planets for the day in question in the outer circle. Aspect lines in the center indicate aspects between the two charts. This method also shows clearly which planets are transiting which Houses, giving an indication of the general flavor of happenings in those areas at that time.

For this example, the person is within a few days of their Mars return since transiting Mars is within 7 degrees of natal Mars. Pluto is in their 5th House, indicating power issues that could relate to children or perhaps a romantic situation with the square to natal Neptune suggesting deception or perhaps drug or alcohol issues. More than likely on this day the person is not being realistic with transiting Mercury, which is also retrograde, conjunct Neptune implies rethinking old information in a compassionate way. The transiting Moon conjunct Venus could stir up romantic feelings or also relate to affection toward children. Transiting Jupiter squaring the Moon could inflate emotional reactions. Transiting Mercury sextile natal Pluto could bring out information that was previously hidden. Transiting Mars trining natal Mercury could bring a new action plan that derives from the subconscious level.

The slow-moving outer planets (Jupiter, Saturn, Uranus, Neptune, Pluto, the asteroid, Chiron) set trends in our lives as those transits can last for years. Events related to these trends are then triggered by the faster moving inner planets (Mercury, Venus, Mars). It's common knowledge that everyone goes through certain stages in life, whether it's the "terrible twos" as a toddler, the teenage years, a midlife crisis or what-have-you. These, too are influenced, as you would expect, by transits, especially planetary returns, which is when a planet returns to its natal position. Several of these cycles, including those we all encounter as adults, are covered in the Parenting with Astrology and Planetary Returns sections. Of course, being able to interpret the meaning of these aspects and transits is what astrology is all about.

Today's astrologers are not the somewhat deranged gypsy down the street with a crystal ball, as they've been viewed for far, too long. The understanding of the planets, their movement, and how each of them relates to the human psyche that is required to be a credible astrologer is astounding. The world's original counselors thousands of years ago were astrologers. Today an increasing number of individuals trained in human psychology and counseling augment this modern knowledge with what astrologers have known for millennia about the influences the planets have on us every day of our lives, including past and future lifetimes. The International Academy of Astrology (www.astrocollege.org), my astrological alma mater, offers everything from lectures to advanced classes for everyone from stark beginners to those aspiring to be professional astrologers.

Most skepticism about the predictive side of astrology arises from the lack of agreement between tabloid horoscopes and people's lives, though many of them are amazingly accurate in spite of their limitations. This is largely due to the lack of detail available when you're casting a horoscope for everyone born under a given Sun Sign. Generate one for an individual using their specific birth date, time and place and you'll see a significant difference. Put that information in the hands of an experienced astrologer who can interpret house information and other factors and you'll see they correlate in significant ways. Another element that doesn't even show up in personal horoscopes is the effect of lunations, or the phases of the Moon.

The real trick is reading predictions in advance. Similar to the Bible Code, it often only works in retrospect, *i.e.*, you need to know the date of an event in order to find it. Astrologers generally agree that for major events there will be several influences working together, not just one or two, and that these are usually to be found in the Natal Chart as part of the "Natal Promise." When they actually occur will depend on a combination of lunations and transits as they aspect the Natal, Progressed and Solar Return charts. An aspect can lie dormant for months or years and then be triggered by a tight aspect to a Full or New Moon or, better yet, an eclipse.

One of my personal research projects relates to the astrological influences in effect at the time of NASA's three major accidents, *i.e.* the Apollo I fire, the Challenger disaster and the Columbia accident. What I found was astounding. Sports teams, corporations, states and countries all likewise have influences wrought upon them by the planets. Astrologer Eileen Grimes has also done some very interesting work on the astrology of the Titanic disaster in her book "Titanic Astrology."

Horoscopes written for all of those with a common sun sign cannot possibly address all the details in each person's life, though certain common themes can usually be found based on the major aspects operating on each sun sign. For details relative to your own personal situation, consider ordering one of our personalized horoscope reports which is cast specifically for you as an individual based on your natal chart data. The degree of accuracy in these will greatly exceed what is possible with mass horoscopes.

NATAL CHARTS

A Natal Chart shows where the Sun, Moon and planets were at the time of your birth. The planets and Zodiac signs are shown using symbols with the position of each planet measured by its degree location within the sign. In the example below, the Sun (which looks like a circle with a dot in the middle) is at 17 degrees 47 minutes Scorpio. The lines in the middle connecting some of the planets indicate specific angular measurements called Aspects. Using this data as well as their knowledge of in the various Signs and Houses, astrologers can often determine detailed personality traits for that individual. Linda Goodman's *Sun Signs* is an excellent book on the basic personality traits for each sign.

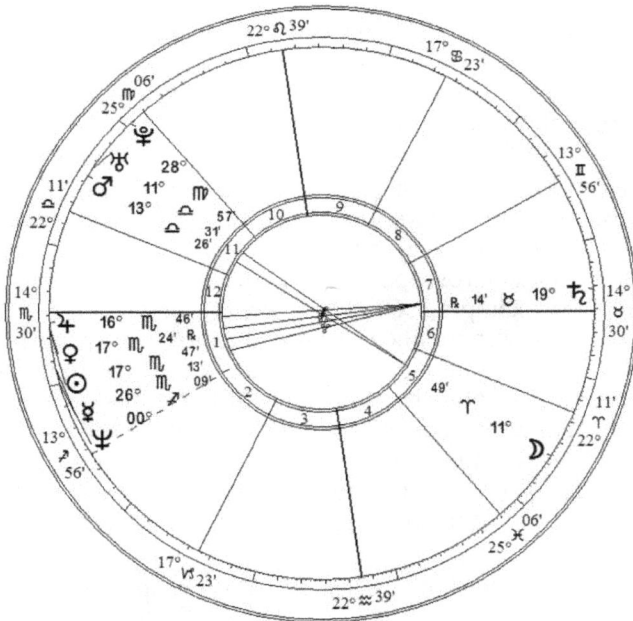

Figure 13 Natal Chart

Generally, the Sun, Moon and Ascendant determine the foundation of personality. The Sun will represent the core personality, the Moon will affect the emotional nature, and the Ascendant, which is the Sign that was on the eastern horizon at the time of birth, defines the outward appearance and how the person interacts with the world. The example shown is an individual who is a very strong Scorpio due to the fact that the Sun, Ascendant, Jupiter, Venus, and Mercury are all in that sign.

If a person seems to be "out of character" with his or her sign it could be caused by heavy planetary influences elsewhere on their chart. For example, a stellium, which consists of three or more planets clustered together in another sign, can create a significant influence that can shift their personality more toward that sign. In the chart below, this person has their Sun in Virgo, yet with Saturn, Jupiter, Mercury and Pluto in Libra, will show many characteristics typical of Libra.

If your birth time is not available, the chart will not be as accurate. I have seen the Natal Charts of twins differ when there was only a three minute time difference in their births. Often their personalities are remarkably different. This occurs because the planets are constantly moving as well as the Ascendant, which can cause major aspects to change, even in a short time. Furthermore, during a 24 hour period, the Moon or even the Sun, can change Signs. Neither conveniently moves into a different sign right at midnight.

Of course the most important element in a Natal Chart is generally the Sun. Almost everyone knows what sign they were born under, though cusp dates (when one sign ends and another begins) may differ, particularly in global horoscopes, such as those found in magazines or the newspaper. For example, someone born on July 22, 2004 at 6:37am would be a Cancer with a Cancer Ascendant, but if they had a twin born a mere three minutes later at 6:40am they would be a Leo with a Leo Ascendant. I've seen global horoscopes list both July 22 and July 23 as the cutoff date between Cancer and Leo, so if you were born on a cusp, your actual time of birth is necessary to know your Sun Sign for certain. The dates for the signs don't change consistently, year to year, either, so it's necessary to check an ephemeris to know for sure.

I've known a handful of individuals born on a cusp who were mistaken about their birth sign until I ran their chart. That's your best bet if you want to know for sure.

While the Sun has a major influence on your chart, the planets likewise contribute significantly, each adding their own particularly energy to the House where they reside, their vibes blending to a greater or lesser degree with the sign in which they're located as well. Also of importance in a Natal Chart is the placement of the major asteroids, *i.e.* Chiron, Ceres, Vesta, Pallas Athena, and Juno.

The Natal Chart is also the basis for much of predictive astrology as well. As the planets move through their orbits they form aspects that can indicate influences in force on a daily and sometimes longer basis. These movements are called Transits and are the basis of Horoscopes.

While your Natal Chart remains in force for your entire lifetime, a technique known as the Secondary Progressed Chart reflects how you evolve as a person with the passing of time. Solar return charts provide a glimpse of what to expect in the year immediately following your birthday.

PROGRESSED CHARTS

We all change with time. As we experience life and our maturity level increases everything about us evolves. These changes can often be found and understood more clearly in a Progressed Chart.

While your Natal Chart has influence for your entire life, a Progressed Chart applies to any given time after that. A Progressed Chart is determined most commonly by what is called the "day for a year" system, a method devised by originally Johannes Kepler back in the 17th century CE. The chart that represents your second year of life is the day after you're born; the third year of life is indicated by the third day; the 20th year is the 20th day and so forth. In other words, if you were born on January 7, 1962 and wanted to know what your chart looked like when you were 30 years old, or your 31st year, you would look at the chart for February 6, 1962.

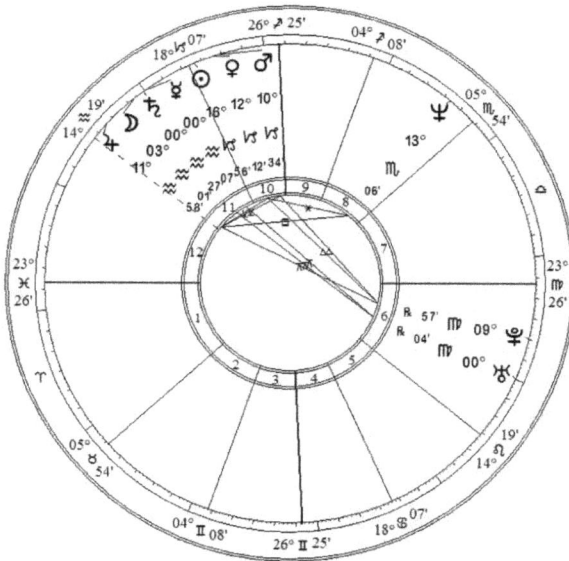

Figure 14 Natal Chart 2

To illustrate what this means, look at the above Natal Chart for this fictitious person. As you can see, the Natal Sun is in Capricorn as part of a stellium. However, there's another stellium in Aquarius, which will give this person many Aquarian traits. Then look at the Progressed Chart on the next page. The Sun, Venus, Mars stellium in Capricorn has progressed into Aquarius along with Jupiter, Saturn and Mercury, which were there natally as well. At this point in life, the person will be under such heavy Aquarian influences it's doubtful anyone could ever guess they were born a Capricorn. There are also many more negative aspects in the Progressed chart than the Natal in the form of numerous squares and oppositions.

While your core personality will always remain consistent with your Natal Sun Sign, progressing to another is somewhat like moving to another state or country. A person born and raised in Texas will always be a Texan, but if they move to another state, for example California, particularly sometime in their youth, they will pick up some of those characteristics. You will often notice the change and feel somewhat confused the first few months. If you're older and think back to a time in your life that was particularly difficult, there is a good chance it was when you went through a sign change.

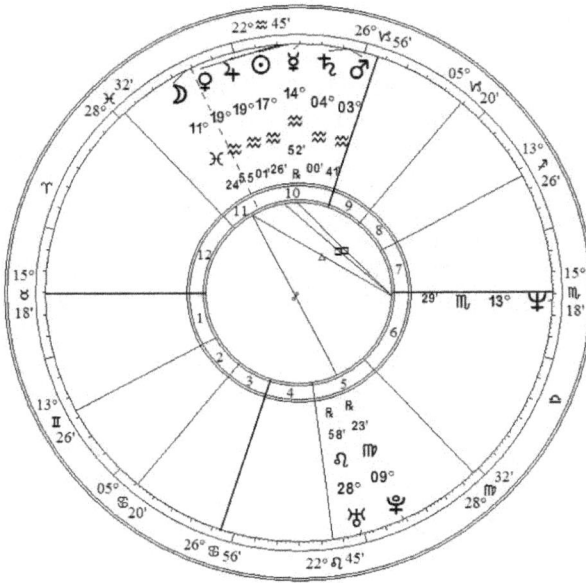

Figure 15 Natal Chart 2 Progression

Depending on whether you were born in the beginning, middle or end of your particular sign, you will progress through two or three or possibly four (if you live long enough) Sun Signs. For example, if you were born on January 21, by the time you're a year old you've already progressed into Aquarius. However, if you were born on January 22, you'll be an Aquarius for roughly 30 years before you switch to Pisces.

One aspect that progresses significantly faster than the Sun, even though it has slightly less effect, is the Moon, which will move through each sign in the progressed chart in about two and a half years. If you know someone well and have regular contact with him or her you can notice this change, which will occur in how they respond emotionally. You are also likely to notice it in yourself.

For example, if your Natal Moon is in Capricorn, logic and practicality will significantly drive your emotional reactions. However, if you're going through a time when your Progressed Moon has moved into Aries, you'll react more quickly and impulsively and you may lose your temper more easily. If it's in Cancer you'll be more emotional, particularly sentimental; in Virgo you'll be more critical, even of yourself, etc. The change is subtle, but if you look at your own decisions and reactions, or those of someone close to you, over several years time there will be a noticeable difference.

It is possible to derive a Progressed Chart for a given day by adjusting the time of the chart as opposed to your birth time. Your birth time will generally represent your birthday. Which one will depend on how many days from your actual birthday the chart is cast. This sounds odd, but consider that if one day represents a year, then 24 hours is also a year. Thus, two hours represents a month or one hour represents approximately two weeks. Taken even further, a half-hour would be roughly a week and a little over four minutes would represent each day. If you're hopelessly confused, don't worry, that is what computers are for and they do a rather nice job of calculating a Progressed Chart.

Progressed charts are not only a tool for determining changes in your personality and view of the world as you grow older but can also be used in predictive astrology as well. Transits affect the Progressed Chart as well as the Natal Chart. However, any major event is usually contained in your Natal Chart; this fact is referred to as the Natal Promise. If it's not there natally, it's unlikely to occur. The Progressed Chart and other factors, such as Transits and Lunations, will simply help pin down the time that it occurs.

Aspects are read in a similar manner to those on a Natal Chart with reports available for the interpretations.

Another chart that changes with time is the Solar Return Chart. This chart is cast based on when the Sun returns to the exact same position it was at your birth around the time of your birthday. The actual date may vary a day one way or the other from your birthday and of course the other planets are in different positions.

This chart provides a very accurate view of what you might expect in the coming year with an approximate three month overlap at the beginning and end. This means you might start seeing the next year's theme come into events in your life starting three months prior to your birthday and it may take approximately three months for the previous year to fade. The Progressed Chart addressed your personal progression and character development whereas the Solar Return chart is more directed at events and interactions to expect with others in the year to come.

PLANETARY RETURNS

As the planets return to the positions they hold in your Natal Chart you experience what is known as a Return; this includes the Sun and Moon, even though they are not by definition a planet. A "Return" initiates another cycle that relates to the issues ruled by that planet; the chart created at the moment of the return is thus in effect for these issues until the next return. A Return Chart is read in much the same way as a Natal Chart except it is only in effect until the next return and will emphasize those affairs that are ruled by that planet. Sometimes the planet goes retrograde and makes three successive contacts to the natal planet. In this case, the charts are in effect until the next contact, which may only be a few days or months away.

The planets, which for these purposes include the Sun and Moon, each move at their own speed and thus take different amounts of time to return to the position they hold in your Natal Chart. The Moon, which moves through the Zodiac approximately every 28 days, provides a Lunar Return each month. Pluto, on the other hand, takes 248 years to make one trip around the Sun, implying that it's highly unlikely that you'll experience a Pluto Return during your lifetime; a Pluto square is probably all you'll experience, which, knowing Pluto, is more than enough.

This does not mean, however, that some houses don't have the benefit of a return chart. Rather, this is where those that are ruled by the "modern" planets with long orbital period revert back to their ancient rulership. Thus, if you're wondering about something that relates to your 11th House, you don't have to wait 84 years for that Uranus Return; your Saturn Return will do the trick. As it is, they only come along about every 29 years but that's better than 84.

The typical duration of the respective return cycles and what they represent is below. For example, the Mars Return will represent those activities you're pursuing as well as Mars-related events such as accidents and surgery. While in effect, Return Charts supplement the Natal Chart. As the return planet continues on its path and makes contact to the planets and aspects of the Return Chart by transit, it will trigger events in the same way as transits work upon a Natal Chart; in fact, transits in general will work upon the Return Chart, but the respective planets will generally have the most influence. By simply following the transits of the Return Planet the timing of events and general theme of that return period can be identified. If you're a serious student of astrology, *"Identifying Planetary Triggers: Astrological Techniques for Prediction"* by Celeste Teal is an excellent reference on planetary returns. Note that more information pertaining to the various cycles is also included in the section on Astroparenting.

When angles and aspects appear in the Return Charts that are similar to those in the Natal Chart, this indicates that the upcoming period will be quite eventful due to the "double whammy" effect. The Natal House brought to the Ascendant on the Return Chart also has a strong bearing on what will be most important during the return period. For example, if the 8th Natal House were brought to the ascendant of a Venus Return, it would indicate an emphasis on shared resources and possibly debt and/or sex issues in relationships. If the return planet is in an angular house (1, 4, 7, 10) the first third of the return period will be emphasized. If it's in a succedent house (2, 5, 8, 11) the second third will have the most activity and for cadent houses (3, 6, 9, 12) it will be the last third.

The Return Chart Ruler (ruler of the ascendant) is another strong indicator of what to expect during the return period. Comparing the position of natal planets to the Return will further reveal the types of events to expect. Timing is affected by the Return Planet as it transits the Return Chart. All of the transiting planets will influence the chart, but simply tracking the Return planet and its contacts to the chart planets, particularly major aspects such as Yods and T-squares, will provide insights into the theme for that period. Chart points such as the Vertex and Part of Fortune are also significant and should be included in interpreting transit activity. The Vertex typically relates to karma or a fated encounter/event while the Part of Fortune relates to where we'll find happiness and joy; when activated it usually denotes a one-time opportunity.

Return charts are an incredibly useful tool and frequently reveal details that Natal, Solar Return, Solar Arc, or Secondary Progressed charts lack; at the least they supplement them with stronger indications of the period's theme. Particularly when you're looking for something specific, you can count on finding a wealth of information, especially when you factor in the transits.

Planet: Moon
Sign Rulership: Cancer
Cycle: 27.5 days

Influence: The Moon rules your emotional nature and the Lunar Return indicates the issues you'll be dealing with for the coming month. These apply to not only individuals but to relationships, cities, and corporations. For example, the Lunar Return for New York City for September 2001, which is described in "Lunar Returns" by John Townley, quite accurately explains the Big Apple's reaction to the terrorist attacks of September 11, 2001. The Lunar Return Chart will describe the general character and timing of events that will affect you emotionally during that cycle. The Moon also relates to your mother or wife and can be useful with regard to her as well. If your Sun, Ascendant or Moon Sign is in Cancer these cycles will be even more pronounced. Whichever natal house contains the ascendant of the Lunar Return will be emphasized that month.

Planet: Sun
Sign Rulership: Leo
Cycle: ~365 days

Influence: The Solar Return or "Birthday Chart" provides a template for the coming year, though there is typically an overlap period of up to three months at both the beginning and end as one year transitions to the next. It is read like a Natal Chart, except it's only in effect for a year. Since the Sun rules the 5th House which includes your ego, self-expression, creativity, children, romantic interests, entertainment and speculations these are the types of activities that will be emphasized.

Even as the Moon can represent your mother or wife, so the Sun can also represent your father or husband. Note that the areas covered by the 5th House and thus the Solar Return are those that relate to you at a very personal level. Personal growth will be greatly reflected through how you respond to the year's events; a Progressed Chart also reflects your evolution as an individual thought it changes in a more consistently manner.

The Sun is the center of the solar system, however, so it will reflect upon all the major themes coming upon you in the subject year as it transits each house of the Return.

Planet: Mercury
Sign Rulership: Gemini and Virgo
Cycle: Approximately once a year

Influence: Mercury's cycle around the Sun only takes 88 days to complete, but astrology is based on a geocentric view, *i.e.* its position as observed from Earth, not the Sun. From this perspective, since Mercury is between Earth and the Sun, he appears to follow the Sun. Typically Mercury has three retrograde periods each year that are three weeks in duration. When all this is factored in, the actual return period for Mercury astrologically turns out to be approximately once a year.

Mercury rules our thoughts, ideas, communications, negotiations, local travels, transportation, written agreements, and daily activities. The House position of Mercury in the return, the aspects it makes with Return as well as Natal planets, and the Sign location of the angles will help determine what to expect with respect to Mercury ruled affairs in the year to come. As transiting Mercury traverses the chart, special attention will be drawn to those areas where he goes retrograde, which happens approximately every four months.

Since Mercury rules transportation, if you are planning to buy a car it's important to make sure that your Mercury Return contains favorable aspects. If Mercury is retrograde, either in your Mercury Return or in transit, you should wait. If the Return period is going to contain more than one contact with Mercury, it's best to wait until the final direct pass before purchasing a car or anything else that involves paperwork.

It's best to buy a vehicle when all planets are in direct motion, not just Mercury. This is because when you take possession of something it creates a birth chart for that item that will manifest as indicated by the planets' positions at that time. Depending on the time of purchase, retrograde planets could turn up in any house of the item's chart or on the ascendant and thus cause problems.

Planet: Venus
Sign Rulership: Taurus and Libra
Cycle: Approximately once a year

Influence: Venus takes approximately 225 days to travel around the Sun, but like Mercury is between the Earth and Sun, making its return cycle closer to a year. Venus influences our affections, pleasures, needs, what we value, and where we find comfort. Its return cycle will indicate the social contacts we'll make, the objects of our affection, love nature, popularity, and benefits, both social and material. These will be further defined by the sign and house placement of Venus and the accompanying aspects.

Since a Venus return relates to where we find love and happiness if the chart is afflicted it will indicate difficulties in these areas. For example, if you're having relationship problems or getting a divorce it will show up. Financial issues can also be indicated by Venus' placement in the 2nd or 8th House. In the 7th, relationships will be the focus. The 12th can indicate the need for caring for a loved one who is ill or incapacitated in some manner.

As transiting Venus reaches the MC or 10th House cusp there is usually an emphasis in social activity, sometimes the single most important social event for the time covered by the return.

Planet: Mars
Rulership: Aries (traditional ruler of Scorpio)
Cycle: Approximately every 2 years

Influence: Mars reflects our independence and drive to get what we want. The Mars Return will reflect those activities that we initiate, new undertakings, and how we express our individualism. It is very useful for identifying the best times to take action on specific endeavors. The Mars return for a woman sometimes relates closely to the activities of her husband or a male child. As the ancient ruler of the 8th House, Mars also rules our sex drive. Other 8th House issues that will surface in a Mars Return include death, debt and transformational experiences in general.

Favorable aspects to Mars support using its energy in a positive manner, such as manifesting courage and assertive behavior. Conversely an afflicted Mars can result in inappropriate extremes in aggression, passive aggression, or in some cases even cowardice, especially during a retrograde return; fortunately these are not usually in effect for too long. If not properly managed, the Mars energy can also invite aggression or confrontations from others. Accidents will be reflected in the return via an afflicted Chart Ruler, Pluto or Saturn on an angle, the Sun or several planets in the 8th or 12th, and/or Uranus or Neptune in the 1st House.

For example, the Mars Return for Princess Diana had numerous ominous aspects in addition to hostile transits on the day of her fatal accident. On the Return chart the Chart Ruler, Pluto, was in the 1st House squaring Mars, a common aspect for accidents, especially those that involve a fatality. There is also a yod comprising Uranus, Saturn and Mars at the eye, indicating an unexpected, solemn occurrence leading potentially to a violent event. Transiting Mars, the Return Sun and Return Ascendant were all conjunct in Scorpio, the zodiacal 8th House of transformation and death. Transiting Saturn was on the Return 6th House cusp of health indicating a serious threat of injury. Her natal Sun fell in the Return's 8th House with transiting Chiron, the "wounded healer." The Vertex, which is typically active during fated events, was in the Return 12th House of the spirit world, confinement, transcendence, and hidden enemies. There were ominous contacts to the Return from her Natal Chart as well, including Uranus on the MC, indicating an unexpected event that would affect her relationship with the public and Neptune on the ascendant, further implying transcendence to a different state of existence.

When Mars goes retrograde it can bring reversals to the area its transiting on the Return Chart and particularly if it stations on a planet or cusp. The retrograde period lasts for approximately two and a half months. If a retrograde period begins shortly after a Mars Return, there can be three contacts to the natal position and thus three separate Returns; each is in effect only until the next contact. During the retrograde portion progress often slows and requires review. As a rule there is continuity between the three returns that show the shifting emphasis of the activities at hand.

Planet: Jupiter
Rulership: Sagittarius (traditional ruler of Pisces)
Cycle: Approximately every 12 years

Influence: Jupiter reflects upon those areas in our life where we expand and grow and thus the Jupiter Return reflects fluctuations in 9th House matters such as material conditions, religious, educational, and philosophical trends, interactions with different cultures, extended travel activities, as well as people and society in general, especially if any legal issues are involved. As the ancient ruler of Pisces, the zodiacal 12th House, it also includes events associated with that venue, such as spiritual enlightenment, transcendence, encounters with hidden forces or enemies, confinement, and institutions. Thus, a hospitalization that

159

involved surgery would be likely to show up in both the Jupiter and Mars Return.

The house(s) ruled by Jupiter in the Return (cusps on Sagittarius and Pisces) indicate the area where long-term efforts will be taken with regard to Jupiter-related issues and the house occupied will indicate the approach taken to achieve those goals. Placement in angular houses (1, 4, 7, 10) indicate turning points and deeply personal affairs; succedent (2, 5, 8, 11) indicate events involving resources or personal values and usually also bring endings or conclusions; cadent houses (3, 6, 9, 12) show transitions, changes and preparation.

Planet: Saturn
Rulership: Capricorn (traditional ruler of Aquarius)
Cycle: Approximately every 29 years

Influence: Saturn rules how you view, respect and respond to authority. It's about restrictions, delays, your sense of responsibility, how you handle your obligations and life's hard lessons, through which you gain wisdom. The 10th House includes your career, reputation, public image, and status. "Status" is a rather vague term which includes such things as graduating from school, getting married, becoming a parent, buying a home, running for public office, receiving an award or promotion or, conversely being fired or arrested. Anything that changes how you are viewed by the public will be reflected in this area. It's interesting to consider that in Biblical times a man wasn't considered a mature adult until he was 30, which coincides closely with the first Saturn Return. This is often when you finally feel as if you're grown up. I have frequently noted that by this age someone who had a hard time during their teens and early adult years is either straightened out, dead, or in jail.

The 11th House, which was ruled anciently by Saturn, includes all your interactions with groups and organizations, which ties in easily with the public, though you'll still be a slightly different person, depending on whether you're in a private, group, or public setting. The 11th House also comprises your goals, hopes and wishes which are often dependent on your interaction and the response of others to achieve. In other words, it would be difficult to find fame and fortune if others didn't recognize your accomplishments as well. No matter how satisfied and happy you may be with yourself, it's not the same if you're not recognized by your peers and/or the public, thus placing these types of goals in the 11th House.

Saturn returns come at major turning points in your life, one at around 30 when many are either settling into a career or considering a change, and then again around the late 50s or early 60s when retirement or another career change often looms. The second return ushers in the "croning" years where you assimilate your knowledge and life experience and mentor others, passing the baton to the next generation, so to speak.

Planet (Asteroid): Chiron
Rulership: Not assigned but some relate to Sagittarius
Cycle: Approximately every 50 years

Influence: Chiron influences the various hurtful experiences we encounter in life and how we use them to help others. These can be of a physical, mental, emotional or even financial nature, depending on the natal house placement. If Chiron is retrograde in your natal chart, you may have a more difficult time processing these hurts, making it harder to "forgive and forget" or simply accepting the lesson and moving on. While this tendency may stick with you, perhaps because it has become a habit, a Chiron Return with more favorable placement and aspects may help relieve that hyper-sensitivity. For example, Chiron in the 3rd or 9th House may help you be more rational or philosophical about a situation and thus not internalize it as much as you would in one of the more emotional Water Signs such as Cancer or Pisces. Chiron retrograde in the 8th would incline a person toward being vengeful.

The Chiron return, which occurs around age 50, often marks the time when you assimilate those early hurts and assume the role of healer in a figurative sense, sharing your wisdom with others similarly afflicted to help them navigate the rough waters and find comfort. A Chiron return can also reflect your determination to rectify those hurts incurred earlier in life in one way or another. Placing the Natal Sun on the return chart often reveals by its House placement what area such issues reside within. There is the possibility at this time that as you seek to resolve old wounds that it is you who imposes wounds and hurts on others according to the planets' sign placement and the houses they rule. For example, if relationships have been a source of pain and disappointment, this is a time when your quest to escape these old wounds inflict the same on others and you attempt to escape old patterns as well as individuals.

COMPATIBILITY

One of the most difficult yet important things we need to deal with in this life is relationships. They start before we're born and continue until the day we move on to another existence.

We get along with some people instantly, recognizing them as old friends from another dimension a long time ago, and others we can't stand, no matter how hard we try. Unfortunately, some of these people in the latter category cannot be avoided; they're our close relatives, in-laws, coworkers, bosses, and so forth. As with everything else, astrology can explain a lot, and with understanding we often can better control our reactions. The basic sign characteristics alone explain a lot about a person's temperament as well as many of their likes and dislikes. This section is dedicated to helping you understand how you interact with others. Hopefully you'll have a few laughs and learn a few things as well.

Synastry Charts

A synastry chart compares your Natal Chart to someone else's. This can identify things you have in common, including your emotional compatibility, how you handle conflict, etc. Some Signs are naturally more compatible than others. However, any combination can have a good relationship, though it may be more challenging and require more maturity, understanding and commitment to maintain.

If you're just starting out in a relationship and see some troublesome issues already, you may want to see how compatible you are astrologically before investing too much emotional energy. At the least you can find out what to expect to see sooner or later.

In theory, Sun or Moon signs in square to one another will be much less compatible by nature than those in trine. These are easy to identify via the Modes and Elements, *i.e.* Modes (*Cardinal, Fixed, Mutable*) square each other and Elements (*Fire, Earth, Air, Water*) trine each other. Signs that square each other will usually find at least one trait in the other that drives them crazy. Whether or not it is tolerable depends on numerous other factors. You

can forgive a lot if you really love someone. If you're together for other reasons, it's usually not that easy. Signs in trine will have a generally harmonious nature, regardless of whether or not they are madly in love with each other. But there are exceptions to every rule and any time you get two human beings together there are no guarantees.

Being a lot alike can be a good or bad thing, depending on other chart elements, but this is a place to start. If the Sun Signs are not naturally compatible this can be balanced out if the Moon Signs are, since the Moon rules our emotional nature and that is one of the most important elements of a good relationship. Compatible Ascendants can likewise temper any conflicts since this is the face we show to the world. However, this can also cause an initial attraction that later is found to be based on inaccurate information as the two people come to know each other well enough to let go of their initial facade and show their true colors. This can be particularly the case if one of the parties was under heavy Neptune influences when they met.

Signs that sextile one another often are compatible, also, i.e., those that are two away from yours. For example, if you're a Pisces then Capricorn or Taurus would be a comfortable match and you're likely to have numerous friends with those signs. Note that Pisces is a Water sign while Capricorn and Taurus are Earth. Water and earth work well together for growth. As they say, Earth stabilizes Water and Water nourishes Earth.

If your sign is Aries, then Aquarius or Gemini would be comfortable companions. Aries is a Fire sign while Aquarius and Gemini are Air signs. Fire needs Air to burn. However, too much of a good thing can cause either a major mudslide for the first example or conflagration of Biblical proportions for the second.

Sextiles - Compatible (Fire/Air and Earth/Water)		
Sign	Compatible with either:	
Aries	Aquarius	Gemini
Taurus	Pisces	Cancer
Gemini	Aries	Leo
Cancer	Taurus	Virgo
Leo	Gemini	Libra
Virgo	Cancer	Scorpio
Libra	Leo	Sagittarius
Scorpio	Virgo	Capricorn
Sagittarius	Libra	Aquarius
Capricorn	Scorpio	Pisces
Aquarius	Sagittarius	Aries
Pisces	Capricorn	Taurus

Table 5 Sextile Compatibility

As with everything else in life, there are no guarantees, balance is essential and free will rules. This is not to say that Fire and Water or Earth and Air cannot have a good relationship because it's simply not the case. There are too many variables when the entire chart is considered, to say nothing of the human heart.

Fundamentally, each sign is naturally compatible with at least four others. But human nature being what it is, it seems most the time we wind up with someone from the other eight! However, this is not as black and white as it may seem because compatibility does not have to come from the Sun Signs alone.

Generally, if you look at each person's "Big Three" (*i.e.* Sun, Moon and Ascendant Signs) you can get a fairly good view of the relationship's potential, both positive and negative. Probability alone would indicate it's very likely for compatibility at some level when comparing two "Big Threes" but some people don't have three different signs.

For example if they were born early in the day and their Sun Sign and Ascendant are the same or if they were born during a New Moon where the Sun Sign and Moon Sign will be the same. This, of course, strengthens the sign characteristics they have. But like previously stated, maturity, understanding and commitment exercised with a determined free will can conquer just about anything, provided BOTH parties are willing to work it out.

We can always learn something from another person, whether it helps us to grow or simply illustrates the old saying, "No life is ever wasted. You can always serve as a bad example."

Other Chart Techniques

One textbook method for determining who a person will be attracted to is to look at the sign where Mars is located in the woman's Natal chart and conversely, the location of Venus in the man's Natal chart. The odds are high that they will find themselves drawn to members of the opposite sex with either a Sun Sign or Ascendant in that sign. The caveat here, however, is that just because they're attracted to them doesn't mean they'll be compatible! Taking it a step further, any aspects made to the Ruler of the 7th House of Relationships can hold clues as well. Planets aspecting the Ruler may be the ruling planets of those with whom they're inclined (or possibly destined) to have a serious relationship.

Another thing to look for is Sun or Moon signs located in reciprocal Houses. For example, for a Pisces man and Leo woman, if his ascendant were Aquarius then his 7th House would be Leo and for hers to be reciprocal she would have a Virgo ascendant and her 7th House would be Pisces. These can result in strong attractions, even if other compatibilities are missing. For 7th House reciprocity you may have a strong feeling of belonging together or a strong sense of partnership. For the 8th House, there could be a very strong sexual attraction that can't be explained by any other aspect. When these two people look each other in the eye everything disappears but the attraction between them. However, not all problems can be solved in bed (though it's not always a bad place to start....)

Composite Charts

Composite Charts combine the Natal or Progressed charts of the two individuals and create a single chart comprised of the midpoints of their individual planets. This chart delineates the relationship itself as a living entity and captures areas of focus, emphasis and the general personality of the partnership, based on the blending of energy each person brings. The House placement of the Composite Sun will reveal the relationship's foundation.

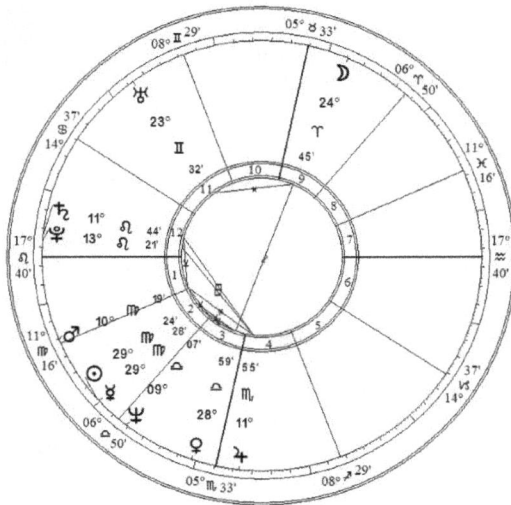

Figure 16 Composite Chart: Bill & Hillary Clinton

The example chart to the left is the composite chart for Bill and Hillary Clinton. The Sun and Mercury in cazimi (in the heart of the Sun), i.e. a conjunction within 17 minutes of arc, implies they were focused on similar goals, given the Sun rules the ascendant and Mercury rules both the 11th house of goals and the 2nd of possessions. Saturn and Pluto in the 12th suggests hidden power, control and authority as well

165

as a few secrets including some big ones based on the square to Jupiter, traditional ruler of the 8th. The Moon in the 9th house of legal matters suggests their common background in law though the opposition to Venus in Libra, the sign that rules fairness and justice, implies it needs to be balanced with their drive for success. Fame and fortune were clearly their shared ambition.

House	Relationship Focus based on Sun Placement
1	Personal gratification, ego. "Arm candy" would fall in this category. Appearance or education could be a significant driver for one or both parties.
2	Accumulating possessions or other assets. Both desire a comfortable life style, early retirement, etc. Probably quite materialistic, may forego children in lieu of possessions. Pleasures a priority including gourmet food and fine wine.
3	Mental compatibility, joint endeavors, busy and involved with neighborhood issues. Common career interests will often bring these people together or they could also have been childhood sweethearts.
4	Creating a comfortable home. Want the stereotype "ideal" family setup. Time and energy will be devoted to the children and home environment as the first priority.
5	Children, hobbies, creative endeavors. Could be unconventional; Idea of fun could be the entire family going to conferences or shows relative to a common interest, *i.e.* rock hounds, camping, writing, genealogy.
6	Work interests, health issues, shared interest in pets. Could work in the same industry, share common health challenges or possibly even have an interest in pet breeding.
7	Fulfilling relationship, strong partnership, inseparable. Lifelong companions, possible soul mates. Also business partnership a possibility.
8	Sexual compatibility, inheritance issues, entrepreneurial pursuits, major transformation. Strong sexual attraction, could also indicate marrying for money, possibly where one party wants to start a business and marries someone who can be the primary investor. Possibly could call for a major transformation in one or both of the parties involved.
9	Intellectual or higher education pursuits, travel, legal issues or entanglements. Both may be highly educated or devote a lot of time to travel abroad doing research, such as two archeologists. Could also be law partners or meet when one is the other's attorney.

10	Social recognition & status, pillars of community. Social climbing a definitely possibility or simply a logical match of similar social or economic classes.
11	Heavy involvement in groups and organizations. Similar interests in any area that involves others. Could be pioneers of some sort or working for social change.
12	Institutions, spiritual attraction, karma. Could be a very unusual relationship without any logical explanation. Possible a very strange couple, such as two handicapped or disabled individuals who meet and marry in an institutional setting or with a spiritual or mystical mission in life to accomplish together.

Table 6 Composite Relationship Focus

Relationships are never easy. Sometimes the most challenging are also the most rewarding. Not to quote another cliché, but often the course of true love does NOT run smoothly. Who knows what karma you may be dealing with? There are no hard and fast rules regarding who will make a fantastic couple as opposed to who won't. Like they say, rules are made to be broken. However, the general principles of astrology hold true and provide numerous insights into the behavior you can expect from another person. Understanding why they're the way they are and act the way they do can be tremendously helpful. Of even further assistance is knowing what transits are in force for that person at the time, which could also be affecting their behavior. Once you know what's operating astrologically, whether or not you'll be able to deal with it is entirely up to you.

A NOTE TO THE GUYS

Let me guess. It happened again. As an astrologer I know what the planets are doing out there and it's obvious when their misbehavior is reflecting on relationships. While you undoubtedly get sick of women generally and probably swear them off at least two or three times a year, you eventually realize that your relationship with Carmen Electra is really too superficial, even for you, and decide to try again. In an effort to apologize on behalf of the planets and facilitate your conciliatory efforts I'll try to explain some of her behavior below. Hopefully knowing what to expect will help and if you have some damage control to take care of, go to the *Meltdown Repair Guide* below for more ideas.

However, let me preface all this with a reminder that in spite of what you may believe, some and possibly all of the problem is undoubtedly looking at you from the mirror. Yes, *you*, butthead. Let me give you an example that is probably simple enough even for guys to understand. I have a birdfeeder in my yard. My favorites are the cardinals. During most of the year, the males couldn't care less if the females get their share and will even chase them away. However, come spring, when their very tiny bird brains are thinking how nice those female tail feathers really look and how much they'd like to ruffle them a bit suddenly they change their attitude. Then, rather than chasing their female counterparts from the feeder, it's common to see the males actually *feeding seeds* to their selected female.

Do the math, buddy. If a bird can figure it out, you should be able to, also.

So, that said, let's get started. Regardless of what your sign or your sweetie's happens to be, as all guys know there are times where she just starts speaking *feminese* and you're not going to have a clue what she's talking about. That gender barrier has been there since the beginning of time and never, I mean *NEVER*, entirely goes away. [NOTE: Unless, of course, you happen to be in a relationship with someone of the same gender. But even then if one of you is logic based and the other emotion based, there will be misunderstandings as noted earlier on sign compatibility.] Further complicating a male's understanding of a female is the fact that, even within the *feminese* language itself, are various dialects, making it even more difficult for males to understand. In the context of astrology this means that there are sign-related differences in how a girl reacts emotionally. I'm sure you'll recognize some if not all of them in the primer below.

If she's a **Watergirl** *(Cancer, Scorpio, Pisces)* there will be lots of affection and warmth and all sorts of sweet femininity that wins your heart. Conversely, there will also be lots of tears. If she really gets upset there will probably be episodes that involve her throwing herself down on the couch (or floor or bed or even ground, but hopefully not in Wal-mart), all accompanied with heart-wrenching sobs. You may need to buy tissues in caselots. This behavior will mess with everything about you that's male, similar to throwing water in an electrical outlet. More than likely you'll be willing to do just about anything to get her to stop. *(P.S. She knows this.)*

For female **Earth** *(Taurus, Virgo, Capricorn)* signs, you'll rarely see her cry, if at all. She's generally cool and logical and the most you'll probably see is her eyes gradually disappear behind a wall of tears (and only if you're attentive). You'll barely begin to figure out she might be upset when she'll either get it under control and wipe her eyes, saying her allergies are kicking up again, or if it's really serious she'll leave the room and go underground. If you try and get her to talk about it she'll refuse and more than likely you won't even know what "it" happens to be. Furthermore, she'll hold it against you because you DON'T know. Just because you seldom if ever see her cry doesn't mean she's not emotional. Ice queens definitely exist, but more often she just doesn't want to carry on in front of you, or anyone else, for that matter, except maybe her mother. And if she's a Capricorn, probably not even her mother. (If YOU happen to be a water sign yourself, she'll be more logical about emotional issues than you are and drive you crazy in an entirely different way.)

Classic female **Air** *(Gemini, Libra, Aquarius)* signs can generate lots of sobs and sniffles, combined with incessant talking. No, make that jabbering or maybe blubbering because you probably won't be able to understand a word she's saying. She'll go on and on and when you've run away screaming because you can't take anymore, she'll be on the phone with all her friends, relatives and coworkers telling them what a sleezebag you are. But don't worry, they won't be able to understand a word, either. Once she gets past that stage, she will want to talk endlessly about it until she understands everything possible to understand. This could involve delving into your childhood, past life regressions, astrological transits for the two of you for the time in question, and possibly consulting her psychologist as well as yours. (If you don't have one now you probably will by the time you're through.) Once she gets to the point she thinks she knows what happened she'll be amazing unemotional about it all, especially if she's a Gemini. They distract easily, remember?

If your beloved is a **Fire** *(Aries, Leo, Sagittarius)* sign, well, your best bet with this chick may be to get out of Dodge as quickly as possible. Really. When she's hot, she's hot, but this is when you're really going to pay the price. You'll not only get all the tears but lots of yelling, a stanza or so of screaming, and more than likely hitting, either you or something else. She'll probably throw things, too, so be prepared to either catch it or duck, both of which will infuriate her even more. We're talking real drama queen here. You are not too likely to feel sorry for her but rather have a much less benevolent reaction. Try to bear in mind that she's really hurting. And therefore, wants to hurt you. Whatever you do, don't laugh. In her mind, that would make it justifiable homicide.

While I know that no guy likes it when his girl cries, knowing what to expect may help some. And though I hate to betray my gender by letting out one of our secrets, some females know the power of their tears and will use them to exploit you. (Not to point fingers, but the Watergirls are probably some of the most qualified experts. Air girls are next, but Earth signs will seldom do this since they won't display emotion in the first place.) You also need to remember that very few people are purely one element and you are likely to see a mixture of these behaviors, depending on her Moon sign and other chart elements.

So what's a guy to do? There is no panacea for all feminese displays of emotion, but one that comes close is the *"Hold me"* solution. Unless your life would be physically in danger by getting that close it's usually worth trying. But let me warn you right now not to get the mistaken notion that "hold me" is synonymous with "let's have sex." Granted, if you execute it properly that could be a possible side benefit, but if you go into it with that intent it could exacerbate the entire situation and result in you being cutoff entirely for a significant amount of time.

So if you opt out of "hold me", then your best bet is to remain calm, tell her you're sorry she's so upset and that you love her (if you really do) and that you'll talk later. Then leave. Don't be too surprised if the pitch within rises behind the closed door or you hear the sound of objects hitting it as you retreat. This is entirely normal. While you're out, you might want to pick up some flowers or some other peace offering for when you return. In the meantime, go have a beer. I'm sure you can find a sympathetic ear at your favorite bar. Chances are you won't be the only one there for that reason. And more than likely THEY will understand!

Then when you start missing her, check the following *Meltdown Repair Guide* for further suggestions on how to make things right.

MELTDOWN REPAIR GUIDE

Forgot birthday, anniversary, Valentine's Day, etc.

Her sign element: Fire (Aries, Leo, Sagittarius)
What she said: "How could you possibly forget something like that!"
What she meant: "You really hurt my feelings."
What to do: Flowers. Lots of them.

Her sign element: Earth (Taurus, Virgo, Capricorn)
What she said: <Possibly nothing but a glare, but she's thinking you're a total idiot.>
What she meant: "You really hurt my feelings."
What to do: Something that sparkles. (Jewelry, butthead, not a fishing lure, except under rare circumstances.)

Her sign element: Air (Gemini, Libra, Aquarius)
What she said: " How could you do that? How many times do I have to remind you? Don't you ever listen to me? Do I ever do that to you? I don't understand how you could forget something so important!"
What she meant: "You really hurt my feelings."
What to do: Dinner in nice restaurant. (Hint: She can't talk as much when she's eating.)

Her sign element: Water (Cancer, Scorpio, Pisces)
What she said: <Sob, sob, sniffle, sniff, sob!>
What she meant: "You really hurt my feelings."
What to do: Hold her. (Remember this doesn't mean *"let's have sex"*), then go shopping for new clothes. (For *her*, idiot, and NOT a sporting goods store unless it's her idea.)

Hour late for dinner date.

Her sign element: Fire
What she said: "Where the hell have you been?"
What she meant: "I'm starving! Where could you have possibly been that was more important than being with me?"
What to do: Arrive with peace offering, *e.g.* flowers and show tickets.

Her sign element: Earth
What she said: <Nothing but a glare.>
What she meant: "You're 61 minutes and 38 seconds late, dumbass. "What am I doing with such an inconsiderate clod?"

What to do: Admit you're an idiot and take her to a nicer place than originally planned, *i.e.* spend more money. Be sure to get an expensive bottle of wine w/dinner and tell her how beautiful she is.

Her sign element: Air
What she said: "Hey, you're here already!"
What she meant: <She just barely finished getting ready because she was on the phone or texting with a friend.>
What to do: Kiss her nice and long and soft and have a nice evening.

Her sign element: Water
What she said: <Sob, sniff> "I've been waiting for you for hours!"
What she meant: "I feel totally neglected and unloved. You're going to pay for this in spades."
What to do: Hold her (remember, this isn't the same as sex), then make sure the evening's even more special than planned.

Whoops, my bad! I forgot you're a guy and don't know what that means. Okay, take her to a really nice restaurant, then rent a movie, preferably a romantic comedy. You know, one of those foo-foo chick flicks. Hold her hand the whole time, except maybe when you're eating.

Forgot to call all week.

Her sign element: Fire
What she said: "Who is this again?"
What she meant: "Don't expect me to sit around and wait on you, buster. Who wouldn't want to be with me?"
What to do: Ask if you can come over; bring flowers and a bottle of wine. Skip the movie, it would be better to concentrate on her. She needs attention, not competition from the TV. Don't even go near that remote control, even if she has cable and you don't. Suck it up, buddy. It'll be worth it.

Her sign Element: Earth
What she said: "So, what's going on?"
What she meant: "So you finally decided to call, jerk. This better be good or you're history."
What to do: Ask if you can come over and bring a movie, preferably something with some depth like Troy, King Arthur, Avatar, stuff like that. Has blood and guts for you and a romantic element for her. Be sure to hold her hand, especially during the romantic parts. Better yet,

173

look at her during those scenes since you probably don't want to watch that mushy stuff anyway. Note that this simple gesture might pay off in spades.

Her sign element: Air
What she said: (No problem. She'd call you.)
What she meant: "Don't even think about ignoring me!"
What to do: Smile a lot. Include lots of eye contact and act interested while she tells you everything she did last week.

Her sign element: Water
What she said: "Why haven't you called me? What did I do wrong?"
What she meant: "How could you? This calls for a major guilt trip!"
What to do: Ask if you can come over; bring Chinese takeout and a bottle of wine.

Cancelled date to play poker & drink beer with the guys.

Her sign element: Fire
What she said: " How could you? Man, are you cut off, buddy!"
What she meant: "Why didn't you invite me? I love poker!"
What to do: Arrange the next poker party at her house. Expect to lose lots of money, but it will be worth it. You'll probably have to supply the beer.

Her sign element: Earth
What she said: <Glassy-eyed glare.>
What she meant: "You think I'm no fun. Fine. Time for me to find either a new hobby or another man."
What to do: Take her fishing. Bring champagne or white wine instead of beer. It might not hurt to bring a blanket. ;-)

Her sign element: Air
What she said: "Why on earth would you do that? You told me we had a date. Why would you rather be with your friends than me? What's so appealing about sitting around in a smoky room and farting all night? What's the matter with you?"
What she meant: " I can't believe you broke our date for something so stupid! We always have so much fun together!"
What to do: Help her plan a party at her place. "Help" probably means your checkbook since she'll already know how to plan a party and a good one.

Her sign element: Water
What she said: <Sob, sob, sniffle, sniff, sob.>
What she meant: : I can't believe you'd rather be with them than me! Don't you know how much I need you?"
What to do: Hold her, (remember, not synonymous with sex) then take her to play pool. Make sure you put your arms around her a lot and take your time showing her how to make those bank shots.

You have no idea whatsoever.

Her sign element: Fire
What she said: "How could you do this to me?"
What she meant: "I don't understand why you don't think about me 24/7. I need more attention!"
What to do: Tell her how beautiful she is and that you want to show her off somewhere. Dancing is good.

Her sign element: Earth
What she said: <Nothing but a glare>
What she meant: "You don't care about me at all or I wouldn't have to tell you all the time what I want. By now you should be able to read my mind."
What to do: Hold her and ask her what's wrong. (Note that "holding" does not mean sex.) When she doesn't answer, take her to your favorite restaurant and then rent a video such as those mentioned earlier for Earth girls.

Her sign element: Air
What she said: "You know, I really get sick of this. I thought we talked about this and you said you wouldn't do that again. Why can't I count on you? Why don't you care about me as much as I care about you?"
What she meant: "I expect you to remember everything I say and do everything you say you'll do, no exceptions."
What to do: Resistance is futile. Take her to a movie, a serious one where the characters have REAL problems, like a disaster flick. (Hint: Her talking will be minimized in a movie. Note I said TAKE HER TO A MOVIE, not rent a video!)

Her sign element: Water

What she said: <Sob, sob, sniffle, sniff, sob>

What she meant: You don't love me! If you did you wouldn't be such an ass!

What to do: Hold her for at least 5 minutes (behave yourself, buster!), then take her out for a nice dinner.

GUY GUIDE FOR GALS

Fire (Aries, Leo, Sagittarius)

What he likes: Attention, praise, excitement, telling jokes and stories, impressing people. He wants you to act like a woman, the more feminine the better. Let him be smarter and more competent, don't beat him at anything or do anything to threaten his masculine "superiority."

What he hates: Boredom, criticism, being outdone in any way whatsoever, waiting in line.

Gift Ideas:

Aries: Weapons; books about weapons; Rambo video collection; alcohol in any form; NRA membership; gift certificate to local shooting range.

Leo: Anything related to his favorite hobby or pastime; movie passes or event tickets.

Sagittarius: Barnes & Noble gift certificate; subscription to *National Geographic*.

Earth (Taurus, Virgo, Capricorn)

What he likes: Bargains, security, practicality, sincere admiration, nature and the outdoors. Needs more time to himself than others. Likes it if you're self-sufficient and can share responsibilities. Wants you to be clean and neat but not necessarily beautiful. Being frugal and appreciating a good bargain is a plus.

What he hates: Frivolity, excessive glamour, whining, extravagance, spending money, meanness or pettiness.

Gift Ideas:

Taurus: Soft shirts; gourmet food or wine; gift certificate at local nursery if he likes to garden; subscription to *Money* magazine; a massage.

Virgo: Gift certificate to Home Depot, Lowes, Sears or Autozone; tools; How-To, fitness and herbal healing books.

Capricorn: Career clothes (he may actually LIKE ties); concert tickets; investment guides.

Air (Gemini, Libra, Aquarius)

What he likes: Trivia, sports and sports statistics, hanging out with friends, staying busy, talking, rock concerts. If you don't like these things you're with the wrong guy. He likes you to be his "buddy" as well as his "girl."

What he hates: Stupidity, shyness, too much seriousness, sulking, emotions in general. (Libras dislike contention of any kind.)

Gift Ideas:

Gemini: Sudoku; remote control toys; hockey game tickets; Trivia games.

Libra: Symphony or ballet tickets; Skating, dance or gymnastics exhibitions; clothes (probably preppy).

Aquarius: Sports event tickets; New baseball hat for favorite team; case of his favorite beer.

Water (Cancer, Scorpio, Pisces)

What he likes: Movies, television, staying home for a quiet evening, understanding his moods (which may be worse than yours), quiet weekends. More inclined to like strong women than other elements. These guys are deeper than most, are often in the Mr. Sensitive Guy category, and need to be appreciated as such. If you don't like the fact they're somewhat emotional, find someone else.

What he hates: Conflict, arguments, too much logic, being insensitive to his feelings.

Gift Ideas:

Cancer: Home cooked meal; casual clothes; the ultimate TV/stereo/DVD integrated remote control.

Scorpio: Anything that has to do with sex. *(Yes, anything...)*

Pisces: Science fiction, fantasy, martial arts or metaphysics books; *Star Trek, Star Wars* or *Lord of the Rings* video collection.

LIFE IS FILLED WITH CYCLES

Everyone knows that kids go through "stages." What you probably don't know is that everything from the terrible twos to the trying teens and that threshold of adulthood crisis at 21 has an astrological explanation. Knowing what these influences are can increase your understanding of your child, give you more patience, provide guiding wisdom to help them navigate through it, and also inspire hope that yes, this, too shall pass. And don't think for a moment that once you get past 21 that these major events cease! That mid-life crisis and "empty nest syndrome" have astrological corollaries as well.

Those infamous yet predictable life stages come about primarily as a result of outer planet transits, *i.e.* Jupiter, Saturn, the asteroid, Chiron, and Uranus. Neptune and Pluto move very slowly and are primarily responsible for the "generational effect" where children born over the course of several years have these planets in the same sign, giving them similar characteristics as noted on the specific planet pages linked above. When a child is very young, the inner planets have the most noticeable effect. For example, around the age of 22 months a child will have his first Mars return, which is when Mars returns to its natal position on the child's Natal Chart. Obviously this coincides quite closely with the advent of the "terrible twos."

Of course the most obvious "return cycle" is our solar return, more commonly known as our birthday. This marks the beginning of a new life cycle every year of our life, the specifics of which can be read in a solar return chart which is cast for the exact moment when the Sun returns to the degree it was in when you were born. This may be on your birthday or sometimes the day before or after. The Sun represents our ego and each birthday this gets redefined, either consciously or subconsciously.

Children identify very closely with age, and this is part of the reason; we know intuitively that we've reached another milestone relative to who we are and progressed accordingly. Children tend to look up to those who are older and look forward to the additional privileges available as they get older, whether it's to start kindergarten, first grade, middle school, high school, get a driver's license, be able to vote, smoke, drink or whatever. We even look forward to 25 when our insurance rates usually go down! After that we tend to pay less attention because societal influences are less obvious. Nonetheless, the even decades such as 30, 40, 50, 60 and above are typically recognized, even for those of us that tend to try to ignore the years in between.

I would hardly represent myself as the perfect parent. If I even attempted to do so I'm sure one or all of my six offspring would jump right in to quickly correct the record. One thing I've noticed, however, with not only my own but other people's children as well is that by the time they get through that first Saturn return around 29, they are usually either dead, in jail, or straightened out.

I realize that is very representative of my Cappie "gloom and doom" nature of which I'm reminded on a regular basis by those close to me, but that doesn't change the fact it seems to work. Fortunately, the vast majority are in the last category. This undoubtedly relates to our first Saturn return. At that time, as well as a few stops in between as denoted below, we take a careful look at how we feel about authority figures, responsibility, our obligations, and the various restrictions imposed by bureaucracies and other large entities such as corporations.

Back in the 60s the prevailing advice was not to trust anyone over 30. The implications of that sentiment reflected on the concept of a Saturn return where after that age people would have a higher regard for authority and "The Establishment" as it was derisively called back then. Now the "baby boomers" who grew up with that are twice that age! However, as a member of that particular group, I'm not sure we have that much more respect for authority than we did back then, particularly regarding this most recent crop of politicians.

The following denotes some of these key cycles and the associated influences you'll probably recognize, from your own experience growing up if nothing else. Since this section is largely about children, I haven't included much detail about cycles past the 20s, but rest assured that they continue throughout your life. Also note that I've only included the "hard" aspects, such as the square and opposition since they are the most noticeable. Favorable influences such as the trine are seldom noticed by virtue of human nature, which takes the good times for granted while resenting the bad.

Note that the early to mid teens and around 21 contain overlapping cycles that often manifest as difficult times in the child's life and naturally this splashes on the parents stress level as well. If a difficult cycle for one or both parents is in effect at the same time it will be a very trying time indeed for all concerned, for example if one or both parents are having their mid-life crisis at the same time they're trying to raise a teenager.

More information about planetary cycles is also available in the Planetary Returns section.

☿ Mercury

Mercury completes one orbit around the Sun in 88 days, but astrology is based on a geocentric view. Thus, it appears to follow the Sun other than its retrograde periods which occur approximately every 4 months.

Mercury rules the brain and is thus all about our ideas, thoughts and communicating as well as eye-hand coordination and motor control (or lack thereof). A child's survival depends on being able to communicate and move. Each of these aspects will mark a milestone in the child's ability to communicate with his environment and his physical development then continue at regular intervals of approximately 1 year's duration. During Mercury retrograde periods, progress will typically slow down considerably.

1st Quarter (Square)

~3 months: Responds to loud noises; recognizes parents' voices; coos, smiles and responds to attention; rolls over and interacts with others. By this age is it fairly easy for an adult to understand what the child is trying to convey.

Half Cycle (Opposition)

~6 months: This is about the time when a child starts to crawl and explore his or her world in a more mobile way. His curiosity is awakened and the child can become bored if s/he doesn't have an interesting toy or person to keep him or her occupied.

Last Quarter (Square)

~9 months: At this point the child is usually pulling him or herself up and may stand unassisted or even walk. They are occupied greatly with movement and are doing so during nearly all their waking moments. Even if they can't quite walk, they usually are adept at crawling and getting to where they want. If their efforts are frustrated, they are likely to protest very loudly. Their vocabulary is starting to form with simple words.

Return to Natal (Conjunction)

~1 year: Most likely the child is walking and communicating quite effectively with numerous words and actions. They are fascinated by various toys and devices such as the television or cell phones, which they understand are for communicating so will mimic talking on one, even if you don't know what they're saying; they do! At this point the toddler is rapidly becoming a "miniature person" with his or her own style of investigating their world and communicating with it.

Ω Ω Ω

♀ Venus

Venus has a 225 day cycle, but like Mercury is between Earth and the Sun, so astrologically its cycle is closer to a year. Venus influences our affections, pleasures, what we value, and where we find comfort. During the first year an infant shows distinct stages of development as he determines his needs and responds to whether or not they're being met. The ability to receive and give love is developed during this time.

1st Quarter (Square)

~ 3 months: Realizes that eating is more than just to satisfy hunger but is also enjoyable; may take a pacifier refused earlier or nurse for comfort long after milk is gone.

Half Cycle (Opposition)

~ 6 months: Interested in food, openly affectionate, responds to love and attention; may start to show preference for a certain toy or blanket as a comfort device.

Last Quarter (Square)

~ 9 months: Is more aware of his senses as a way to experience the world; everything starts to go in the mouth; pays attention to music and cries when it stops; voices pleasure or displeasure.

Return to Natal (Conjunction)

~ 1 year: Shows clear preference for certain toys; may have a favorite blanket or stuffed animal that is soft and no substitute will do. Shows affection with kisses and understand what they mean, *i.e.* will withhold them if unhappy.

Ω Ω Ω

♂ Mars

Mars has a 687 day cycle. Mars is all about independence and our drive to get what we want. These cycles represent the child's efforts to assert himself and do things he hasn't done before. They motivate him or her to seek out experiences that provide more autonomy. How dramatic or difficult these stages may be depends on how Mars is placed in the natal chart as well as in the return chart. If Mars is in a Fire Sign, on their Ascendant, the Chart Ruler, or the Sun is in Aries, this will be more pronounced.

1st Quarter (Square)

5 - 6 months: Sits up independently, crawls.

Half Cycle (Opposition)

~11 months: First steps, unassisted. Mars and Mercury work together for mobility with Mars providing the motivation and drive for independence while Mercury supplies the motor skills to accomplish the action.

Last Quarter (Square)

~ 17 months: Walking unassisted. Often resists help or direction.

Return to Natal (Conjunction)

~22 - 23 months: Aware of own identity; *Terrible Twos!* Wants to do things in his or her own way and shows considerable resistance when restrained.

2nd Mars Return

~ 4 years: Interested in new experiences; develops more complex motor skills such as riding a tricycle and possibly simple sports.

3rd Mars Return

~ 6 years: Starting to think on his or her own and take action based on own experience and ideas. This is the true difference between kindergarten and 1st grade! [Corresponds with Jupiter opposition]

4th Mars Return

~ 8 years: Various religions consider this the time when a child becomes accountable and knows the difference between right and wrong. They are likely to no longer ask permission as often or even be openly rebellious. [Correlates with Saturn square.]

Subsequent Mars Returns

Approximately every two years. Parents have often noted that a child's even-numbered years tend to be more challenging than the odd-numbered years; this is easily attributable to Mars returns when a child's will is renewed, new drives are introduced, and different experiences pursued.

Ω Ω Ω

♃ Jupiter

Jupiter has a twelve year cycle. Jupiter is known as one of the "social planets" and rules your expectations, beliefs, and your philosophy of life. You will notice that your child's understanding of the world around him changes significantly at each of these milestones. They are learning not only rote knowledge, which falls under Mercury, but learning how to put it together and form their own opinions. Jupiter also influences your confidence. Note that at all these junctures s/he thinks he knows it all.

These returns continue throughout your life with each one representing a time when you pull it all together in some area of your life, depending on the House placement of the return Jupiter. Jupiter rules such things as politics, religion, higher learning, relocation, long-distance travel, and legal matters, any of which can become a new focus with a Jupiter Return. A new awareness of something and its meaning in your life will be the hallmark of each one.

1st Quarter (Square)

About 3 years: Curiosity increases and wants to learn; answers simple questions.

Half Cycle (Opposition)

About 6 years: "Why?" Synthesizes information and begins to form own opinions from discrete information

Last Quarter (Square)

About 9 years: Socializing increases with other children; stronger interest in learning; likes and dislikes more pronounced; "Best friends."

1st Jupiter Return (Conjunction)

12 years: Begins to realize place in society; "Cliques"; starts to discover world outside immediate environment; interest in other lands and cultures increases. [Correlates with Chiron square.]

2nd Jupiter Return

1st Quarter (Square)

About 15 years: Thinks s/he knows it all and everyone else, especially adults, are stupid; peer pressure strong and influential.

Half Cycle (Opposition)

About 18 years: Graduates from high school; strong opinions of how world works; begins to interact with society outside peer circle.

Last Quarter (Square)

About 21 years: Graduates from college or getting established in some sort of vocation; attains new level of understanding of how the world works, based on learning and own experience. [Correlates with Saturn square.]

2nd Jupiter Return (Conjunction)

About 24 years: After living in the world on his own for a few years (hopefully) further grasps how it all fits together beneath the social umbrella.

3rd Jupiter Return

~ 36 years: Re-examines life and its direction; dramatic changes ensue if things don't add up. Many individuals return to school, change jobs, or get more actively involved in politics or religious organizations at this time. [Correlates with 3rd Chiron square.]

4th Jupiter Return

~ 48 years: Reassessment time again that will result in attitude adjustments and change. Many people at this age enjoy travel now that the kids are gone and their income is likely to be more stable than the earlier years. A mid-life crisis is possible if beliefs and expectations not being met, though this is more likely to occur at a Jupiter opposition, *i.e.* 42 years or 54 years.

5th Jupiter Return

~ 60 years: Enters the "croning" years when life experience is displayed as a panorama expressed by every wrinkle and grey hair. Perspective is deeper as well as understanding of the world at large. What needs to be done to improve the world seems intuitively obvious to you and yet the rest of the world hasn't caught on. At this point many of the individuals with whom you interact such as your physician, legal advisor, broker, and so forth will be younger than you are and you may begin to doubt whether they really know what they're doing. [Correlates with 2nd Saturn return.]

$$\Omega \; \Omega \; \Omega$$

♄ Saturn

Saturn has a cycle of 29 years. Another "social planet," Saturn rules how you view, respect and respond to authority. It's about restrictions, delays, your sense of responsibility, how you handle your obligations and those hard lessons we all experience, through which we gain wisdom.

1st Quarter (Square)

7+ years: Recognizes right and wrong and need to follow established rules. Rules are "black and white;" may not obey but doesn't modify them. [Correlates with 4th Mars return.]

Half Cycle (Opposition)

14-15 years: Questions restrictions and boundaries; redefines and interprets rules.

Last Quarter (Square)

21-22 years: Accepts, adapts or rejects rules of childhood as s/he is now an adult and no longer answers to parents. [Correlates with Jupiter square.]

Return to Natal Position (Conjunction)

29 1/2 years: Recognizes the need for rules, that lack of responsibility will have a price, and fighting against the world is an exercise in futility. In Biblical times, a man was not considered an adult until he was 30 years old.

2nd Saturn Return

~ 59 years: At your first Saturn return you learned responsibility and with your second you begin to gain wisdom. In concert with the 5th Jupiter

Return, an entirely new outlook begins to form regarding responsibilities, authority, and anything else that has been a stern instructor in your particular life. Regard for authority is likely to change as respect is expected from others more than you're inclined to give it to those around you. [Correlates with 5th Jupiter return.]

Ω Ω Ω

⚷ Chiron

The asteroid Chiron has a cycle of approximately 50 years. Chiron influences the various hurtful experiences we encounter in life and how we use them to help others. These can be of a physical, mental, emotional or even financial nature, depending on the house placement.

1st Quarter (Square)

12-13 years: Hormone and growth influx brings a wealth of potentially painful experiences such as discovery of the opposite sex and body changes.

Half Cycle (Opposition)

25 years: By now realizes that the world is a difficult place and can be cruel and responds to his experience, perhaps in a violent or self-defeating manner.

Last Quarter (Square)

37-38 years: Mid-life crisis; seeks meaning in life. Contemplates mistakes, their price, and corrective action. [Correlates with 3rd Jupiter return.]

Return to Natal Position (Conjunction)

50 years: Has just about "seen it all" and integrates experiences into psyche; desire to help and mentor others. Any unresolved hurts from the past may demand absolution.

Ω Ω Ω

♅ 𝓤ranus

Uranus has a cycle of approximately 84 years. Uranus is about sudden change, freedom, rebellion, disruptions, and the unexpected after which our life is never the same. These are typically times of our life when we experience major changes, perhaps of our own making.

1st Quarter (Square)

21 years: Determines own path that may be significantly different than the way he or she was raised. Parents can't do much about it and s/he knows it.

Half Cycle (Opposition)

42 years: A different type of freedom ensues with kids leaving the nest; time to reassess and redefine life's direction with changes likely. This is also right around a Jupiter opposition time which could result in a mid-life crisis and breaking away from previous restrictions, particularly if unsatisfied with life to this point.

Last Quarter (Square)

63 years: Retirement countdown begins; leaving a career or work behind represents another type of freedom. Ambition is likely to wane or be redirected to another area (i.e. retirement) if you're caught in a "grind."

Return to Natal Position (Conjunction)

84 years: Onset of old age, more social and physical changes. Freedom at this point may be lost due to physical limitations.

Ω Ω Ω

Other Cycles

Progressed Sun and/or Moon signs are other possible reasons for personality and behavioral changes you may observe in your child, other family members, or even yourself. If a child is born toward the end of an astrological sign, his or her Sun Sign will change at an early age. For example, based on the "day for a year" formula for advancing a birth chart, a child born at 25 degrees Pisces will display all the dreamy and typically gentle attributes of a little Fish for the first five years of life, then about the time s/he enters school, will become more aggressive and active than previously. Their interests will change, they'll become more bossy, have a lot more raw energy and be more drawn to or in need of physical outlets for their exuberance.

It would be natural to "blame" this on the school environment whereas in reality it's the sign change. Thus, it's a good idea to take note of when this will occur and be prepared. Your child may wonder why s/he feels differently as well, even to the point of wondering *"What's wrong with me?"* which can be very disconcerting, especially if they're already at a difficult age. While they may not be able to understand or even belief in the astrological effects, you can and thus have a better idea how to help your child because of the veritable window astrology can give you into their deepest feelings and motivations.

Conversely, if someone is born at the beginning of a sign, they won't undergo a sign change until adulthood. In other words, there are thirty degrees per sign, so if you were born at zero degrees, you will be 30 before you progress into the next one. No matter what age this occurs, it can be quite disconcerting to the person as well as those close to him or her. This can have an effect on all relationships but particularly marriages when one of the partners suddenly changes their personality.

This is not to say that they leave their entire previous persona behind, only that another layer will be added. The beauty of this evolution is that it teaches us to understand others as we get to view the world through various zodiacal knotholes. While we never leave our birth chart entirely behind, these progressions add another layer of experiential wisdom. As an analogy, if you were born and raised in Montana you'll always possess the traits and paradigms you acquired from that culture. If you move to Connecticut you'll assimilate certain elements of that culture though at heart you'll still be a Montanan.

Even Moon Sign changes are noticeable, sometimes even more so, at least once you know what to look for. I've had adult clients come to me asking why they cry more easily than before and react more emotionally to stress; this is usually explained by their Moon progressing into Cancer or Pisces. If someone suddenly becomes more worrisome, critical, complains more, has to blame everything on someone or something, and is more organized, maybe even to the point of being a neat-freak, the odds are good their Moon has gone into Virgo.

Moon signs change approximately ever two and a half years. The lunar phase changes as well, which also affects a person's emotional nature and quest for learning. It's a very good idea for a parent to keep track of their child's Moon Sign since it has such a strong effect on their emotions. Especially during times that are highly charged anyway, such as the teens, it provides one more piece of data to help you understand your child and help him or her grow into a responsible adult.

About the time each person reaches approximately 30 years old, they will experience their first Progressed Lunar Return, meaning that they will have experienced the entire zodiacal emotional spectrum, further adding to the wisdom they assimilate with their first Saturn Return. This has a lot more meaning and learning value when the person recognizes the different effects of each excursion so s/he can use it for understanding others' emotional natures. The Natal Moon Sign will still be in force, but the Progressed Moon will manifest itself somewhat similar to the way cumin will manifest itself when you add it to a pot of chili. It's still chili and maintains its basic character as such, but there's a new dimension to its flavor that gives it more authenticity.

PARENTING WITH ASTROLOGY

It's important to know the general theme of each astrological sign so you can understand how your child is "programmed, where s/he is going and thus prepare him or her for the journey. These are elements that will be ingrained in their psyche and will be there whether you like them or not; your child cannot do anything about his basic nature and neither can you. Ignoring this will not make those irritating qualities or behaviors go away; it will simply drive your child to other sources for whatever you don't provide.

I don't have any problem admitting that I would do any number of things differently if I were raising my six children today. I wish I'd had the benefit of astrology; it would have changed my tactics in a plethora of ways if I'd had that insider information about what made each of them tick. Maybe they would have fewer hang-ups and be happier today if I had, who knows? Clearly that is water over the dam at this point, but perhaps I can improve some of my karma by sharing this information mingled with my experience.

♈ Aries Kids

Aries children are so full of energy that they'll wear you out just watching them. If you recall the old comic strip, Dennis the Menace, there is little doubt in my mind that he was a little Aries.

Channeling all this raw Fire Sign energy into positive activities is absolutely essential. That energy is going to be expressed one way or another so it's in your best interest to direct it accordingly. Independence is another challenge to the parent of an Aries child. When they're knee-high to a grasshopper they'll wander off without a backward glance, not afraid of a thing. If you've seen parents in the mall with their toddler harnessed to a leash, there's a good chance that child has an Aries Sun, Moon, or Ascendant. They are impulsive and fearless, and having a child with those traits can mean numerous premature grey hairs for mom and dad.

Driven, self-motivated, and independent are a few other common Aries traits that are best refined through parental attention and love as opposed to suppressed. Whatever you do, don't put a damper on that natural fire. Encourage it, but in a responsible way. Being impulsive by nature, you'll have to remind your little Aries a dozen times a day to look both ways when crossing the street and not to talk to strangers. They're not afraid of taking chances, so it's up to you to give them challenge and adventure within a safe realm. Otherwise, they'll define it themselves, which could lead to disaster.

One of the first things you probably noticed about your Aries as an infant was the little dickens had a temper. Patience is not one of his or her strong points. Aries is ruled by Mars, the God of War, and is often expressed as aggression. Discipline is essential, but don't do so in a cruel way that will simply feed that natural combative nature. Again, find creative and constructive outlets for that aggression. Sports are a great vehicle for this, no matter how young they are.

Have plenty of options in the house and backyard to keep this active child moving in a positive direction. Noise and boisterousness goes with the territory. That isn't going to go away any time soon, so about all you can do is set boundaries upon it. Make it a matter of whether it's appropriate behavior in a given setting as opposed to making it entirely forbidden. That independent streak is not going to coexist well with anything associated with the word "No!" "Not here" or "Not now" may fly, but never "no." Trust me on that one.

Aries is a Cardinal Sign, meaning they don't have any difficulty making their own decisions, which will hail from an early age. You can see how this coupled with that independence will be a challenge to direct. Notice I said "direct" and not "control" since that would be an exercise in futility. Your little Aries has tremendous potential for success. This may be hard to appreciate when he or she is in the midst of the "terrible two's" or numerous other stages of growing up.

However, if you try to suppress that ambition it will not end well. That Aries energy is going to assert itself one way or another and if you aren't supportive and direct it in positive channels you probably won't like where it comes out. You also run the risk of alienating your child for a long time to come if you persist in that style of parenting. Remember that they're represented by a horned animal that excels at butting heads. They tend to be brutally honest and direct in their communications, so sensitizing them to the effect this can have on others is a good idea once they reach school age; tact won't come naturally.

Being self-motivated is a great asset so your charge as a parent is to make sure that you provide plenty of acceptable outlets for your child to choose from. They're great starters but often burn out before finishing, so encouraging perseverance is important to their future success. Reward it heavily, starting with short-term projects that they can handle comfortably then celebrate when they complete it. Allow them to make their own decisions as much as possible, don't expect to suppress their competitiveness, and provide socially-acceptable outlets for their natural aggression. Aries are drawn to careers that allow them to express their independence, courage, and natural drive. When these kids say they want to be a fireman when they grow up there's a good chance this will indeed come to pass. The military is often attractive as well as just about anything where they can compete. Sports of all types are also good ways to direct that competitive energy.

One thing you probably don't ever have to worry about is your child being lazy. Providing enough activities to keep them occupied in a constructive manner can be a definitely challenge, but it will pay huge dividends later. Again, bear in mind, that if you don't provide appropriate outlets and stimulation, that your child will find it somewhere and it may not be where you'd prefer. Foster all that energy is a positive direction, however, and s/he will make you proud someday.

Aries Primary Need: To be #1

Ω Ω Ω

♉ *Taurus Kids*

Taurus children tend to have an easy-going nature and not be in a hurry about anything. If you remember the children's TV show, Mr. Rogers, you may remember him singing "I like to take my time..." This was undoubtedly inspired by some little Bull moving at glacial speed.

Like their polar sign, Scorpio, Taurus children have a penetrating gaze that projects wisdom beyond their years. They have a certain look in their eyes that tell you they can't be fooled. As a practical, ground-based Earth Sign, they're going to want the facts. While they'll enjoy fictitious stories and movies as much as anyone, no one is going to fool them into thinking that they're real. Bear this in mind when you introduce your child to Santa Claus and see who's fooling who with that one. Little Bulls like nice things and if they think that believing in Santa will bring them more goodies, they will play that game. But watch that look in their eye, because regardless of what you may think, you're not the one who's in control.

Taurus rules the zodiacal 2nd House which includes possessions, finances, comforts, pleasures and needs. These kids will like their "stuff" and will also demand comfort. They are patient by nature and slow to anger, but they'll simply commandeer what they want in a quiet, unassuming way. Like crawling into bed with you in the middle of the night and then proceeding to push you out. As they grow up they'll particularly enjoy good food, possibly even exotic things that kids aren't usually interested in such as sushi. They tend to be quite possessive and probably won't like sharing their toys with other kids. They're another one that will tend to be "entitlement minded" and not have any problem asking or taking whatever you care to give. This is fine when they're young, but bear in mind that they will someday grow up and expect the same treatment, except by then the cost will be far beyond that of their own TV or a new bicycle.

Little Bulls like to take it easy and can be lazy if you allow it. While it may be pleasant to have a child that is not bouncing off the walls, at the same time they need to be taught discipline and to work. Don't allow them to indulge in that bowl of ice cream or curling up on the couch with the remote control until they have put away their toys or done any other chores you may have assigned. They have a whole lot of charm thanks to being ruled by Venus, such that they could sell ice to an Eskimo, but don't fall for it or you'll live to regret it later. At some point they need to learn that the National Bank of Mom or Dad closes at a certain age, the younger the better.

Once they start earning their own money, or even if you give them an allowance, they will probably hoard it and not let go of it easily. They won't even want to spend it on stuff for themselves, which they'll expect you to pick up the tab for. This is good in the long-run because they will become frugal, practical adults. Just make sure you let them know the bank is closed, however.

One Taurus trait you're probably already aware of is stubbornness. As a Fixed Sign, there is no question that they don't change their mind easily, if at all. Thus, you need to train them right when they're young and impressionable. You are not doing yourself or them a favor by spoiling them at a young age because once they hit adolescence the mold is going to be largely set.

One way to get them to thinking in their slow, methodical way is to use a textbook marketing approach and point out what's in it for them. This is about the only thing that will come even close to them changing their mind about anything. You will get very good at luring and bribing with time, but it's your most effective approach. Simply trying to assert your authority or control will simply push the Stubborn Button and you can bet they can out-wait you, unless you're also a Taurus or have strong Fixed Signs in your own chart, in which case you may wind up with an irresistible force and an immovable object. However, make sure that your bribing doesn't turn against you. Once they figure out what you're doing they will use it to get anything they happen to want. If you fall into that trap the results will not be in your favor. Little Bulls can appear to be slow learners, but they spend a lot of time thinking about how to get out of work and get what they want.

They like clothes that are soft and comfortable and will tend to hang onto their favorites, even after they outgrow them. They won't be particularly fashion-conscious unless they have a Leo, Virgo or Libra Moon or ascendant, but even then comfort will be essential, regardless of how stylish it is. Also note that bribing them with food is probably not a good idea. They tend to love good food and drink and if they aren't physically active, they will develop a weight problem. Thus, bribing with activities is better, though it will also have less appeal. They do tend to like the out-of-doors and nature, however, so going for a walk or to the park when they're little is a good plan, provided it's practical.

If taught to work in order to get what they want, they will be hard workers. Their calm and patient personality usually assures them of lots of friends and getting along with their teachers as children and supervisors as they get older. At least until one of these individuals asks them to do something they don't want to do in which case they may encounter some hard lessons along the way. The main thing to bear in mind is not to spoil them and do your best to stay one step ahead of them. Taurus is one of the strongest astrological Signs so don't let their leisurely pace or lack of aggression fool you.

Taurus Primary Need: Comfort & Security

Ω Ω Ω

♊ Gemini Kids

If there's one sign that's the most likely to at least appear to have Attention Deficit Hyperactivity Disorder (ADHD) it has to be Gemini. Ruled by speedy Mercury and hailing from the 3rd House of mental activity, ideas, neighbors and short journeys, these miniature human RAM chips absorb data like the proverbial sponge.

I kid you not. These kids thrive on data of any description and if there's nothing new to ponder they'll find something. If you think of most individuals' thought processes in terms of computer processor speeds, most of us are probably in the megahertz range; Geminis, on the other hand, are running in gigahertz. Your challenge, therefore, as the parent of such a wonder, is to keep your child stimulated intellectually without giving yourself a brain hemorrhage. These are the kids who can learn to read by the time their two and perform algebraic computations by second grade. They love to learn and see it as a game. As a logical Air Sign, their ability to synthesize information is also highly developed. I don't know what percentage of PhD recipients are Geminis, but from my knothole, I've known more PhD's from this astrological persuasion than any other.

If you're a bit of an intellectual yourself, you can have a tremendous amount of fun with your little Twin. There is little they won't enjoy as long as it's new. Whatever you do, don't discourage them from learning. If you burn out providing a steady flow of data for their mental consumption, then make sure you provide them with toys and games that will do the same. However, bear in mind that most toys will become boring after about four minutes, max. As they become old enough to do puzzles and play word games, Suduko and so forth, you can find some respite. Expect questions galore; you will probably think that no child ever born asked "Why?" as many times per hour as your own.

Geminis are typically unemotional as far as it goes, but this will also depend on their ascendant and Moon Sign. However, unless they have a Water Sign moon, for the most part they will be driven by logic. This is not to say that they don't have emotions, only to point out that they will be more inclined to make their decisions with their head as opposed to their heart. Yes, they will cry and be upset like any other child, but it's more likely to be out of boredom or frustration than emotional hurt. For example, if you had a Cancer child and a Gemini child in the same room and both were crying, the little Crab would be bawling because someone looked at him funny while the little Twin would be wailing because he had nothing to do. The worst thing you can do is underestimate how quickly these kids can learn. They consume information at a rate that boggles the mind.

One of the things little Twins need to accept is the fact that not everyone is as quick and intelligent as they are, neither do they enjoy learning as a pastime. This does not mean the other kids are dumb, only focused on different pursuits. While a little Crab may become the teacher's pet for all those hugs he freely dishes out, the little Twin will become the teacher's pet because he or she takes credit for how quickly and easily s/he learns and how much s/he enjoys it.

The one problem you'll have with a Gemini child as they get old is keeping their interest on something. They tend to be jacks of many trades and masters of none, so to speak. If they've not found some pursuit that holds their interest or don't have an inborn passion for something, it will be difficult for them in school simply because they get bored easily. While their ascendant or Moon Sign can help, generally speaking they will have a difficult time maintaining interest on something they find boring. They will learn much quicker than other children and thus while the teacher plods along trying to instill the subject at hand to the non-Geminis in the room, those hailing from the 3rd House of data will be fidgeting, throwing spit wads, texting someone, or surfing on the iPhone. In all likelihood they'll be doing these things even if they *are* interested because they're masters at multitasking.

Note also that Geminis are known for having two personalities. This is probably because they absorb so much information that their brain splits or possibly the result when their processor goes into sleep mode. Seriously, this is a Gemini trait. What triggers or defines them is no doubt a function of other elements of their Natal Chart. At the least they are very comfortable with two different personas. For example, if your child is one of many whose parents are divorced, it's likely that s/he will be a different person for each parent. While this will be the case with most children as they acclimate to different environments, a Gemini child could easily thrive on the stimulation of two homes, two schedules, two sets of rules, and so forth. Even as adults Geminis are very comfortable with two careers, two homes, two jobs, etc.

For those born without a single driving interest regarding what they want to be when they grow up it behooves the parent to make sure that their little Twin is exposed to as many different career options as possible. Scouting programs do an excellent job of this and if that is not available, make sure you child understands all the many things there are to learn. Since what they're taught in school is going to be limited by the intelligence of the other children in the class, they are likely to be bored and not see the more interesting side of things that comes past the basics. These kids need to jump right to the "good stuff" to keep their interest long enough to challenge them, then they'll back-track as necessary to learn what they need to so they fully understand. Being slightly above their head is preferable to boredom.

What ever you do don't mistake their activity level for misbehavior. If you keep them busy with things to learn and do, they'll have no interest in misbehaving, unless it's primary purpose is to learn something new. Also make sure that your little Twin does not simply become addicted to computer games or TV because it provides the stimulation they need. They may eventually become whizzes that know every possible question on Jeopardy, but it's not going to prepare them to be a productive citizen. Encourage hobbies, participating in sports, reading, and educational games and both of you will probably survive just fine.

Gemini Primary Need: Mental Stimulation

Ω Ω Ω

♋ Cancer Kids

Cancer is the zodiacal 4th House of home environment, providing Crabs with a strong attachment to home, especially their mother. This will persist throughout their life, which can either be seen as a blessing or a curse since severing the umbilical cord may take decades to achieve.

It shouldn't be surprising, then if your little Crab is a bit clingy. This is not necessarily a problem unless they happen to be over the age of 35. Then again, if you can get them to hand over their paycheck this can be a good thing. Another item to bear in mind, however, is that Crabs are ruled by the Moon, which rules everyone's emotions according to which sign it's in. This gives Cancers a double-whammy, however, as far a personal planets are concerned. The Moon is the fastest moving astrological entity and makes its rounds through the Zodiac every 28 days or so, which brings an emotional peak to each house ever few days. Cancers are very sensitive to the Moon and its phases and especially eclipses. Thus, if your little Crab (literally and figuratively) seems out of sorts, it's a good idea to check what's going on with the Moon before overreacting.

Cancer is also a Water Sign, all of which are driven by emotion, even without all that lunar activity; others in this group include Scorpio and Pisces. They're all sensitive, intuitive, and feel their emotions so intensely that it is going to take a long time for them to learn to control them. One thing that helps, however, is when their Natal Moon progresses to another sign. This may have such a dramatic effect that you wonder or possibly even worry what happened to change your child. Either that or you may have the false hope that s/he is gaining control, only to find out at a later date that it was only a passing phase (pun intended).

Depending on their ascendant and Natal Moon sign this can be either increased or mitigated, but the important thing to bear in mind is that your child is very sensitive, will get his or her feelings hurt easily, needs a lot of affection (which he or she will return generously), and is likely to lose control fairly easily. The bottom line is s/he cannot help it and if you get too angry or frustrated it will only make it worse because there's a good chance they will pick up on your emotions in addition to their own.

Cancer is a Cardinal Sign so little crabs have no problem making a decision. They like to be in charge and you can bet if they play "house" when they're little, they will run things quite decisively. The down side, of course, is that they will not always agree with what you want them to do and won't have any trouble resisting. On the surface this has the look and feel of defiance, but the good news is that they're using their brain to make a decision, which will come in quite handy later in life. Your best bet when this happens is to employ the art of negotiation and reason. Depending on how old they are, you may not get very far with this tact, however, and it may result in a noisy and tearful scene. This is when you need to remember your child's deeply emotional nature and keep your own in check. When they calm down be sure to reassure them of your love and explain to them why they couldn't have it their way. They still may not agree, but over time the rationale will stick with enough repetition.

Since Cancers have such a strong attachment to their family, it's important to involve them with their extended family as well. They are likely to have a special attraction to their grandmother(s), who can lend much assistance toward teaching them proper behavior since they probably won't see them as someone they need to compete with as much as a parent. Experiences and lessons involving their grandparents will be well-remembered and integrated into their lives. This comes in very handy as a respite for parents who need a break occasionally, particularly if you have trouble dealing with an emotional child. If you are less emotionally inclined, this is not something that you will understand naturally and it will undoubtedly get on your last nerve from time to time.

Another thing to consider regarding their attachment to family is that if you have a family business, chances are quite good that your Cancer child will be the one interested in taking it over someday. If this is your situation, your child will probably show an early interest in it and involving him or her in everyday operations as soon as they're old enough to understand will be beneficial all around.

The most important thing to remember is your child's deep, emotional nature. If you're not comfortable with displays of raw emotion, it will be easy to hurt your child's feelings repeatedly and cause significant damage to their self-image and your relationship. It's certainly okay to be angry from time to time, but always make sure that you show an increase in affection after any unpleasant scenes to reassure your little Crab that s/he is loved. Never forget that hugs and kisses are as important to them as balanced meals and clean clothes, maybe even more-so.

Cancer Primary Need: Affection

Ω Ω Ω

♌ *Leo Kids*

Leos are born knowing that they're royalty and expect to be doted upon as such. They're confident by nature, being a resident of the 5th House of ego, creativity, romance, speculation and entertainment, yet surprisingly sensitive and caring.

Leos are easy to spoil. They just expect it in such an unpretentious way that you feel as if it's your duty to provide them with anything they need. They are generally good natured, but like that cute lion cub, can have quite the tantrum when displeased. After all, they are a Fire Sign and can display a healthy temper when provoked. Remember that Leos are ruled by the Sun which is the center of the solar system. Thus, if they get plenty of attention and believe that they're the center of the universe, chances are things will go well. However, if they're not your only child or you have other distractions such as a day job meaning they have to compete for attention they can get pretty creative in how they obtain it. Just remember that a Leo child needs attention and praise every bit as much as s/he needs food, clothing and love.

Since Leos truly believe they are royalty, they tend to have a bit of an entitlement mentality. Again, they aren't always demanding, though they can be, but they definitely have high expectations. The older they get, the higher the expectations. That appetite for attention can also increase with age.

They like to be noticed so don't be surprised if your little (or not so little) Lion dresses quite outlandishly once they reach adolescence. Now lots of kids will dress in a manner that parents frown upon, sometimes because they can't match their clothes, others because they have a favorite shirt they won't allow to be laundered, or they just have weird taste. Leos, however, will have generally good taste except they'll want to be stylish. They also like bright colors. In fact, it's a good idea to paint their room in nice sun-shiny colors, even something like red or orange that you might not be able to stand yourself. Even if you have to put on sunglasses to go in there, accommodate them in this way. They can't stand a dull environment, which they'll find horribly depressing, so it's in your best interest in the long run to indulge them, like it or not.

Leos are natural leaders, which shouldn't be surprising, and as such they tend to be bossy. Depending on other influences in their Natal Chart, they may accomplish this is a brassy or loud manner but they may also take control in a less assuming way, but they will get their way, whatever it takes. Since they like to be surrounded by their adoring subjects, they tend to get along reasonably well with other children, especially those who tend to follow rather than lead. Whatever you do, don't discourage your child from being a leader. They're going to do so as second nature anyway so accept it and do everything you can to teach him or her the responsibility it entails. Teach them honesty, kindness, and understanding so they don't lead others astray.

Don't underestimate how sensitive your little Lion is. They get their feelings hurt quite easily and can lick their wounds for a long, long time. They tend to be creative and like to make presents for their loved ones. Always accept them as if they have given you the Hope Diamond. Foster their creativity however you can. Whatever they take a liking to, let them pursue it and show off their work. Even if they're only a toddler, it will mean a lot to them to have their work of art displayed proudly on the refrigerator. Brag about them in front of others and watch them shine.

When they reach adolescence and their teens be sure they have something to keep them busy and to obtain that limelight they crave. Sports, dance, martial arts, music, whatever, encourage them to develop their natural talents, which are many, and direct their ego in an appropriate manner. Leos have a natural grace that lends itself well to physical activities. They may not be the fastest one out there, but they will look the best, effortlessly. They may not be terrifically competitive or need to come in first; they can tend to be a bit lazy, especially if something comes easily. Given a touch of Aries or Capricorn, they'd more inclined to compete heavily, or possibly even some Virgo, which would throw some perfectionism in there. The fact of the matter is they like to think they're the best and don't need a medal or trophy to prove it. If they get overly competitive it might just be because they aren't getting enough attention as it is.

Just don't forget if they don't get enough attention in an acceptable way, they will get it however they can and you probably won't like it. Some kids may not care that much whether or not you show up at their games, concerts, competitions and so forth, but a Leo will expect it and if you don't they'll be quite hurt. They probably won't say anything, because even at a young age they tend to be on the private side, but it will hurt their pride and self-worth in such a way that it could cause lasting scars.

It's important to understand that their need for attention and praise is not because of conceit. They truly need to be validated, overtly loved, and receive their energy from others. This is just the way they're wired. This is not to say that some of them won't be on an ego trip, because in some cases they will, but this is more likely if they're not getting enough attention. All kids need attention, but a young Lion or Lioness **NEEDS** attention. Lots of it. If you have other children you'll obviously have to be creative yourself in how you accomplish this. Your best bet is to teach them to help you in whatever way they are capable and then lavish them with praise. If the other kids want to help to get their share, all the better. Just remember they can't help needing attention any more than a Cancer child can help being moody or emotional.

Teach them to work so that they understand its benefits and rewards. Remember that tendency toward an entitlement mentality and steer them away from it gently but firmly. Praise is even more important than payment; they need to learn that a job well-done is its own reward, anyway, and if they get plenty of attention they won't complain. As they grow older they will like nice things. While some teenagers are happy with an old, beat-up car as their first vehicle, your Leo will probably expect something new; if it has to be used, then it will need to be something classy like a BMW, Mercedes, or Porsche.

Typically Leos are good kids, at least if they get the love and attention they require. They need some alone time, but generally love to be front and center. Give them the emotional support they need and they will be loyal, loving and make you proud.

Leo Primary Need: Praise & Attention

Ω Ω Ω

♍ Virgo Kids

Little Virgos can be finicky, impatient, critical and ornery like a miniature adult. They don't even know what will make them happy because what they're looking for is perfection. They have their own view of how things should be and if they're not, it's wrong.

They may go their entire life seeking perfection, which of course they'll never find and only frustrate themselves and everyone around them trying. Thus, it behooves you as the parent of a little Virgo to help them understand that there is something called "Good Enough." Ordinarily, this would NOT be something you'd want to teach your child for fear of making them satisfied with mediocrity. This is not something you need to worry about with a Virgo because they will always strive for perfection. However, in spite of how they see things, they need to realize that being a perfectionist is NOT a virtue.

On the positive side, they have a natural sense of order. Their Sign Ruler is Mercury, which gives them excellent eye-hand coordination, spatial recognition, the ability to learn quickly, and understand how things work. As soon as they're old enough they'll do well with such things as Legos, puzzles, and models. They're interested in how things work, so focus on games and activities that demonstrate a flow of events or actions to a logical conclusion. If it's not logical, they'll get frustrated and think it's stupid.

Little Virgos like to be clean. They may think a bath is a nuisance or an inconvenience, but they will like the result. This is a good analogy to use when trying to reason with them to do something they don't like, that the result will be something good. As an Earth Sign they are logical and have a hard time grasping abstract concepts. Since they usually have excellent eye-hand coordination, activities such as coloring are good for them, though they'll probably fuss or criticize themselves if they go outside the lines. Encourage creativity, but don't force the issue if they get frustrated. It will make them think that they're stupid anytime they can't do something exactly right the first time.

For example, if they decide they want to learn to play a musical instrument, they may expect to be able to sit down and play symphony-grade numbers within a week, maybe two. Teach them the principle of natural progression and learning line by line, precept by precept, and striving for a goal. Let them know it is okay not to be perfect. Mistakes will happen, but we learn from them. Emphasize to them that then they're smarter, which should help them accept them more readily. Virgo is a Mutable Sign, meaning they can change more easily than others.

Their attitude toward school can be less than positive. They learn quickly, but in their impatience and tendency to rush through things, thanks to Mercury, they tend to make mistakes. This, of course, results in a less than perfect result, in this case a grade, so they'll be frustrated and disappointed. Teach them to slow down and check their work. If they don't get all A's let them know this is okay. Again, point out the principle of progression, *e.g.*, they're smarter now than they were a year ago, or when they had their first lesson, or played their first game, or before they tried at all.

Virgo rules the Zodiacal 6th House which comprises work, health and pets. It's usually not too hard to teach a little Virgo to work, even though as a child this will be largely through their play. As noted earlier, putting things together is a great activity for them and they can enjoy a sense of accomplishment when they're finished. Health and its companion, fitness, are also important to Virgos. Encourage them to participate in sports, even though they're not usually naturally competitive. If necessary, emphasize the fitness side of things, which they can appreciate. Teach them to eat right and they probably will for the rest of their life. Cleanliness fits in with both work and health. Let them help with chores around the house and teach them how to keep their things in order, which they'll like. In most cases, Virgos will keep their room reasonably neat without being nagged. As far as pets are concerned, most Virgos like animals better than people, so bear that in mind as well.

Virgos are witty, have a wry sense of humor, and generally get along with others. Since they're perfectionists, they tend to behave fairly well, at least for others; they don't put on façades for family though there will be times when you wish they would. Nonetheless, they have a lot of charm and their honesty can be quite refreshing. They call 'em like they see 'em, which isn't always pretty, but they can be trusted. What you need to do as a parent is make sure that the positive side of that perfectionistic nature is preserved while teaching them to deal with the self-defeating parts. They have a tremendous amount of potential and usually grow up to be responsible, productive adults. You know, the kind that support themselves and move out before they're thirty.

Virgo Primary Need: Order

Ω Ω Ω

♎ *Libra Kids*

Libras are typically mild-mannered and pleasant, largely because their cosmic programming has instilled them with the inherent need for balance. They need other people as much as a Leo needs praise and do not like conflict or discord.

We have all heard a child at some time or another express the notion that "It isn't fair!" If you were to tabulate how often a child of each Sun Sign persuasion were to utter this phrase, you can bet that the Libran would win, hands down. They want everyone to be happy and if they're subjected to an environment where this is not the case, it will frustrate and depress them. If their parents or siblings are constantly in a contentious frame of mind, the little Libran see this is constant interference and noise and will try to rectify it. If they're fighting a losing battle, they'll withdraw, not quite to a fetal position, but their social development will more than likely be impaired.

No astrological sign does a better job of seeing the world through someone else's knothole, undoubtedly aided by the fact their Sign Ruler is Venus. Their interest and concern for people seeks for understanding. They will listen to everyone else's point of view and even if it differs substantially from their own they won't argue. Rather, they will find a way to agree. As time goes on and they grow older they'll eventually be perceived by someone as two-faced, simply because they can agree in perfect honesty with two opposing views. Some people may even feel betrayed, when all the little Libran was trying to do was preserve the peace and really could see both sides.

Fairness will be a reverberating theme for their entire life. If they're ever involved personally in some sort of situation that they believe wasn't fair, it will bother them tremendously, even though they're very unlikely to confront the other party. They will remember it for a long time and be bothered by it with the only possible resolution if they can eventually learn the "why" of it and thus understand. An apology usually works well for this peace-loving sign.

In today's society where divorces are the norm, you can see what a mess this could create. Too many parents use their children as pawns and will also try to influence their feelings toward the other parent. This can be harmful enough with virtually any child of any astrological birthright, but to a Libran this will be horribly painful. S/he simply won't want to hear it. At first, depending on their age, they might try to speak on behalf of the absent parent but will usually learn to keep quiet because of the reaction it evokes. They want to be on good terms with both and when a parent maintains that "the friend of my enemy is my enemy" with regard to their former spouse, this can have very damaging and lasting effects on the child. Thus, if you're in this situation, it behooves you to consider your child's inherent happiness and mental health and not indulge in bashing your ex. This is advisable in all cases but critical for little Librans.

Not only do they like peace with respect to the people in their lives but they also need order. This isn't the compulsive, perfectionistic order a Virgo may seek, but a predictable, peaceful balance. Naturally, not everyone is born with this ability, but Librans will be more receptive to it than others, particularly if they discover that keeping their room picked up or neat makes mommy or daddy happy. On the other hand, "order" does not only mean that everything is put away where it belongs. It can also means things are left alone, undisturbed. A Libran can tolerate a mess provided no one else is bothered by it and he can find what he needs. Again, it all comes back to wanting everyone to be happy. If lack of order upsets another family member, it will be the frustrated family member that upsets the Libran, not the mess itself.

The Sun, which astrologically represents our ego and personal identity, is in a condition known as "fall" when it is in Libra. This means that it can't operate to its fullest and implies the challenges a Libran has defending his ego. This is also why s/he is so dependent on others, for companionship as well as validation. They *need* to be liked. They *need* other people.

Libra is a Cardinal Sign with inherent leadership abilities. These can arise in childhood as they strive to get everyone to get along. They usually get along with just about everyone and are non-controversial and non-competitive. Unless they have an ascendant or Moon Sign that instills jealousy they'll be truly happy for the winner, whoever it is. If their best friend comes in second they will try to console them and possibly even make the mistake of trying to explain why the winner deserved to come in first. In trying to keep the peace, they get themselves in trouble more often than their behavior itself.

Since they don't like to argue, it's important that you make sure they associate with the right kids. Even though they have what it takes to be in charge, they won't fight or argue with someone for that role and can fall into being an obedient follower to avoid conflict. If they're hanging with a well-behaved crowd this is great; they won't tip the boat. But if they're hanging with a questionable crowd, they won't either, which can mean trouble. Librans have an inherent appreciation for beauty and do well with the finer things in life. They will like music, art, good books, and appreciate refinement and be uncomfortable with coarseness of any kind.

Little or even medium-sized Librans may not care too much for team sports because the competition tends to result in contention of some form, even if contained. As they get older and you want to keep them in the right crowd, sports like swimming or track are usually good bets along with anything else where they're part of a team but their individual performance counts more. They tend to do very well in debate where they can easily take up for either side and as adults do well as attorneys. As an Air Sign they are more logical than emotional, but their seemingly logical need for fairness can drive their emotions. Again, this will depend a lot on their Natal or Progressed Moon Sign.

One of the most important lessons that all Librans need to learn is that life isn't fair. While they may eventually be able to understand that intellectually, they will still have a hard time with it emotionally and try to even the playing field however they can. On the other hand, if they discover in a harsh or bitter way that life is *not* fair they could become vengeful or retaliatory, especially with a Fire or Water Sign Moon. However, in most cases, they become attractive, pleasant, hard-working adults who are very well-liked. They main thing they need to learn is to stand up for themselves and realize that they don't always have to be the one to make concessions so everyone is happy.

Libra Primary Need: Harmony

Ω Ω Ω

♏ Scorpio Kids

Even as a baby your little Scorpion will possess an amazing intensity. You can see it in their eyes. As a Water Sign they are deeply emotional, intuitive and often psychic. One thing you need to know about Scorpios is that they know everyone's secrets and have plenty of their own. This will become apparent even when they're a child.

This comes from having Pluto for a planetary ruler whom I repeatedly refer to as the Zodiacal roto-rooter. Pluto's job is to exhume old, buried, rotting issues, and expose them to the light of day for resolution, which can be compared to the mythical Phoenix that rises from its own ashes. This is ultimately a good thing that effects healing, but getting there can be a bit frightening.

I'm telling you this so that you recognize the general theme behind Scorpio which will ultimately reflect in all its constituents. Your child will derive things from his or her experiences that go way beneath the surface. They will ask you deep, probing, and possibly weird questions. They may be interested in occult subjects at an early age and may also demonstrate a fascination with death. Your best bet is not to react to their queries in a shocked manner but to answer them as matter-of-factly as you can manage. These are normal questions for a Scorpio. I kid you not. They also tend to be obsessive, so whatever you do, don't encourage that. You're not going to be able to eliminate that particular tendency, but by all means don't give them a reason to be, either. Again, being matter of fact is likely to be your best bet. If you appear upset by their questions, they may obsess on being weird or different. In fact, take note of the fact that their passionate nature predisposes them to be making obsession into an artform.

Nonetheless, Scorpios tend to be very affectionate and benefit greatly from a lot of love. Along those lines, however, another thing you need to know is that Scorpio rules the Zodiacal 8th House which comprises sex, death, transformations, debt, and other people's money. So another thing they have a strong affinity for is sex. You need to bear this in mind early in their upbringing so as to educate them about the birds and bees in a straight-forward and honest way. If you wait too long they'll probably know more about it than you do. They need a strong moral code to live by, especially if you don't want them to engage in recreational sex from an early age. As a Fixed Sign they're set in their ways so it's best to assure that their "ways" are as above-board as possible.

Another thing you probably cannot program out of a Scorpio is their sense of entitlement. While they usually have a strong work ethic as a result of all that passion, they have no problem availing themselves to other's assets. If someone has more money than they do they will expect them to share. As they mature they will be very comfortable around wealth and luxury and will be constantly looking for their share of the pie. They probably invented the phrase "What's mine is mine and what's yours is mine." Teach them to handle money, earn their own, then guard yours as if its Fort Knox.

This is not to say that Scorpios aren't loving and loyal to their families, because they are. You will be an important role model to your little Scorpion because they will be fiercely protective and close to their own offspring someday. However, you need to know that they are not to be trifled with and arm them with the emotional tools they need to deal with their problems in ways that don't involve a snap of their lethal tail. Under most circumstances they won't do this to family members, but for the sake of the rest of the world it would be a good thing to prevent any carnage you can.

With their incredible knack for uncovering secrets, they do very well in occupations that harness that particular talent, for example, forensics, computer security, and any kind of research. Of course whatever they decide to do their ability to discover information, no matter how deeply buried it may be, will come in handy; but if they lean toward something that is clearly a good fit for the astrological nature, then encourage them, even if it's something unconventional like a medical examiner or mortician.

One thing you need to remember is that beneath that shell your little Scorpion has a soft heart. They are deeply emotional and need a lot of affection, especially hugs. Make sure s/he has a strong moral compass and plenty of constructive outlets for that natural passion. They are loyal, caring, never dull and will truly make your experience as a parent an interesting one.

Scorpio Primary Need: Mysteries to Solve

Ω Ω Ω

♐ Sagittarius Kids

Your little archer hails from the 9th House which comprises higher education, legal matters, other cultures, long-distance travel, beliefs, expectations, politics and religion. They have a natural sophistication and affinity for complex matters. Start saving early for their college education because they are probably going to spend a number of years within those ivy-covered walls.

Thus, you should begin preparing them for this experience at a young age. Of course the best means for learning is "field trips" but if you can't afford lengthy vacations abroad, at least introduce them to what you can.

Little Archers are likely to have a multitude of interests but you might be able to identify their primary interest before they're out of elementary school. If so, feed him or her everything you can about it. One thing Sagittarians tend to all have in common is world travel. They're fascinated by other cultures, even those within their native country. They are people watchers and interested in what makes them tick in different ways. Thus, let them watch things like the Travel Channel from an early age. As soon as they're old enough give them a globe and talk about it. They will soak it up like a sponge.

As a Fire Sign they will have a lot of enthusiasm. They will be optimistic by nature, thanks to Jupiter, their Sign Ruler, though this could be mitigated by their ascendant or Moon Sign. They may tend to be over-confident. Of course you don't want to squelch this entirely, but you may have to teach them to tone it down a bit. As they mature, they do tend to be pompous. Somewhat like Leos, who believe themselves to be descended from royalty, Sags believe themselves to be descended from Einstein. They have a temper with a character all its own. They're not aggressive like an Aries

Sagittarius is a Mutable Sign. As intelligent as they are, they are not natural-born leaders. They tend to talk over people's heads as they get older and don't relate well to common folk. They may become a recognized expert in their chosen field and have a lot of potential for success. Since they love learning they could become obsessed with it, especially if they have any influences from neighboring Scorpio. They are adaptable, also, which helps them to be open to learning and experiencing the world. In some cases they may zero-in on a single field of study but in others they may become an information junkie, so to speak, and become the proverbial jack of all trades and master of none. They have a good sense of humor but not everyone can understand it and there will be numerous times that they may not understand yours, either.

All Fire Signs have a lot of energy with their physical and mental energy closely matched. Thus, encourage physical activity and sports. Their thirst for knowledge and understanding can make them outstanding athletes; learning the rules won't bore them, though they may question them from time to time. They may enjoy sports where they can excel as an individual, such as martial arts with their success in their own hands rather than dependent on a team. They will also enjoy sports statistics which they'll see as brain candy. Scouting, which offers a wide variety of experiences, is also a worthwhile activity. It's unlikely that a young Sag will want to spend hours on end playing Halo or some other video game; they rather be doing something real.

Since they thrive on new experiences, their teen years can be a bit rocky. Again, keeping them fully engaged and occupied with appropriate activities will help steer them away from less appropriate endeavors. If possible, keep them focused on a higher education and the college experience and all the positive things they don't want to miss. Keep reminding them that the world is an exciting place with lots of cool things to do besides checking out the drug or alcohol scene.

The thing to remember is that your little Sag will bore easily and will want to be on the move learning new things. Here is another child where a substantial investment in truly educational toys will most likely pay outstanding dividends. To save your own sanity you'll want to teach them how to entertain themselves at as early an age as possible because you won't be able to keep up otherwise. Feed their mind as well as their body, encourage that natural optimism and make sure they have something to look forward to; a bored or depressed Sag is truly a sad sight to behold. Whatever you do, don't smother their *joie de vivre* but take advantage of their natural curiosity and need to explore as an excuse to enjoy life more yourself. Parenting is a grand adventure and a little Archer can truly show you the way.

Sagittarius Primary Need: Knowledge

Ω Ω Ω

♑ Capricorn Kids

Capricorn children often seem older and more mature than their years. They are typically serious, well-behaved, and follow the rules. The only time they might break them is when they think they're stupid, in which case they'll have no problem pretending they don't exist.

For example, if you teach your Cappy child to look both ways when crossing the road, but then tell him or her to never cross a busy street alone, s/he may carefully look both ways, cross the street safely, then wonder why s/he gets in trouble. I know this to be true because I did it when I was three years old. I truly couldn't understand what all the fuss was about since I had been careful, looked both ways, and nothing bad had happened.

This sign has a sense of humor, but you can bet that it's not silly or sophomoric. Rather, it's quite dry, even at an early age. Their appearance and persona is typically serious, though they enjoy just about everything other kids enjoy once they get into it. In most cases they won't be mischievous, though they may get into trouble at the prodding of someone else showing them how it's done. This does not come naturally to them as they seldom have trouble following the rules, provided they understand their rationale and they make sense. If they're stupid they'll say so and probably dismiss them.

Cappies are conscious of status and appearance and have little regard for something that isn't the best of the best. For example, getting second place just doesn't do it; no silver metals here, it's the gold or rated as a complete failure. It is thus important to instill in your little Cappy the concept of making progress in a methodical way. They need to understand that in order to get to the top it takes work (which usually isn't a problem) but being number one is part of a process. Even those people on TV who seem to accelerate to the top overnight have been working on their respective talents for years prior to being discovered. They will tend to admire success and naturally want it for themselves. Your challenge as a parent is to teach them how to get there because they probably won't know how as intuitively as they know what they want.

The amount of patience a little Goat has is greatly influenced by their ascendant and Moon Sign. For the most part they won't have a problem with moving forward in a methodical way, once it's explained to them why it's necessary. Those with other Earth Signs predominant will be even more serious about where they're going. Taurus will give them a lot of patience and determination and Virgo will give them a critical eye and perfectionism, which can actually hinder them if they expect too much of themselves and discouraged as a result.

Capricorn is a Cardinal Sign, meaning Goats don't have trouble being in charge. They aren't as presumptuous about it as an Aries can be, but quietly take the helm and run things as less ambitious individuals step out of their way. There are exceptions, of course, particularly if they have strong Fire Sign influences.

Conversely, if their Sign Ruler, Saturn, is retrograde in their birth chart this can inhibit them from stepping in and taking over, but it won't stop them from wanting to get to the top of that proverbial mountain. They'll just expect their inherent ability to be recognized by others who will reward them accordingly without them specifically asking or pursuing it. This can work to a certain degree, but to really get what they want in life will require conscious, confident, persistent action on their part, particularly is there is strong competition. Teach them that they have to follow the rules early in life; if you want <blank> then you need to do <blank>.

Like their polar sign, Cancer, Cappies have a strong loyalty to their family. However, if their family is somewhat of an embarrassment for any reason, this will bother them considerably. They won't necessarily abandon them, but they won't exactly bring friends home to dinner, either.

Encourage your little Goat to have fun and play. They usually like to read or, in this day and age, surf the web, and they don't usually have any problem with being alone. However, it's good for them to interact with other children so encourage their participation in group activities such as sports, dance, scouting or anything else in which they show an interest. Encourage their creativity and keep an eye out for any outstanding talents that bear development. Like all children, they thrive on love and affection but will not be as demanding in attaining it as other signs.

Reward their progress in whatever pursuit it may be and point out to them how much they've learned along the way. Build their confidence and encourage them, even if whatever it is they are going after seems foolish to you. They like structure, security, stability, and generally don't have a problem with rules and restrictions, provided they make sense to them.

These are likely to be the kids who grow up and take care of you in your old age, firstly because they're likely to be successful if you do your job as a parent, and secondly because they are loyal to their family. The one thing you want to avoid is putting them down, alienating them, or discouraging their sense of ambition. That desire to get to the top is not going away and it's in your best interest to make sure they're headed in a good direction and know how to get there.

Capricorn Primary Need: Status

Ω Ω Ω

♒ Aquarius Kids

Even if you didn't live through them yourself you are probably familiar with the Flower Children of the late 1960s and early 1970s who declared they were living in the Age of Aquarius.

During this time we saw a significant revolution in the area of social change, civil rights, and technological innovation. All of these and more can be credited to Uranus, who rules Aquarius. Hippies were all about being unconventional, altruistic, rebellious, and unfettered. They were nonjudgmental and frequently lived in communes. Is someone looked like a hippy but was a loner, they were just a bum because hippies hung out in groups. They were eccentric to say the least. All these and more are elements of the Aquarian mindset. They don't blindly follow the rules but will question them.

For example, Aquarian children typically have a lot of friends and thrive on their interactions with them. They are quite social, often at an earlier age that other children. As they grow up they're likely to have friends of all ages, not sticking to those in their immediate age group. This may seem a bit strange, but rest assured it's quite normal for an Aquarius. Remember that Aquarius rules the 11th House which comprises groups, associations, coworkers, friends, hopes and wishes, meaning these things will be inherently important to all Aquarians. They are prone to find their identity through their friends and associations, so it's obviously very important to make sure your child is hanging out with the right people, especially since s/he is more likely to be a groupie than a leader.

If an Aquarius child is not receiving enough social interaction they are likely to find it through video games, online chatrooms, or even books. These are the kids that are most likely to have the TV on while they're doing homework or home alone because they can't stand quiet. Banishing an Aquarian child to his or her room or to "timeout" is more difficult for them than those who are comfortable being alone.

Needless to say, team sports of whatever variety he or she is best suited for are an excellent activity. While it's probably not a good idea to impose solitude on an Aquarian child, it doesn't hurt to encourage them to entertain themselves once in a while. It's also important to instill goals and ambitions as much as possible, though these will be most successful and likely to stick if they involve lots of interaction with other people. Without a specific goal they may while away their time hanging out and be perfectly happy doing so. They don't care that much about impressing others and will be perfectly happy as long as their basic needs are met.

Aquarius is a Fixed Sign, meaning that its fellows will be opinionated and not inclined to change their mind or anything else about themselves on a personal level, even if they're out there trying to change the world. Instill good habits in them early because it will be like pulling teeth to get them to do it later. Neatness in particular is usually not one of their virtues unless they're blessed with some serious Virgo influences. They don't much care what others think of them. Their clothes tend to be unconventional, though this can be greatly influenced by their Ascendant, which deals with outward appearance. If they are a dyed in the wool Aquarius they may use clothes to express themselves, in which case it will be colorful, possibly won't match, and is likely to be slightly unconventional. They probably won't care if something is out of style as long as they like it.

As a rule Aquarians are emotionally detached, though this can be greatly affected by their Moon Sign, especially if it's a Water Sign such as Pisces, Cancer or Scorpio. Barring that, they'll seldom share emotions or feelings, though they'll be very willing to listen to others and show concern for those in need. As an Air Sign they like to talk and communicate, no matter how young they are. They can be loud and boisterous, but not necessarily, since there are so many other chart elements that can put a damper on such traits. They like surprises and unique experiences, the more the better. It's also a good idea to emphasize and encourage development of their individuality so they're less likely to be lost in the crowd. Aquarius children are usually easy going and their friendliness extends to family as well.

The best way to communicate with an Aquarian child is to use others as a positive example. Since he or she is inherently interested in other people, this will get and hold their attention. Don't compare them to others in a derogatory way, however, because they'll probably just tune you out. This is when the fact that they're a Fixed Sign becomes readily apparent. If you persist in criticizing them it can cause serious harm to their self-image because they don't believe they can change. Another means of getting something across would be to explain the affect their behavior has on others.

As far as career guidance is concerned, Aquarians like work in which they can be allowed to find their own way of doing things. They don't like to be micromanaged, even by their parents, and can be quite inventive when left to their own devices. High tech fields and technology are good fits, particularly communication fields where they can interact with others. They also do well in social work or promoting charitable causes due to their inherent concern for mankind. An Aquarian will find making a difference in society very satisfying. This is something they comprehend at an amazingly young age.

Aquarius Primary Need: Friends

Ω Ω Ω

♓ *Pisces Kids*

Little Pisces are usually peace-loving dreamers who are more likely to have an imaginary friend than just about any other sign. They are sensitive, intuitive, and easily hurt by the harsh realities of life. They will naturally seek to escape from unpleasantries of any kind and seek solace in a fantasy world.

Pisceans tend to be idealistic and absolutely loaded with questions relative to the imperfections around them. This won't be done in the critical manner of a Virgo, but with genuine disappointment that the world is not a better place. They will be emotionally affected to the point of tears over a dead bird or other example of Nature's brutality. They will love animals but won't like the fact they kill and eat each other. They could even turn into a vegan at a very tender age once they find out where that hamburger really originated. They typically don't want to hurt anything and anthropomorphism is assumed to be reality. They will talk to animals at a level that astounds you and be enthusiastic about sharing its reply.

Pisces are gentle and sensitive by nature and, as a Water Sign, are deeply emotional, intuitive, and often have psychic abilities as well. They are ruled by dreamy Neptune and sometimes have a hard time differentiating between what's real and what's not. These kids will really get into things like fairy tales in any form they're delivered whether it's between the covers of a book or on DVD. They can transport themselves to another world and use their extremely vivid and active imagination to become part of it. If they don't particularly like the real world, and few of them do, they will escape whenever they can.

Fish are very much of the mind that *"All you need is love"* and can't understand why everyone can't get along. One keyword that is associated with Pisces that you need to remember is "transcendence." This is something they will seek throughout their life as they strive to find a higher plane of existence. Your job as a parent is to provide this in an appropriate way when they're very young and show them the way to find socially acceptable "escapes" as they grow up. As a Mutable Sign they are adaptable and while they don't like to be told what to do, they don't necessarily care to be in charge, either.

Their vivid imagination often provides a lot of fuel for any talents they may have, such as for art, music, dance or writing. Any of these media provide an acceptable escape vehicle that can serve them well throughout their life. If they're not interested in creating their own, they will nonetheless have a strong appreciation for that of others. Having a Pisces child can be a wonderful experience for a parent who also needs an escape from a harsh and unpleasant world. Don't be afraid to thoroughly enjoy getting away from the mundane and unpleasant elements of life and running away in a figurative sense with your little Fish. Indeed, the biggest challenge you will probably encounter as a parent is teaching him or her to exist successfully in the real world.

Since little Fish are tremendously emotional, they are easily hurt, particularly since they hold the world to such high standards. If they are exposed to too much reality, especially if it involves any form of brutality, it will drive them to escape in any way they can. This could be to books, movies, video games, or any alternate reality, and they won't want to leave it. If they have a bad experience at their daycare or school they'll resist going back but may not be able to explain why. It may be too painful to talk about or they simply may not understand it themselves.

While obviously they aren't going to have a choice about returning, it's important to deal with the real issues so you can help them cope with reality. Otherwise they may withdraw into their own little world more and more. If you see this happening, you may tend to ignore it or even enjoy having such a "nice, quiet child who's so good at entertaining himself." At the least, share his or her world with him from time to time and invite them into yours. Being optimistic about the world is essential or they're likely to retreat even deeper into fantasy.

You need to accept the fact they can't handle a 24/7 dose of reality. It's really not even good for the most strongly grounded, well-adjusted Earth Sign. This is why it will do you good to join them from time to time. Don't be afraid to get into it for fear they'll be less likely to come out of it themselves. This need of theirs is not going to go away; what they need to learn is how to balance it with existence in the real world. Learning, working and coping are skills they need to learn and this is not always easy. And it needs to be done with a gentle, understanding hand.

For example, if they're spending too much time playing video games, rather than take them away entirely, stress that they need to spend a certain amount of time doing their chores or homework and then they can spend a designated amount of time with their games. You have an obvious reward system going which you should exploit. Also do whatever you can to show them the positive side of the world. They typically love nature, so help them explore it in all its wonder. It's okay if they think fairies live in the forest, a game you can even play with them. Feeding their imagination will do less harm than forcing them to focus on reality. They can have their little world, but they need to realize that they can't stay there all the time. If you forbid them from going there at all, they will withdraw even further and be even less engaged with real life.

These kids will love places like Disneyworld. You should make at least one excursion there or a similar place while they are young because they will never forget it. As they grow older introduce them to acceptable ways to escape and let them know it is okay to do so, provided they fulfill their responsibilities. I have known adult Fish who engage in a variety of escape mechanisms. Sports and such things as a "runner's high" are quite popular; I know one Pisces who is not only a marathon runner but ran one in Antarctica. Other activities include being a pilot and this particular one also was very much into Star Wars, where I'm sure he found his inspiration. Mountain climbing is another pursuit I've known Pisces to engage in. Anything that provides an adrenalin rush transports them closer to where they want to be.

221

Of course one of the biggest dangers you need to steer your child clear of is drugs. Drugs are ruled by Neptune and Pisces is also ruled by Neptune. Their ability to create another reality can be a tremendous temptation to a Fish. It is extremely important that you provide acceptable, lawful substitutes to fulfill their need for fantasy and getting away from reality. Providing worthwhile and challenging activities is extremely important for keeping them on track. If they are bored or depressed, the temptation will be far too strong for them to handle. Helping them achieve a balance that keeps their Pisces soul fed is essential.

Pisces Primary Need: Escaping Reality

Ω Ω Ω

REAL LIFE APPLICATIONS

The reason that astrology has endured for literally thousands of years is that it works. Furthermore, the challenges we face today are often not much different than those that mankind has faced for the entire time they've been on the Earth. There are numerous areas of everyday life where astrology can be useful, other than the personality and predictive side. There are even specialties within astrology, such as karmic astrology and financial astrology to name a few, which have obvious applications. The original counselors were astrologers, and even today more and more in the counseling professions are augmenting their formal education in psychology with certification as an astrologer because it can be so effective at determining what factors are active in a person's life and thus causing them trouble.

The following sections look at some of those areas where astrology can provide some assistance with everyday life decisions which frequently cause a dilemma, namely choosing a career and when and how to go on a diet as well as a quick look at a place where astrology is used, but in disguise.

Choosing a Career

If you find yourself in a job that you don't like, yet aren't sure why, it doesn't hurt to look at it from an astrological viewpoint. Sometimes you hate going to work, but know exactly why, in which case it's easier to fix. But sometimes you just can't figure out what makes it so frustrating or unsatisfying much less what you'd really like to do. Sometimes you accept a job simply because you need one without regard to whether or not you'll find any enjoyment in it. This is all well and good to pay your bills, but some individuals, especially those who have their Moon in the 6th or 10th house, will be very unhappy in an unsatisfying job. Personally, I think there are precious few individuals who can honestly say they love their job. Astrologers frequently do career readings which can help you identify a profession you can enjoy.

[NOTE:--While this section is intended to help you figure out what career choice is best for you, it's also useful if you're a supervisor or manager looking for an employee. The closer you match a person's inborn traits with the job description the happier you'll both be. It's also useful for seeing how your manager or supervisor sees you. No matter how hard you work or how flawless your work is, if you're viewed as "high maintenance" it can work against you. I've been a supervisor and manager for over a decade in my day job and I've found that a mediocre employee who gets along with everyone is preferable to someone who's a perfectionist but criticizes and complains constantly. While asking for birth information is illegal due to its implications in job discrimination, if you direct your interview questions such that they reveal the traits described below, you can get enough information to extrapolate their Sign or Ascendant and thus determine if a person is a good fit. This, of course, depends on whether or not they're telling the truth and not just saying what you want to hear because they're desperate for a job.]

Astrological Indicators and Career Choice

Numerous astrological factors come into play regarding what career choice is best for an individual. While the Sun Sign is a major driver, other key chart influences such as the natal Ascendant and Moon Sign are also significant players. Three house cusp positions that enter the picture as well are the 2nd House of possessions and finances, the 6th House of work, and the 10th House of career, status, and reputation. The 10th House cusp is known as the MC, which stands for *medium coeli* and is also known as the Midheaven. This represents the part of the sky that was directly overhead when you were born and figuratively represents whatever "heights" you can reach in your life. When you do the math on how many different combinations are possible with just those factors alone, you can see there are no easy answers. In fact, there is at least one entire book on the subject of astrology and career choices that I'm aware of and I'm sure there are others.

Some people stay in the same line of work their entire life and are perfectly happy while others evolve through several careers in their lifetime. Some people get bored and enjoy the stimulation of learning and doing something different while others value the security of experience. Some people plod along in a nothing job their entire life and find their joy and satisfaction elsewhere while others are more than miserable if they don't feel as if they're contributing something of meaning every day. One thing that's worth considering is that in medieval times the 6th House (which in modern times includes your work, health and pets) comprised indentured servants and slaves. If that's how you feel about your job, then you need to start looking for a career.

What do you want to be when you grow up?

It's very common to not have a clue what you want to do for a living when you graduate from high school. It's not terribly uncommon in college, either, which is often a problem because when the going gets rough, if you're not strongly motivated by what's at the end of the road it's all too easy to drop out. Everyone knows at least one person who knew from the time they learned to use an adult toilet that they wanted to be a doctor when they grew up, or maybe a plumber for that matter. Many of us, on the other hand, evolve through numerous choices, usually without experiencing any of them.

I've found that in many cases if there was something you wanted to do when you were a child, but drifted away from it over time, oftentimes it bears a second look later if you're lacking a sense of direction. First of all, determine why you gave up on it. If you let it go because you investigated the job description and decided that really didn't sound very appealing, then you're in good shape. On the other hand, maybe you thought you weren't smart enough, didn't have the means to go to school, or were distracted by some other factor, such as ridicule by someone whose opinion you valued. If any of those ring a bell, then it's time to discount that original rationale and take a second look. If you allow a dream to die, part of you dies with it. If you really want to do something, regardless of your age, at least find out what it would take before you throw it away. Your inner compass is probably trying to tell you something so listen!

It's more troublesome if you don't have a foggy clue what you want to do. If you're in a serious quandary regarding what you want to be when you "grow up," your best bet is to consult an astrologer who can take a look at your specific natal chart and synthesize all the elements involved so they can give you a comprehensive answer. We offer this service, so if you're interested, feel free to contact Whobeda. I will look at all those things noted above and see what the stars and planets seem to say about the matter.

Just as an example of how strongly a natal chart can reflect career, in one of the classes I took from the International Academy of Astrology we spent the better part of a semester studying charts without knowing who they belonged to. Rare was the instance in which we didn't have a fairly tight handle on what that person did for a living. In fact, after looking at one chart following class, I decided it belonged to Ernest Hemingway and was correct. What are the odds of looking at a natal chart with no dates or other identifying information other than if the person is male or female and being able to tell who it is? Celebrities in particular typically have indicators all over the place. The essence of who you are is imprinted on your natal chart and what better way to determine your life's work (or works) than to look at that?

Working with the Stars

If you read your horoscope on a regular basis, you've noticed that one of the things I typically address is which house the bulk of activity will be in each month. While it's always more accurate to know the house structure of your own natal chart, the natural houses for your particular Sun Sign still have a strong bearing. In other words, when the Sun is in your 6th or 10th House, chances are there will be a lot going on with your job/career.

For those of you who may be wondering why your job is in one house and your career in another, the best way to describe that is to say your work (6th House) is your day job and your career (10th House) is where you leave your mark on the world. The 2nd House comes into play as your house of possessions and finances, which determines how you'll feel about material possessions and thus implies how you'll earn your living. In other words, if you have a strong need for luxury or foreign travel, you won't do well in a job where you're repeatedly asking, "Do you want fries with that?" or "Welcome to Wal*Mart."

The planets natally placed in these Houses on your personal chart affect how you will behave in that area as well as any aspects they make to other planets. As the planets move in their daily transits and go through these areas of the chart, this will also stir up action in that part of your life. For example, Venus transiting your 2nd House implies good financial fortune, especially in positive aspect with Jupiter. Mars in your 6th House implies increased drive, though if it's in hard aspect (square or opposition) with a planet like Pluto, it indicates power struggles and covert actions. A slow mover like Uranus in your 10th by transit will generate various long-term career changes and/or disruptions or perhaps just a very hectic pace.   In other words, if there are auspicious aspects to your career houses it's time to exploit them in your favor and if they're less positive, you need to take appropriate action to protect your interests.

All that said, there are still some basics for career choices based on your Sun Sign, even if it's no more than a daily task characteristic that applies to a variety of industries. If you haven't looked at "Who Ya Gonna Call?" you might want to read that over as well since it will give you some more ideas based on how the different signs react to emergency situations. Meanwhile, here's some food for thought, starting with the modes and elements. Read all the basic traits that apply to your Sign, then combine them into a job description that allows them all to function.

The section below flows from the most basic (Modes and Elements) to the more specific (Signs and House Cusps). A few suggestions are included to help you along. See if anything rings a bell for you.

Cardinal Signs (Aries, Cancer, Libra, Capricorn)

Cardinal signs are good at making decisions and like to be in charge. They don't do well having to take orders from someone, especially if they think they're smarter than their boss. Definitely avoid "Do you want fries with that?" unless you own the place.

Tip for Managers: *These folks are comfortable making decisions and should be allowed to do so as much as possible. Micromanaging will be ineffective and probably drive them to seek employment elsewhere.*

Fixed Signs (Taurus, Leo, Scorpio, Aquarius)

Fixed signs like stability and dislike change. A job with a consistent daily routine with few if any surprises is usually quite comfortable for these folks, though a challenge is nonetheless dealt with effectively, according to the specific Sign in question.

Tip for Managers: *These folks tend to be stubborn but usually make very loyal employees. If they must implement change, allow them to be part of the decision process and expect it to take plenty of time.*

Mutable Signs (Gemini, Virgo, Sagittarius, Pisces)

Mutable signs are flexible and adapt well to change and variety. They like to stay busy and are happier in a job that isn't the same every day. They enjoy learning and new experiences and may change jobs or careers frequently as they become saturated with one and find their interests shifting in a different direction.

Tip for Managers: *Don't put one of these folks in a dull, routine, boring job. They need to be mentally active at the least, i.e. required to use their brain. They learn quickly, so if they express an interest in doing something different, they probably can.*

Ω Ω Ω

Fire *(Aries, Leo, Sagittarius)*

Fire signs require some excitement in their job as boredom is poorly tolerated. The same-ol', same-ol' day after day will get to them in short order. Sitting behind a desk pushing paper for forty hours a week is seldom for them, unless there's something really interesting on that paper regarding which they need to take action.

Tip for Managers: *Stay in touch with these folks. They have good ideas and lots of enthusiasm, which is contagious and helpful if you want to implement something new.*

Earth *(Taurus, Virgo, Capricorn)*

Earth signs like stability and practicality. This often translates as job security, including a good salary. They excel at careers that involve tangible results so when they go home at night they feel as if they've accomplished something.

Tip for Managers: *These folks have a lot of common sense and their judgment is sound, so they can provide good insights into any project or situation. You'd do well to listen to them. They will tell it like it is, whether you like it or not.*

Air *(Gemini, Libra, Aquarius)*

Air signs like to communicate. They tend to talk a lot and be "people persons." If they are in a job where they were isolated most the day, such as a forest ranger or independent computer programmer, they will think they've died and gone to Hell.

Tip for Managers: *These folks thrive on daily challenges that allow them to learn something. If they don't stay busy enough or interact with others as part of their job description, they will probably be on the phone talking or texting friends and family instead. It's hard to give them too much work, so load it on until they scream in protest.*

Water (Cancer, Scorpio, Pisces)

Water signs are touchie-feelie types who thrive on emotion. They are good listeners and often get involved socially with their coworkers. They do well in a career where they feel needed and can help others in some way.

Tip for Managers: *Water signs can be very persistent, so if there's something that requires perseverance, look their way. Since they are quite emotional, if they're in a negative environment it will affect them deeply with stress. They usually don't handle conflict or criticism very well and need a fair amount of TLC. If they don't agree with you, they'll quietly and persistently ignore of even undermine your efforts. If you think these folks are weak in any way, remember that water carved the Grand Canyon and sank the Titanic.*

Ω Ω Ω

Aries

Aries are self-directed and thrive on excitement. Sitting at a desk all day doing the same thing over and over would drive them to a rubber room. They are well suited for the military, police work, field work of numerous kinds, emergency medical technicians (EMT's), rescue work, emergency room work, surgeons, etc. A certain amount of freedom to structure their daily routine themselves is required.

Tip for Managers: *It's important that a Ram's natural drive be properly directed so that it doesn't leak out as aggression. Otherwise, they'll be spending a lot of time in the HR office. Give them plenty to do, but let* them decide when and how, as much as possible. They don't like to be told directly what to do and absolutely won't tolerate being micro-managed. If you're a Virgo, you may have a hard time dealing with a Ram.

Taurus

Taurus' like security, are stable, slow, methodical, and usually quite patient. They typically make sound decisions, but it may take them a while to get there, so they need to be in a career that allows them to mull things over sufficiently without causing a problem. They love land and are often found in careers involving real estate or construction. They also love money and are often found in banks.

Tip for Managers: *Make sure that any Bulls in your midst have a well-structured job description and accountability for completing their work as they can tend to be lazy if not properly motivated. While many are hard-working and dedicated, this is not always the case. If you're not careful, they can be the highest paid and lowest producing people on your team.*

Gemini

Geminis love data and get bored easily. They usually have multiple projects going at any one time, but also distract easily so don't always finish what they've started if something more interesting comes along. They require a lot of variety and mental stimulation. Being a researcher of some sort or journalist is well-suited for their natural abilities for communicating.

Tip for Managers: *Unless Twins are kept busy and have sufficient variety in their work they're likely to spend way too much time at the coffee pot, visiting with coworkers, surfing the Internet, or anything else they can get away with to break the monotony. If you can't offer them variety as well as a career path to other more interesting jobs, don't expect them to stay onboard for too long. The good news is that they learn quickly.*

Cancer

Cancers tend to be moody, but as a rule are people-oriented and caring. Interacting with others on a regular basis, particularly if they can use their nurturing abilities, will bring them the most satisfaction. They make good daycare providers, nurses, massage therapists, medical technologists, and social workers as well as anything else where they can feel as if they're helping others.

Tip for Managers: *Being emotionally driven, Crabs will probably spend a lot of time in your office complaining. They can be moody and sometimes ornery and irritate their coworkers, but are usually kind-hearted and hard working, which helps balance it out. They're happiest when they feel needed and as if their work is valued, so be sure to tell them if they're doing a good job as it will mean the world to them.*

Leo

Leos are another sign that likes some excitement. They're natural leaders and do best when allowed to do so. They thrive on attention, praise, and credit and have no problem being in the spotlight; a bit of drama is welcomed and even sought after. They make great salespersons and entertainers, plus they have a very creative side as well, but look out for that Leo temper if they get frustrated.

Tip for Managers: *Leos need attention and praise. They will work very hard for you when this is provided and if it's not, they'll get it somehow, perhaps in a very negative way. They don't like to be told what to do, much less micro-managed. In spite of their outward appearance of confidence, they get their feelings hurt easily and this can trigger that leonine temper if you're not tactful with any criticism. They love to lead, but don't always have the necessary people skills to do so effectively as their basic philosophy tends to be "My way or the highway."*

Virgo

Virgos are detail oriented and meticulous. They don't tolerate sloppiness of any description and their critical nature is best put to work in a constructive way. They make excellent auditors, accountants, engineers, database administrators, and anything else that requires thought and precision. They tend to be good with their hands and make excellent mechanics and carpenters. Service industries are also good choices. However, their critical eye can not only get them into trouble with their targets, but also destroy their morale if they feel overcome by mediocrity. They don't always take direction well as they think they have a firm grip on perfection.

Tip for Managers: *Virgos are hardworking, dedicated, meticulous and critical by nature. However, they don't always get along well with their coworkers as they'll see every flaw and tell you as well as the offending party all about it. They do a good job, but can be high-maintenance if you want to keep them happy. They do well in an environment where they can do most of their work independently and interface with people who can take criticism in stride. Accounting and engineering are two fields that offer numerous opportunities. If possible, training in communicating in a positive, tactful way is a good investment as they're usually right, but tend to express themselves in a manner that puts others on the defensive.*

Libra

Libras are fair by nature and very people-oriented. They do well in a career where they can interact with others on a daily basis. They love to talk so it's best that this be included in their job description in some way. They're very sociable and don't like too much solitude. They have a strong appreciation and need for aesthetics and beauty so prefer a pleasant work environment. A noisy, hectic office or industrial setting would upset their sense of balance. They like people, but not conflict, which will stress them out as they try to smooth things out. Negotiating comes easily and they are often lawyers or counselors.

Tip for Managers: *Libras are hard working and usually self-directed. They are good problem solvers, since they excel at looking at all sides of an issue and weighing them objectively. Unfortunately, their sense of fairness can result in their being indecisive, but they're great at bringing in all the options for consideration and make excellent executive assistants. They generally possess good people skills.*

Scorpio

Scorpios are deeply passionate by nature and are drawn to secrets and mystery. They are natural detectives and do well in forensic work. They also make good auditors or investigators due to their ability to ferret out hidden information. If it's not part of their job description, they'll unearth quite a wealth of potential blackmail material on their coworkers (and maybe their boss) instead.

Tip for Managers: *Scorpios are hard-working, but tend to be opinionated. If they don't get their way, they will probably remember it forever in the form of a grudge and do what they can to sabotage it, whatever it might be. While they tend to throw themselves into life generally with a passion, they'll do a good job at just about anything, but they'll be much happier if there's an element of mystery or intrigue of some sort involved.*

Sagittarius

Sagittarius' have a couple hallmarks that are usually reflected in their careers. One of these is their love of other cultures and foreign travel and another is their love of waxing philosophical. Being an anthropologist or archeologist is a natural. They're another one that doesn't want to sit behind a desk all day, unless it's as a travel agent. They need to travel, have the opportunity to pontificate from time to time, and feel a bit superior or they'll be miserable. Definitely not a "Do you want fries with that?" candidate.

Tip for Managers: *These folks tend to be a bit flamboyant and opinionated, which can irritate their coworkers (and you); others tend to find them offensive, even when they don't intend it that way. Like all fire signs, they're enthusiastic and like attention. They usually think they're smarter than everyone else and they definitely do have a different take on the world that is usually worth listening to. Nonetheless, their tendency to be opinionated and verbal about it doesn't always make them team players or good problem solvers who work in your favor. They're another sign that will not do well in a boring job. They are also prone to changing career as their interests are very dynamic and easily take them in a different direction. Not keeping these people occupied and challenged intellectually can make them high-maintenance.*

Capricorn

Cappies like structure and discipline and prefer to work within a known framework. They make good leaders, are comfortable with authority, and do well in careers with the government. They're ambitious and aspire to great heights. Their organizational skills and common sense assist them in excelling as project managers, administrators, and Human Resource managers.

Tip for Managers: *The Goats in your midst probably want your job, so bear that in mind. They do well with their own turf and opportunities to expand it accordingly. They're ambitious and hard-working but make sure their pursuits don't include bulldozing your office.*

Aquarius

Aquarius' tend to be altruistic and thrive in groups. They don't require a lot of variety, as a rule, but they do need to feel challenged, stimulated, and needed. They'll be friends with their coworkers and expect to fulfill some of their social needs in the workplace. They do well organizing activities outside of work such as happy hours. In spite of their surface friendliness, they have a private side and can be emotionally detached. As such, they make excellent social workers, teachers, and psychologists.

Tip for Managers: *As another Fixed sign Water Bearers can be opinionated and hard to convince if they think otherwise. They tend to gather allies if opposed, which is usually easily accomplished since they're friends with so many coworkers. They're hard workers and can have unconventional ideas, some of which are very innovative and worth soliciting from time to time. If they're bored or unhappy they'll be on the phone, visiting with coworkers or on Facebook.*

Pisces

Pisces are found in a variety of jobs but their common factor is the need for something that helps them escape the real world in some manner. Hum-drum, boring, routine jobs will make them crazy and then they'll make you crazy. Depending on other factors in their chart, they may look for this via excitement, such as in the military; living in a fantasy world such as writing; or seeking spiritual summits such as yoga or new age pursuits. The key word is "transcend" to another level of existence. If it's too down to Earth, it won't work.

Tip for Managers: *Remember that Fishies are always striving to escape the real world. They have vivid imaginations and thrive on experiences that take them one step beyond reality. The more you can utilize their visionary tendencies, the happier you both will be. They can view the world through rose-colored glasses, however, and be deeply disappointed when it doesn't measure up. If they're not comfortable with the status quo, they may try to change it in a slow, persistent Water Sign fashion, though if it's a formidable obstacle, they will probably be* *overcome by stress, which they don't handle particularly well. This is another sign that can be high maintenance if not properly matched with the task description.*

𝕻utting 𝒥t 𝒜ll 𝒯ogether

We've all known people, perhaps even ourselves, who are entirely different people on a personal level versus in the workplace. This is where the House cusps come into play. The 2nd House will imbue the person with an attitude toward finances and possessions that is characteristic of the sign on that particular cusp; the sign on the 6th House cusp will describe the general work environment that is most comfortable and how they approach their tasks; and the sign on the 10th House cusp will indicate how the person approaches their ambitions or life's work.

Remember that these will be more accurate when based on your personal Natal Chart, so the extrapolations below will have some bearing, but are likely to be a bit "off" unless you were born early in the morning such that your Ascendant (1st House) is the same as your Sun Sign. If you know your Ascendant, then look at both. If you're fairly familiar with astrology you'll notice that the 2nd, 6th and 10th house are of the same element, *i.e.*, Fire, Earth, Air or Water, which will be different than their Sun Sign, giving them characteristics slightly different than their Sun Sign alone. These houses are also known as the "Substance" houses for obvious reasons.

Aries
2nd House: Taurus
6th House: Virgo
10th House: Capricorn

Rams need excitement. They also like to be first. They will actively seek opportunities for advancement and not be satisfied until they reach the top of the mountain, much like their fellow horned-animal and Cardinal Sign, Capricorn the Goat. Part of being *numero uno* includes having the fastest car or biggest house and having a big bank account doesn't hurt their feelings, either, though being in debt a bit doesn't bother them. Since they want to be on top they work hard and do a good job, criticizing others if they don't live up to their standards. This, of course, is another way of saying "I'm the best."

Taurus
2nd House: Gemini
6th House: Libra
10th House: Aquarius

Bulls like to have data that substantiates their payscale and to know that they're being paid what they're worth. They prefer a pleasant work environment with whatever aesthetics are possible. If you've seen that email of the soldier in Iraq who had his wife send him American soil and grass seed, which he cultivated outside his barracks and lovingly trims with scissors, this fits this description and I suspect that soldier is either a Bull or Taurus ascendant. Bulls also want to distinguish themselves as being unique in their field in some way.

Gemini
2nd House: Cancer
6th House: Scorpio
10th House: Pisces

Twins often enjoy working at home and tend to be emotionally attached to various items that have sentimental value. They excel at research of any description and enjoy uncovering previously hidden information through synthesizing data. Many are drawn to pursue advanced degrees and will go on learning for their entire lifetime. Idealism regarding their role in making a positive difference in the world in some way is an ongoing driver. Most twins typically have at least two major interests which may reflect in their career or perhaps an avocation.

Cancer
2nd House: Leo
6th House: Sagittarius
10th House: Aries

Crabs know they're worth every penny they're paid, plus some, and can become very offended and emotionally wounded if they know they're underpaid. They enjoy intellectual stimulation that will possibly lead them to involvement with foreign countries, different cultures, unusual industries, or academia in some way. Crabs will actively pursue promotions and more responsibility such that they work circles around their coworkers.

Leo
2nd House: Virgo
6th House: Capricorn
10th House: Taurus

Lions like only the best and expect to have it, whether or not they can afford it. They will normally keep their work areas clean and organized and prefer some structure in their work environment, whether it the way of procedures, processes, or other guidelines that are well-defined. They pursue success in a slow, patient, but determined manner and are likely to stick to one career field throughout their lifetime as they value job security and experience.

Virgo
2nd House: Libra
6th House: Aquarius
10th House: Gemini

Virgos crave an orderly, pleasing environment with an artistic flair and their work area will reflect this. Even if they work as a mechanic, at the least they'll have a calendar that features artwork from the masters, leaving the girly versions to their Scorpio coworkers. They expect fairness in their payscale and can be very insistent about it. They know they work hard and that its quality is high, so expect their paycheck to reflect as much. They tend toward innovative and high-tech fields, but are likely to change careers numerous times, though they're likely to be related in some manner so they can draw from past experience and information gained.

Libra
2nd House: Scorpio
6th House: Pisces
10th House: Cancer

Libras like to maintain some hidden resources which could manifest by hiding money around the house or having alternate sources of incomes, such as a hobby, avocation, or second career. They possess a touch of idealism regarding their work and if it provides escape of any kind from the real world, all the better. They tend to be somewhat emotionally involved with their work and those around them and usually get along well with others.

Scorpio
2nd House: Sagittarius
6th House: Aries
10th House: Leo

Scorpions are fascinated by anything mysterious and foreign lands fit that description. Even if they don't ever visit one, they're likely to have either foreign investments, work for a foreign company, or decorate their homes with items that reflect other cultures. They tend to be driven and sometimes aggressive in how they approach their work and expect to be publicly recognized for their accomplishments.

Sagittarius
2nd House: Capricorn
6th House: Taurus
10th House: Virgo

Archers are practical about financial matters and expect to be paid accordingly. They won't be entirely satisfied until they reach the top of their payscale, whatever that may be. They approach their work in a methodical way based on their own experience and resist change and outside direction. They are likely to have a detailed career plan and schedule with well-defined milestones. More than likely they have a globe, world map, or other similar entity representing the world at large in their work area. Working on foreign soil at some time in their life is highly likely.

Capricorn
2nd House: Aquarius
6th House: Gemini
10th House: Libra

Cappies approach their finances in an innovative, matter-of-fact manner and will do whatever is necessary to get where they want to go. A specific career field is less important than the opportunities it provides. They like variety in their daily job description and expect fairness regarding promotions and recognition; they don't condone favoritism or nepotism, but expect a person to earn their way to the top.

Aquarius
2nd House: Pisces
6th House: Cancer
10th House: Scorpio

Water Bearers aren't always realistic about their finances and also tend to be drawn to jobs in an unusual field that challenges reality in some way. They tend to look upon their coworkers as extensions of family and get somewhat involved in their lives. Happy Hours with coworkers are often at the core of their social life. Their career aspirations can be ruthless, once they know what they want, and if anyone gets in their way they have reason to watch their back.

Pisces
2nd House: Aries
6th House: Leo
10th House: Sagittarius

Impulsiveness with their financial dealings, *i.e.* spending money freely on items that serve their need to transcend, can result in Fishies frequently being on the edge of being broke. If they're getting what they need, however, this isn't a problem; they can tolerate a daily lifestyle that is quite Spartan provided they're getting their ya-ya's. They require recognition for their work and prefer creative involvement as much as possible. Pursuit of their career ambitions frequently includes foreign travel or academia.

DIETS

The two times of year when folks are most likely to think of dieting is at either the start of the New Year or the swimsuit season. Ironically, both fall when the Sun is in reality-based Earth Signs, *i.e.*, Capricorn (January) and Taurus (May), which should actually be of some help when we vow to lose weight and/or exercise more. The question, however, is whether or not we actually do.

All of us have had the experience of making a solemn assessment (emphasis on the *ass*) in the mirror, yet in spite of our momentary disgust we can't seem to muster the needed self-discipline or motivation. Occasionally, we may even find the willpower through sheer, brute determination only to be frustrated when the results simply don't measure up to our efforts. *The good news is that those times of year may not be the best times for you to start. So when is?*

In general, if one of the luminaries, *i.e.* the Sun or Full or New Moon, is transiting an area of your Natal Chart that corresponds to any of the weight-loss motivators below it should help you get off your dead butt and "git 'r' dun."

As with everything else, there is a time and a season which are keyed to the *reason* you want to lose those extra pounds. This isn't intended to give you an excuse for blowing off those season-based aspirations, but for the sake of effectiveness and planning for your highest probability of success. There is nothing more discouraging than feeling as if you've starved yourself for days only to find you've lost a lousy pound. Your personal House structure on your Natal Chart could possibly add another window of opportunity. Determine which of the statements below most closely denotes your reasons for wanting to lose weight then read that section to find out how you can use astrology to help you reach your health and fitness goals.

Diet Category #1

As a perfectionist, I'm embarrassed if I'm overweight
or
I really need to lose weight for my health

If you're dieting because you're a perfectionist about your appearance or because you're concerned about your health, these both relate to the **6th House**. The 6th House rules our work ethic, health and pets and is the throne of perceived inadequacies and self-flagellation for personal imperfections. If this is where you're coming from you'll want to initiate your diet when there is significant astrological activity in your Natal or Natural 6th House. Your Natal 6th House depends on what time you were born and is shown on your Natal Chart. If you don't known, then you can get some help from your Natural House, which you can determine from the chart at the bottom of this section.

Fad diets may give you a jump-start, but obviously keeping the weight off once you get to your goal weight requires permanent changes to the eating and exercise habits that made you store all that fat in the first place. The good news is that approaching your diet through this House has the highest likelihood of success.

Personality traits related to the 6th House are also reflected in the Sun Sign, Virgo. As we all know being organized, paying attention to details and a methodical approach are all required to change your eating habits, initiate an exercise regimen and then stick to it religiously enough to shed those pounds. Paying attention to those details can make the difference between success and failure, e.g. keeping a list of everything you eat, counting calories/carbs/ fat grams and to track your weight.

6th House Diet

Diet Type: Healthy low fat/low carb w/common sense exercise; Weight Watchers; Rotation Diet

Hints: Keep fresh fruits and vegetables and healthy snacks such as almonds and walnuts in the house.

Find easy substitutes for when you're too tired to cook, *e.g.* soup and salad, low calorie frozen dinners, ingredients for low fat veggie wraps, etc.

Replace your favorite no-no foods with healthy substitutes. For example, if you have a sweet tooth eat a bowl of fresh fruit topped with a dab of yogurt. If you like salty snacks, try those mini-bags of microwave popcorn.

Subscribe to a diet newsletter, blog or magazine such as *Prevention*.

Pitfalls: Being too extreme in what you allow yourself to eat and eventually falling off the health food wagon.

Being too strict about exercise and either getting bored or burning yourself out.

Appeals to . . . because:

Capricorn: Practical, sensible and disciplined.

Virgo: Attention to detail comes naturally as well as interest in good health and nutrition.

Cancer: This is a diet where the entire family can eat the same food and be better off for it.

Pisces: Usually comfortable with self-denial.

Here are the best times to give it a shot. Your monthly horoscope will have the exact dates of the lunations in question.

Your Sign	Your Natural 6th House	Sun in 6th House	Full Moon in 6th	New Moon in 6th
Aries	Virgo	August 24 - September 22	February/March	August/September
Taurus	Libra	September 23 - October 23	March/April	September/October

Your Sign	Your Natural 6th House	Sun in 6th House	Full Moon in 6th	New Moon in 6th
Gemini	Scorpio	October 24 - November 22	April/May	October/November
Cancer	Sagittarius*	November 23 - December 21	May/June	November/December
Leo	Capricorn	December 22- January 20	June/July	December/January
Virgo	Aquarius*	January 21 - February 18	July/August	January/February
Libra	Pisces	February 19 - March 20	August/September	February/March
Scorpio	Aries	March 21 - April 20	September/October	March/April
Sagittarius	Taurus	April 21 - May 21	October/November	April/May
Capricorn	Gemini	May 22 - June 21	November/December	May/June
Aquarius	Cancer	June 22 - July 22	December/January	June/July
Pisces	Leo	July 23 - August 23	January/February	July/August

Table 7 The 6th House Diet Schedule by Sign

*Be aware that some aspects may actually be contrary to losing weight, especially if they involve Venus or Neptune, which can make you lazy or delusional respectively. This pair is likely to make you think you can take off that flab by eating nothing but chocolate as long as you watch Oprah everyday. Currently Neptune is in Pisces, sign of his modern rulership, which makes him quite powerful, which doesn't bode well for Libras.

To overcome this particular problem, try using the good feelings these planets emanate to visualize yourself the way you'd like to be when you lose that weight and then use your Virgo detail-oriented, critical attitude to stick to your diet and exercise regimen as if your life depended on it. Since Venus moves fairly quickly and doesn't stay in any sign too long (except when retrograde, in which case she could be there roughly four months, give or take) she shouldn't be too much of a problem, especially in the 6th House since the love goddess may help you love yourself a little more and thus help motivate you to mind your health and fitness.

Ω Ω Ω

♎ Diet Category #2

I want to look and feel good
Or
I'm too cheap to buy new clothes

If you want to lose weight because you're finally fed up with feeling tired and not being able to tie your shoes, then you're either pregnant or have a **2nd House** motivation. This House drives your possessions, which includes your body. It also covers sensual pleasures such as gourmet food, fine beverages and hot oil massages. In this House you are only thinking of how you feel about yourself. You're not trying to impress anyone, you just want to feel good and like what you see in the mirror. You're taking care of yourself, as you would any other valued possession; kinda like taking your car in for an oil change.

If this is where you're coming from you'll want to initiate your diet when there is significant astrological activity in your Natal or Natural 2nd House. Your Natal 2nd House depends on what time you were born and is shown on your Natal Chart. If you don't have one, then you can get some help from your Natural House, which you can determine from the chart at the bottom of the page.

The Universal 2nd House belongs to Taurus. As most people know, this sign likes comfort and nice things but is also somewhat cheap. I mean frugal. Very frugal. This puts another spin on diets that relate to this House. For example, those size 5s in the closet are not from Wal-Mart because you like things that are soft and fit well. Right now they don't fit at all. Since your budget won't allow buying more right now, however, you simply need to lose weight so you can fit into existing clothes and save money. (These would obviously be the Slim Fast folks and not those with personal trainers.)

If either of these sounds familiar, then the 2nd House approach is probably for you.

2nd *House Diet*

Diet Type: Preplanned, "eat this" types, *i.e. Nutrisystems*; Slim Fast; "Fat Farms"

Hints: Pamper yourself with harmless indulgences, *e.g.*, a candlelight bubble bath with soft music and incense, on a regular basis.

Find dessert substitutes like fresh fruit topped with yogurt to control cravings.

Take note of what you're eating and the quantities so you can continue to consume a similar amount of calories when you go back to "normal" food.

Don't cut out your favorite foods entirely. Either cut back on quantity or find substitutes. Depriving yourself long-term will result in binges.

Pitfalls: Does not change your eating habits as required for permanent weight loss; tendency to go back to the way you ate before when you decide to quit dieting.

Depending on how long you need to diet, can be expensive or boring.

Appeals to ... because:

Taurus: You like comfort, convenience and being pampered.

Gemini: Who has time to mess with all that menu and calorie counting crap?

Libra: It's too hard to make up your mind with all those choices on other diets.

Scorpio: It's hard enough to diet. Let someone else do as much work as possible.

The exact date for the lunation in question can be found on most astrology websites.

Your Sign	Your Natural 2nd House	Sun in 2nd House	Full Moon in 2nd	New Moon in 2nd
Aries	Taurus	April 21 - May 21	October/November	April/May
Taurus	Gemini	May 22 - June 21	November/December	May/June
Gemini	Cancer	June 22 - July 22	December/January	June/July
Cancer	Leo	July 23 - August 23	January/February	July/August
Leo	Virgo	August 24 - September 22	February/March	August/September
Virgo	Libra	September 23 - October 23	March/April	September/October
Libra	Scorpio	October 24 - November 22	April/May	October/November
Scorpio	Sagittarius*	November 23 - December 21	May/June	November/December
Sagittarius	Capricorn	December 22 - January 20	June/July	December/January
Capricorn	Aquarius*	January 21 - February 18	July/August	January/February
Aquarius	Pisces	February 19 - March 20	August/September	February/March
Pisces	Aries	March 21 - April 20	September/October	March/April

Table 8 The 2nd House Diet Schedule by Sign

*Be aware that some aspects may actually be contrary to losing weight, especially if they involve Venus or Neptune, which can make you lazy or delusional respectively. This pair is likely to make you think you can take off that flab by eating nothing but chocolate as long as you watch Oprah daily. Currently Neptune is in Pisces, and will be for quite a long time, which doesn't bode well for Aquarians. For Aquarians to overcome this particular problem, try using that Neptunian idealism to visualize yourself the way you'd like to be when you lose that weight and then use your Air sign logic to stick to your diet and exercise regimen as if your intellectual future depended on it. Venus moves fairly quickly, so shouldn't be a hindrance for an extended time (except when retrograde, in which case she could be there roughly four months, give or take). To get past Venus, just focus on pleasures other than eating.

$$\Omega \; \Omega \; \Omega$$

Diet Category #3

I'm trolling for a relationship
or
I want people to notice me
or
I want to look "hot"

You need to lose weight--*FAST!*--for a wedding, your 10-year reunion, or you've met someone you like--a lot. You do one of those bright light assessments of yourself stripped naked in front of the bathroom mirror and decide you definitely don't like what you see and there ain't no way on God's green Earth that anyone else is going to see you lookin' like *that*. If this sounds familiar, you're undoubtedly setting foot into the 5th House which governs love affairs, your children, creative expression as well as your self-image; the 5th is represented on the Zodiacal level by Leo.

This is the House where you want to impress others with how you look. You may not only diet, but upgrade your wardrobe as well to reward yourself. There is a bit of ego here; okay, maybe *a lot*. At any rate, losing weight is only part of it. You'll probably do something new and different with your hair and makeup to achieve a general overhaul, *i.e.* the ultimate make-over. You may not care what you actually weigh as much as what size you can fit into. You'll be excited and enthusiastic about what you're doing and how you're going to look when you're through. You may even convert numerous friends to a similar plan.

If this is where you're coming from you'll want to initiate your diet when there is significant astrological activity in your Natal or Natural 5th

House. Your Natal 5th House depends on what time you were born and is shown on your Natal Chart. If you don't have one you can get some help from your Natural House, which you can determine from the chart at the bottom of the page.

One more thing. Not to dampen your enthusiasm, honey, because losing weight is definitely a good thing, but you need to be aware that the only way to attain permanent weight loss is to make serious changes to your eating and exercise habits. *"If you keep on doing what you've always done, you'll keep on getting what you've always got,"* in this case a fat ass. So recognize that this diet plan has serious limitations that you'll need to acknowledge and address if you want to stay in your size of choice.

But who am I to criticize since I'm certainly not in the size of my dreams, either? So have at it with my blessings and the blessings of the heavens as well if you follow the Sun and Lunation table below.

5th *House Diet*

Diet Type: Gimmick diets of all descriptions, *e.g.* Atkins, South Beach, grapefruit, cabbage soup.

Hints: Indulge yourself in designer workout clothes if it will help keep you motivated or better yet buy some new clothes in your "fat" size before you start to improve your self-image. It's easier to diet when you feel good about yourself than when you avoid mirrors!

Learn everything you can about your diet, why it works, which movie stars swear by it, etc., so you have plenty to talk and brag about.

Transition to a healthy, sensible diet that includes regular exercise slightly before attaining your goal weight.

Pitfalls: Easy to regain weight plus some when you stop.

Unhealthy for long-term dieting. Can stress vital organs, mess with your metabolism or cause nutritional deficiencies.

Appeals to...because:

Aries: Fast results, especially if coupled with a lot of exercise.

Leo: Like being special and different and having something new to talk about.

Sagittarius: Another new idea to learn about and discuss, requires less patience than long-term changes.

Aquarius: You're always willing to try something innovative.

The exact date for the lunation in question can be found on your monthly horoscope for that month.

Your Sign	Your Natural 5th House	Sun in 5th House	Full Moon in 5th	New Moon in 5th
Aries	Leo	July 23 - August 23	January/February	July/August
Taurus	Virgo	August 24 - September 22	February/March	August/September
Gemini	Libra	September 23 - October 23	March/April	September/October
Cancer	Scorpio	October 24 - November 22	April/May	October/November
Leo	Sagittarius*	November 23 - December 21	May/June	November/December
Virgo	Capricorn	December 22 - January 20	June/July	December/January
Libra	Aquarius*	January 21 - February 18	July/August	January/February
Scorpio	Pisces	February 19 - March 20	August/September	February/March
Sagittarius	Aries	March 21 - April 20	September/October	March/April
Capricorn	Taurus	April 21 - May 21	October/November	April/May
Aquarius	Gemini	May 22 - June 21	November/December	May/June

Your Sign	Your Natural 5th House	Sun in 5th House	Full Moon in 5th	New Moon in 5th
Pisces	Cancer	June 22 - July 22	December/January	June/July

Table 9 The 5th House Diet Schedule by Sign

*Be aware that some aspects may actually be contrary to losing weight, especially if they involve Venus or Neptune, which can make you lazy or delusional respectively. This pair is likely to make you think you can take off that flab by eating nothing but chocolate as long as you watch Oprah everyday. Currently Neptune is in Pisces, which doesn't bode well for Scorpios. To overcome this particular problem, try using some of that Neptunian idealism to visualize yourself the way you'd like to be when you lose that weight and then use your Scorpio propensity for obsession combined with regular naked appraisals in front of a full-length mirror to stick to your diet and exercise regimen as if the future of world peace depended on it.

Venus moves quite quickly so shouldn't linger in the target house too long (except when retrograde, in which case she could be there as long as four months, give or take). Your best bet is to pamper yourself with something other than food. A good 5th House diversion would be to go shopping and check out all the cute outfits you'll be able to fit into someday soon.

CHOOSING THE RIGHT PLACE TO LIVE

There are two specific branches of astrology which can help you decide whether or not you're in the right place at the right time. One is Astrocartography. The other is Horary, which is discussed in the next chapter. Astrocartography is a technique that examines how your Natal Chart changes when you move a significant distance from your place of birth.

Your date and time of birth remain the same instant in time, but the location changes, relocating your Ascendant and other House cusps to a different position, perhaps improving certain parts of your life. Of course this can work in reverse as well.

Everyone would like to know if there is some magic place where they could live happily ever after. They'd find their soulmate, secure their dream job, and live in the house and neighborhood they always dreamed of. Of course there is no such ideal place, but moving can affect your "luck" and other factors that contribute to certain areas of your life. While you can't change when you were born and the astrological sign position of the planets at that time, moving *can* bring more favorable circumstances your way. Sound crazy? Here's how it works.

When you move to a new place, usually at least a hundred miles away and preferably in an east or west direction, your Natal Chart is "relocated" and calculated for how the sky appeared at your moment of birth from the new place. If the distance is sufficient, your Ascendant will change as well as every other House cusp. Remember that the influence of your Natal Chart comes from not only which planet is in which sign, but which House as well. You can't change the planet or the sign, but you can change its House, which shifts its influence.

For example, if you want to move somewhere to find romance, it would be advantageous to have Venus in your 5th House of romance or 7th House of relationships. If you want to maximize your learning experience when you go away to college, it would be beneficial to locate Jupiter in your 9th House of higher learning. If you want to have strong and pleasant family relationships then the Moon or Venus in you 4th House would be helpful, though of course this wouldn't necessarily solve all your problems.

Many people have experienced the feeling that they needed to move somewhere else. This may be because nothing is working out in a favorable way in their current location or simply an instinct or impression that they need to be somewhere else, a subtle message from their inner compass. It is always a good idea to listen to these promptings. If you don't know why you're being pushed by the Universe to make your home somewhere else, having your Natal Chart relocated may provide some hints. If you're a person who believes that your life is unfolding according to a specific plan or that you have a mission in life to fulfill, it is even more important to pay attention.

When your Ascendant changes to another Sign it will have a subtle affect on your personality, similar to the way it evolves as reflected in your Progressed Chart. You won't notice a dramatic difference, but you may find you're more outgoing or even more of a homebody than in your previous location. Your personality determines a lot about your life, including how ambitious you are, how you present yourself to others, how you interact with others, how easily you make friends, and so forth. Changes to these types of behavior can have an impact on other areas of your life in and of itself. However, as all the Angles of your chart change, not just your Ascendant, different Sign energy is directed to them as well. Of course you won't be able to get all twelve Houses located in exactly the right Sign to make all your dreams come true. You'll have to prioritize what you want and make some compromises.

These effects will also be present if you travel somewhere for a limited time without changing your residence, perhaps for a vacation or business endeavor. For example, if you're looking for romance you could always vacation in a locale favorable for this to happen, but if it takes you halfway around the world, your new found love may likewise live a prohibitive distance from the place you call home. You are even less likely to notice any differences in your behavior during these jaunts since we all tend to wear a slightest different persona when traveling for pleasure as we set our everyday stresses and worries aside. Same goes for business travel, where you likewise get away from your usual routine and escape some of those things that make your life hectic such as picking up your child on time from daycare or dealing with commuter traffic.

Another thing to bear in mind as well is the fact that you may have to move halfway around the world to achieve your objectives. Putting Venus on your 7th House cusp may require moving to Bolivia. Furthermore, placing one planet in a favorable house may put another somewhere that turns out to be less than enchanting, such as

Pluto or Saturn in your 2nd House of finances and possessions, which would probably not have pleasant results. Nonetheless, it's something worth considering. It's always interesting, educational, and transformational to experience a new location with different people, cultures and traditions. Some planets or aspects in your Natal Chart can predispose you to moving around a bit, too. For example, I have Jupiter in my 4th House of home environment and have lived in New York, California, Utah and Texas. Jupiter in your 9th House would spur a lot of long-distance travel, but not necessarily as a change of residence, though relocations typically show up via planetary transits in the 9th.

If you're seriously thinking about moving, obtaining an Astromap will provide some information about how you'll fare. It may also be a good idea to obtain a relocated natal chart report for further information on its affect to your basic personality. When it comes down to the actual decision of whether or not to move, you can also employ Horary Astrology to let you know if the change will be beneficial and meet your expectations. At the very least, astrology can give you a general idea of what to expect and more options for finding what you want in life.

HORARY ASTROLOGY

Horary is one of the most fascinating and unexplainable forms of astrology in which a chart is cast for the time that a person (referred to as the querent) asks a specific question, which the astrologer then answers by reading the chart.

As with other types of astrology, no one knows why this works, but it does and has been in use for hundreds, probably even thousands, of years. Early astrologer, William Lilly, wrote an entire treatise on the subject back in the 1600s entitled "The Resolution of all Manner of Questions and Demands." Whenever I think of Horary Astrology I think of the scripture that states *"Ask, and it shall be given you; seek and ye shall find; knock and it shall be opened unto you" (Matthew 7:7 KJV).*

Anything as complex as astrology would have to come from God so it makes sense that questions could be answered in this fashion. If asked via prayer, the answer would be delivered via the same energy. For those with insufficient faith to "hear" an answer, an astrologer trained in Horary Astrology could help tremendously. The accuracy of guidance I've been able to provide clients through this method astounds even me. Questions that are well-suited for Horary include such things as "When will I find a job?", "When will I sell my house?", "Is this a good time to buy this stock?", "Should I buy the car I test-drove today?", "Will my friend loan me the money I need?", "Where are my car keys?" and so forth. There are few limitations, other than the fact that a Horary chart will never indicate the death of the querent.

The key to Horary is having a solid understanding of which House rules the question. The Ascendant always represents the querent and the 7th House the astrologer; the 7th also rules anyone the querent refers to by name or otherwise fits in the 7th House of relationships. The House that rules the question will be in keeping with the usual definitions. For example, questions about possessions will be ruled by the 2nd; siblings the 3rd; home matters the 4th; children, romance and speculation the 5th; jobs the 6th; relationships the 7th; loans and other shared resources the 8th; legal issues, academia, cultural interactions, relocation, long distance travel the 9th; career, status or reputation the 10th; friends and organizations the 11th; dreams, hidden enemies, and self-undoing the 12th.

Some astrologers use the place, date and time they understand the question whereas others (myself included) use the place, date and time that the querent asked the question. This is a matter of personal preference on the part of the astrologer based on what they have found to work the best. I use the time the querent asked the question because that is when I feel like issue was put to the Universe; I am simply the vehicle for interpreting. However, other astrologers may feel that they're asking vicariously on the part of their client. Either way, it works; apparently the Universe understands the intent and responds regardless. Would you expect anything less?

In a nutshell, the astrologer identifies the planets that rule the Houses related to the question and determines if there's an aspect between them. Applying aspects, or those that are in the process of forming, are the only ones that count and the concept of orbs is irrelevant. The basic Ptolemaic aspects are the only ones used, *i.e.* the conjunction, sextile, square, trine, quincunx and opposition. A favorable aspect (sextile or trine) indicates a "Yes" answer and a hard aspect (square or opposition) indicate "No."

Conjunctions bring things together and quincunxes indicate an adjustment or change of course is needed. Implications of any aspects to other planets other than those directly related to the question are interpreted according to the planet, sign and house in which the planets reside. Timing is a major challenge, but can often be determined. Hours, days or weeks can be indicated depending on which Signs and Houses are involved with the count typically related to the number of degrees before the relevant aspect is exact. Quite often the ruling planets are located in Houses that relate to the question in some way, but if they don't it doesn't necessarily mean that the chart is invalid.

For example, in the chart below, as a possession the lost remote is represented by the ruler of the 2nd House, which is Mercury, a very apropos representative for an electronic device. Mercury is in the 5th House of entertainment, children and games, which was also applicable since the remote was to a Wii. For lost items, the Signs and Houses provide information regarding the location. Capricorn can indicate dark places near the ground and the 5th House indicates a northwest direction. The 5th House also implies a place where you play or are entertained or that a child will find the item or knows where it is.

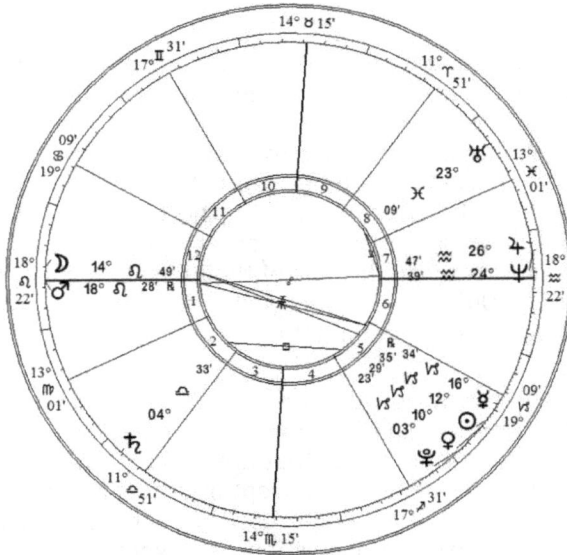

Figure 17 Horary Chart Example: Lost Remote

In this case, a child found the remote on the floor under the couch in the northwest part of the room three days later. The applying quincunx to the Moon implied two days and the applying conjunction to the Sun, ruler of the Querent, implied four; Mercury is retrograde so it was moving backwards. However, if you wanted to discount the effect of retrograde motion, Mercury is about three degrees from the 6th House cusp, implying in three days it would be "working" again plus in two degrees it would quincunx Mars, implying it would be back in the hands of the querent and "back in action." The fact that Mercury was RX was also a strong indicator that the item would indeed be found.

The Moon rules function so co-rules all questions and should always been considered in the answer and timing. The Vertex, which relates to fate, and Part of Fortune, which relates to those things that make us happy, are also frequently relevant. One of the advantages of a Horary chart is that you don't need the querent's birth information, though if it's available it is sometimes useful to compare the two; if the querent's ascendant or any of their natal birth planets conjunct the Horary chart planets, it can have a bearing on the answer, especially if the chart otherwise appears to be invalid due to containing a "stricture against judgment." These are cardinal rules for Horary which indicate that the chart (and/or the question) is probably invalid.

1. If the rising or ascendant degree is 3 degrees or less, it frequently indicates that the answer has been asked prematurely, such as when the querent does not have all the necessary information.

2. When a late degree between 27 - 29 is rising it indicates that the question or matter is already settled.

3. When the Moon is Void of Course it usually indicates that nothing will come of the questions or something that there is nothing to worry about.

4. If the Moon or the ascendant is in the *Via Combusta*, the area from 15 degrees Libra to 15 degrees Scorpio, ancient astrologers considered the chart invalid.

5. If Saturn is in the 7th House, which represents the astrologer, this is another condition that indicates a stricture against judgment. This can mean that the chart was not cast correctly or that the astrologer's judgment is faulty and thus the answer may be incorrect.

Horary charts typically go beyond a simple yes or no answer, providing rationale, alternative approaches to the problem, or further details that an experienced astrologer can identify to provide further guidance. However, conjecture should be used with caution since if it's incorrect it clouds the answer's credibility. I have found that when I see something else that seems important it doesn't hurt to mention it to the client and ask if it makes sense as it has often provided the extra information they needed or further validates the answer. For example, I had a client ask if they should change jobs. The chart indicated there was another choice that involved something that looked like a partnership. I mentioned it and it was exactly what they needed to know since they had been considering that option.

As with any branch of astrology, experience is essential along with a strong background in the basic principles of rulership, planetary conditions such as dignity or debility, and the particulars of color and direction implied by the chart. Three excellent books on Horary Astrology are "Horary Astrology and the Judgment of Events" by Barbara Watters, "The Only Way to Learn About Horary and Electional Astrology" by Marion March and Joan McEvers and "The Martial Art of Horary Astrology" by Lee Lehman.

"GOOD OL' BOY " ASTROLOGY

A farmer or rancher is probably the last image that comes to mind when you think of someone who uses astrology in their everyday life. However, these folks not only continue to use it today but have for centuries, probably even millennia. Much about their work hasn't changed. They still need a lot of cooperation from Mother Earth so she will yield them a good crop, even if they have a combine equipped with air conditioning and a stereo. Surprised?

You shouldn't be. And more than likely you've heard of their primary source for this information, which obviously isn't found in the typical horoscope column. It's been around since 1818 and is known as the *Farmers' Almanac*. I picked up my copy for free in the local feed store and was quite delighted with what it contained, other than a whole bunch of common sense. It has an illustration that includes the parts of the body each Sign rules, the astrological location of the Moon, when the Sun and Moon rise and visible planets can be seen, lunar and solar eclipses, explanation of the lunar phases, and even weather predictions (it's raining as I write, just like they said it would on this date).

Some of the other things this gem contains include the best times for planting and gardening, when to go fishing (at least if you want to catch something) or hunting, and just about everything else you can imagine such as cooking, baking, cutting your hair, quitting smoking, potty training, home repair, working outside, advertising, hosting a party and getting married, to name a few. *I kid you not!*

Of course all they give are the dates, so I did a little bit of cross-referencing with my friendly Ephemeris to see what was going on at those times. For a successful garden, it wasn't surprising to see Water and Earth Signs clearly led the pack. For above-ground crops Pisces, Taurus and Cancer consistently appeared with Libra making an occasional appearance during a waxing Moon. For root crops, Cancer, Libra, Scorpio, Capricorn and Pisces predominated during waning phases.

For transplanting, Scorpio and Pisces predominated with a sprinkling of Cancer and Taurus, all during waning phases. Seedbeds were consistently Cancer and Scorpio after the Full Moon and Flowers favored Cancer and Libra with a sprinkling of Scorpio, after the Full Moon and during the waning phases. Killing plant pests were somewhat inconsistent with three months indicating there were no good

258

days. Generally it looked like Aquarius and Leo predominated during mostly waning phases.

The best fishing days were when the Moon was in Water Signs Cancer or Pisces with Scorpio classified as good. Hunting was best consistently at the time of the Full Moon or immediately after with its Sign also consistent in a Water Sign, though it varied seasonally with it Scorpio for February, March, April and May; Pisces for July, August and September; Cancer for October, November, December and January. Baking will be most successful when the waxing Moon is in an Air or Fire Sign. Home brew will do best when the waning Moon is in a Water Sign.

smoking and weight loss diets generally work best during waning phases in Fire Signs Aries, Leo and Sagittarius as well as health-conscious Virgo and Air Signs Gemini and Aquarius. For potty training, the waning Moon was best from January to June and the waxing Moon for July through December.

The *Farmers' Almanac* has the details and other activities covered that are too numerous to mention, so if you're interested your best bet is to pick one up. If you don't frequently your local feed store very often, you may be able to get one from their website at www.farmersalmanac.com. If you're interested in how astrology operates in the "real world" and would like to use these time-tested recommendations yourself, that is undoubtedly your best resource. For more specific questions, such as whether you should buy the car you just took for a test drive, check out our section on Horary Astrology.

TIMING IS EVERYTHING

If there's one area where astrology is worth its weight in gold it's in timing events. Some situations will come our way, regardless, as the cosmos conducts the symphony of our lives, so if you're trying to accomplish something it always helps if you're in synch with the Universe. As I look back on certain times in my life I could have avoided a lot of frustration if I'd known that the stars and planets didn't agree with some of my ambitions. Conversely, it can also tell you when the time is right.

A very simple way to begin certain activities is to schedule them for when a **New Moon** occurs in the relevant House as defined below; for more detailed information on which areas of life fall under which astrological house go to the House section. Of course other factors come into play, but this is one way to focus on an area that will enjoy a little extra zodiacal help.

On the other hand, if you have something in-work and wonder when it's going to come to fruition, there's a good chance that will correlate with a **Full Moon** in the relevant House. For example, when my daughter was selling her house, she wondered when this would occur. I looked at her chart to see when she'd have a lunation in either her 4th (home environment) or 9th (legal contracts) House. She didn't like the answer, as it was several months hence, but that was exactly when it occurred.

Thus, if you're planning something, the purpose of this section is to give you some idea when it might be the best time to start. *Remember, also, that when Mercury is retrograde it's best to wait until it's over before you start something new.* During those times reworking old issues, making repairs, editing or revising are favored, but moving forward isn't likely to occur. Other planets in retrograde have a similar effect; check the Retrograde Planets section for details.

To use this technique, the first thing to do is figure out which house the activity resides in. A list of the basic matters included in each astrological house follows. When you identify which one you want to target, the next step is to find your sign in the listing that follows to see which sign of the zodiac represents that particular house for you. If you know your ascendant, then look at that sign as well.

After that, you simply have to figure out when the appropriate lunation occurs in that house, i.e. a New Moon for a beginning and a Full Moon for and ending. Most astrological websites, including ValkyrieAstrology.com, tell you when lunations occur and in which sign. A simple guide is that the New Moon occurs when the Sun is in that sign, the Full Moon when the Sun and Moon are in opposing signs. The usual dates the Sun is in the different zodiac signs is found in the Sun Sign section.

To illustrate, if you're wondering about a relationship, a Full Moon in the 7th House doesn't necessarily mean it will end, but it is likely to enter a new level. A New Moon in your 7th House usually heralds someone new coming into your life. Just remember that "relationships" in this context include all one-on-one interactions whether it's your significant other, close friend or relative, business associate, business professional, competitor, cliental or open enemy. If you're in business for yourself, it could mean you'll be getting a new customer or client. As another example, if your Sign is Leo and you want to know when it's a good time to go to Las Vegas to do some gambling, you'd look under "Leo" and your 5th House of speculation, which would be Sagittarius. The New Moon will be in Sagittarius, meaning it would occur some time between November 23 - December 21.

1. Find which house your concern relates to in the chart below.

House	Relevant Issues
1st	Personal goals
2nd	Financial Planning, Major Purchases, Ventures pertaining to income, Vacation for pleasure and relaxation
3rd	Thoughts, Ideas, Neighbors, Siblings, Short Trips
4th	Remodeling, Family Events, Moves, Genealogy
5th	Children, Romance, Creative projects, Entertainment, Speculation
6th	Work, Service, Health Checkups, Pets
7th	Relationships, Clients, Negotiations
8th	Borrowing money, Major life events, Planned Pregnancy, Psychological counseling
9th	Relocation, Legal Matters, Higher Education, Long-distance Travel
10th	Career Planning and Advancement, Public Recognition
11th	Friends, Associates, Group Interactions & Projects, Pursuing Hopes & Wishes
12th	Spiritual Pursuits, Inspiration, Deep Introspection, Seclusion, Hospitalization, Retreats

Table 10 House Issue Coverage

2. Next find your Sun Sign below and determine which zodiac sign represents the house that relates to your issue.

Aries

1st	2nd	3rd	4th	5th	6th
Aries	Taurus	Gemini	Cancer	Leo	Virgo
7th	**8th**	**9th**	**10th**	**11th**	**12th**
Libra	Scorpio	Sagittarius	Capricorn	Aquarius	Pisces

Taurus

1st	2nd	3rd	4th	5th	6th
Taurus	Gemini	Cancer	Leo	Virgo	Libra
7th	**8th**	**9th**	**10th**	**11th**	**12th**
Scorpio	Sagittarius	Capricorn	Aquarius	Pisces	Aries

Gemini

1st	2nd	3rd	4th	5th	6th
Gemini	Cancer	Leo	Virgo	Libra	Scorpio
7th	**8th**	**9th**	**10th**	**11th**	**12th**
Sagittarius	Capricorn	Aquarius	Pisces	Aries	Taurus

Cancer

1st	2nd	3rd	4th	5th	6th
Cancer	Leo	Virgo	Libra	Scorpio	Sagittarius
7th	**8th**	**9th**	**10th**	**11th**	**12th**
Capricorn	Aquarius	Pisces	Aries	Taurus	Gemini

Leo

1st	2nd	3rd	4th	5th	6th
Leo	Virgo	Libra	Scorpio	Sagittarius	Capricorn
7th	**8th**	**9th**	**10th**	**11th**	**12th**
Aquarius	Pisces	Aries	Taurus	Gemini	Cancer

Virgo

1st	2nd	3rd	4th	5th	6th
Virgo	Libra	Scorpio	Sagittarius	Capricorn	Aquarius
7th	**8th**	**9th**	**10th**	**11th**	**12th**
Pisces	Aries	Taurus	Gemini	Cancer	Leo

Libra

1st	2nd	3rd	4th	5th	6th
Libra	Scorpio	Sagittarius	Capricorn	Aquarius	Pisces
7th	8th	9th	10th	11th	12th
Aries	Taurus	Gemini	Cancer	Leo	Virgo

Scorpio

1st	2nd	3rd	4th	5th	6th
Scorpio	Sagittarius	Capricorn	Aquarius	Pisces	Aries
7th	8th	9th	10th	11th	12th
Taurus	Gemini	Cancer	Leo	Virgo	Libra

Sagittarius

1st	2nd	3rd	4th	5th	6th
Sagittarius	Capricorn	Aquarius	Pisces	Aries	Taurus
7th	8th	9th	10th	11th	12th
Gemini	Cancer	Leo	Virgo	Libra	Scorpio

Capricorn

1st	2nd	3rd	4th	5th	6th
Capricorn	Aquarius	Pisces	Aries	Taurus	Gemini
7th	8th	9th	10th	11th	12th
Cancer	Leo	Virgo	Libra	Scorpio	Sagittarius

Aquarius

1st	2nd	3rd	4th	5th	6th
Aquarius	Pisces	Aries	Taurus	Gemini	Cancer
7th	8th	9th	10th	11th	12th
Leo	Virgo	Libra	Scorpio	Sagittarius	Capricorn

Pisces

1st	2nd	3rd	4th	5th	6th
Pisces	Aries	Taurus	Gemini	Cancer	Leo
7th	8th	9th	10th	11th	12th
Virgo	Libra	Scorpio	Sagittarius	Capricorn	Aquarius

3. Now use the following chart to figure out when might be a good time to take action, based on when a lunation occurs in the sign that relates to your chosen house. Remember that New Moons are a favorable time to begin a new endeavor and a Full Moon is the time to finish, culminate or shift to a new phase. The exact date of the lunation can often be found on a simple calendar or check an astronomy or astrological website, including ValkyrieAstrology.com.

Sun Sign	New Moon	Full Moon
Aries	March/April	September/October
Taurus	April/May	October/November
Gemini	May/June	November/December
Cancer	June/July	December/January
Leo	July/August	January/February
Virgo	August/September	February/March
Libra	September/October	March/April
Scorpio	October/November	April/May
Sagittarius	November/December	May/June
Capricorn	December/January	June/July
Aquarius	January/February	July/August
Pisces	February/March	August/September

Table 11 Timing of New & Full Moon by Sign

At this point I need to add one caveat. If you don't like the timing you find, take a look at your 4th house and see if that fits your schedule better. The 4th represents endings and new beginnings so it can often provide the energy you're looking for as well.

THE AGE OF AQUARIUS

If you've ever heard the song from the play, *Hair*, which was popular in the 60s, you have undoubtedly wondered what exactly *is* the Age of Aquarius, anyway?

Most of astrology is based on the motion of the planets through the Zodiac. For astrological purposes the term *planets* includes the Moon and the Sun even though they're not considered such by astronomical definition. Their placements as shown on an astrological chart are based on a geocentric reference frame, in other words, the position these heavenly bodies appear to have from Earth. However, the Earth itself also travels through the 12 constellations known as the Zodiac. One cycle takes an incomprehensible 25,868 years, or approximately 2,500 years to traverse each Sign.

The time spent in a given Sign is what we call an *Age*. Since the Zodiacal constellations aren't all the same size, we don't know exactly when one Age ends and another begins. Nonetheless, even as we can discern "generational" effects as the slower moving superior planets (i.e. Jupiter, Saturn, Uranus, Neptune and Pluto) move through the Signs, we can use the historical record to note major happenings during periods of time that clearly indicate which Sign the Earth was in at the time. Since the Earth moves through these Signs in retrograde motion (*i.e.*, backwards) the order is reversed compared to the way we see the Sun move through the Zodiac. Here are some of the basic indications of these time periods with the Signs as we know them.

10000-8000 B.C., Age of Leo: Prehistoric cave paintings that date back to this timeframe are indicative of man's creativity, even back then. It was the end of the Ice Age, the Sun's importance as a source of life more evident than ever before. Leo, the natural 5th House, is the house of creativity and ruled by the Sun. Its polar sign, Aquarius, and its propensity for invention, was also evident in the use of stone tools.

8000-6000 B.C., Age of Cancer: Cancer, sign of the natural fourth house, is symbolic of the home environment and ruled by the Moon. During this age man began to inhabit homes and the concept of family developed. The Moon has long been associated with motherhood and the female reproductive cycle. As communities and civilizations developed their awareness of the heavens increased along with associations of the Moon with the tides and the Sun with seasons. The polar sign, Capricorn, was represented by the vestiges of security found in the beginnings of agricultural societies.

6000-4000 B.C., Age of Gemini: Gemini is ruled by the planet, Mercury, and is associated with the intellect and communications. At this time the written word was created, as evidenced by Chinese and Egyptian cuneiform writing, and most likely the wheel as well. Civilizations were developing with people beginning to cluster together in larger groups versus small, agrarian communities. Trade began and intellectual expansion was in progress. Sagittarius, the polar sign in this case, was demonstrated by the developing cultures and their interaction with one another as well as the long distance travel involved.

4000-2000 B.C., Age of Taurus: Besides the strong attachment that Taurus has with the Earth itself, beauty and luxury are also associated with this Sign. Egyptian dynasties and other civilizations at this time were known for their imposing and elegant temples and other structures that were so enduring that vestiges of them remain to this day. The polar sign, Scorpio, was represented in the fascination with death and the after-life which manifested itself in mummification methods and elaborate tombs, *i.e.* pyramids. A fascination and appreciation for nature began, including the observation of the stars and the beginnings of astrology and astronomy.

2000 B.C. - A.D., Age of Aries: During this time the Greek culture evolved and the Aries/Libra polarity blossomed. The warlike tendencies of Aries were personified by the aggressive Greeks and the many wars they perpetrated. The influence of Libra was evident in the first democratic governments as well as the continuing development of beautiful structures.

A.D. 0 - 2000 A.D., Age of Pisces: Not surprisingly, this Age began with the birth of Christ. Even the Christian symbol of fish coincides with this Age. Christian beliefs reflect Piscean qualities of kindness, charity and peace as well as self-sacrifice, as shown by early martyrs and even the cloistered lives of monks and nuns, which reflect the Piscean tendency to be reclusive. The polar influence of Virgo is found in the meticulous observance of religious rituals and principles as well as the adoration of the Virgin Mary. The great advances in art during the Renaissance period also reflected an increase in artists' attention to detail.

2000 A.D. - 4000 A.D., Age of Aquarius: We don't know the exact moment when the Earth passed from Pisces into Aquarius, but it is evident that we are now there. The development of modern technology is particularly Aquarian as well as the interaction of the various cultures, particularly noted in organizations like the United Nations and the European Union. The polar sign, Leo, is likewise reflected in the expansive creativity and arts of the time and the renewed emphasis on the importance of caring for children. Leo also likes to rule, possibly influencing the numerous quests for dominance in political and religious arenas that we see in the world today.

Few will argue that we're living in interesting times.

Namaste!

ABOUT THE AUTHOR

"Whobeda," a name which came about in an interesting way, is the pseudonym for Marcha Fox, the story of which she shares with a few select friends and clients with the world at large left to wonder. She graduated from Utah State University with a Bachelor's Degree in Physics in 1987 and worked as a NASA contractor from 1988 to 2009, at which time she retired and came completely out of the closet as an astrologer and began to pursue it full-time.

She studied astrology originally to debunk it, instead becoming converted to its truth, and has thus continued to build upon her knowledge of this amazing, ancient art. At one point in her quest she discovered the online "halls" of the International Academy of Astrology (IAA) (www.astrocollege.org) and hopped onboard for formal training. She graduated in January 2012 and taught the first class in IAA's Natal Studies Module entitled "Examining the Chart's Structure" for over two years, during which time she revised the text of the same name with its original author, Ena Stanley, founder of IAA.

Her website, ValkyrieAstrology.com, first appeared on the Internet in 2006 and has grown significantly ever since. Her clients span the globe, their various testimonials available on the website. The vast majority of material in this book originated on her website, making it available in more convenient form for those who get motion sickness playing "hyperlink bingo." Some material on the website that isn't found here was previously published in ebook format, specifically that on the asteroid goddesses, Lilith, and her research on the astrology of the NASA accidents, the last of which was also published in August 2006 in the International Society for Astrological Research (ISAR) Journal. These books are available on ValkyrieAstrology.com in pdf format with most also available online in Kindle and Nook format.

Marcha is the mother of 6, grandmother of 17 and great-grandmother of (currently) three. For those who are curious, she is a Capricorn with a Virgo rising and Gemini Moon, who at this writing lives in Central Texas, USA.

www.ingramcontent.com/pod-product-compliance
Lightning Source LLC
Chambersburg PA
CBHW072339090426
42741CB00012B/2854